HOOP DREAMS

A True Story of Hardship and Triumph

THE EXCHANGE

How does a
person know
which goals to
pursue?

HOOP DREAMS

A TRUE STORY OF HARDSHIP AND TRIUMPH

Ben Joravsky
Foreword by Charles Barkley

 HAMPTON-BROWN

This book contains mature content. Educators and parents
should read the book and determine its appropriateness
for use with their students.

Hampton-Brown
P.O. Box 223220
Carmel, California 93922
800-333-3510
www.hampton-brown.com

Printed in the United States of America

ISBN-13: 978-0-7362-3195-4
ISBN-10: 0-7362-3195-1

08 09 10 11 12 13 14 15 10 9 8 7 6 5 4

To my parents

CONTENTS

Introduction

William Gates and Arthur Agee lived for basketball. They fantasized about becoming famous basketball stars like Isiah Thomas and Michael Jordan. But more than that, they depended on basketball to get them out of one of the most dangerous neighborhoods in America in the 1980s. Life in their Chicago housing development was a daily battle against **obstacles** that were almost impossible to overcome.

The public housing development was called Cabrini-Green. The city of Chicago built it in order to help people who needed affordable places to live. At one time, 15,000 people lived in the 23 high-rise apartments and 55 row houses. Eventually city officials stopped taking care of Cabrini-Green. There were rats, bugs, garbage, and horrible smells everywhere. This created a very sad and hopeless place for the people who lived there.

Cabrini-Green was known for its poverty, gang violence, and drug dealing. When William and Arthur were growing up, the residents of Cabrini-Green lived in constant fear. Parents feared for the safety of their children when they went to school. Stray bullets from gang fights frequently killed innocent victims. The police were often called to Cabrini-Green for reported beatings, drug problems, and other violence and crime. These **circumstances** led William

Key Concepts

obstacle *n.* something that blocks a path; something that makes it difficult to reach a goal

circumstance *n.* condition, fact, or event that cannot be controlled

9

and Arthur to dream of the day they could get out.

William and Arthur got their golden opportunity when a basketball coach from St. Joseph High School noticed their talent. Coach Pingatore promised to help them get college scholarships if they trained and studied hard. He had helped National Basketball Association all-star Isiah Thomas in the same way. The boys began to work hard and train at St. Joseph's. They soon realized that great dreams require great sacrifices.

The story of William and Arthur's lives was first depicted in a documentary film. Later Ben Joravsky wrote the book version. The film was made by Frederick Marx, Peter Gilbert, and Steve James. It was first shown in 1994 at the Sundance Film Festival and soon became a huge hit. A documentary film tells a story based upon actual events. Critics praised the *Hoop Dreams* film for showing the struggles of inner-city life. It was a very intimate look at the **loyalty** that William and Arthur had to each other and to their dreams. The film made $8 million dollars in 1994. Few documentary films have been more successful at the box office.

Today, *Hoop Dreams* continues to inspire people. The film and the book have been successful in showing thousands of kids and adults that anything can happen if you work hard enough. This real-life story proves that **perseverance** can help anyone **achieve** his or her dreams.

Key Concepts

loyalty *n.* feeling of love and attachment

perseverance *n.* behavior that is repeated to reach a goal

achieve *v.* to carry out a plan with success

MAKING THE
HOOP DREAMS FILM

• • • • • • • • • • •

- The filmmakers spent five years filming William and Arthur. There were 250 hours of material that had to be edited down to less than three hours. The filmmakers spent two and a half years editing the movie!

- It was difficult getting money to make *Hoop Dreams*. Most organizations that fund the making of movies do not take sports seriously. So, it was hard to raise money for a movie about two inner-city boys and sports, but eventually they were able to raise enough money.

- Some people would think that living with a camera crew for five years would change them or cause problems. The filmmakers said that William and Arthur got used to the cameras after the first year. They lived their lives as if a movie were not being filmed.

FOREWORD BY
CHARLES BARKLEY
• • • • • • • • • • • •

I know you won't believe me when I say this, but I wish kids, especially black kids, didn't dream so much about playing in the NBA.

It must sound funny coming from me, since I lived that dream. NBA. Those three letters spell hope, escape, and promise to thousands and thousands of kids across America. And in many ways the NBA is a magical place. Just look around the next time you catch a game. The music, the laser show, the pretty people in their courtside seats. The buzz as multi-million-dollar stars go one-on-one. The roar as the home team rallies to steal a last-second win.

The NBA is dynamic and exciting. But that glamorized view is also incomplete. What you don't see is just as important as what you do. For every David Robinson, Shaquille O'Neal, Hakeem Olajuwon and Patrick Ewing, there are countless names who will never make it. It's not so bad that these kids tried, there's nothing wrong with chasing your dreams. But it's sad when anyone allows themselves to be deluded by glitter and gold. There are so many guys I know who had the intelligence to do almost anything, but all they thought about was basketball. And then when basketball didn't work out, they had nothing to turn to.

Many of the people you will read about in *Hoop Dreams* played the game and had the dream. Most of them had to give it up when their careers were cut short by injury or bad breaks. The thing is—no one's career lasts forever, not even Michael Jordan, and he was the best. At the end of the day, when the game is over, you go home to your friends and your family and your community. The next generation of fans will have other heroes to follow. You'll be lucky if they remember your name.

What's so uplifting about the story of the Gates and Agee families is that almost all the characters, despite their disappointments and setbacks, never lose track of what really matters in life. It doesn't matter how many points you score, or rebounds you grab, or games you win. In the end what will matter is the kind of father, son, brother, husband, and neighbor you are, the closeness with the friends you made, the people you can honestly say you cared for, and who cared for you. That is something the Agees and Gates understand, and if anything makes them special, it's that.

Charles Barkley
February 1995

FRESHMAN YEAR
1987

"If you don't get the grades, you're not going to play. If you work hard at the grades and if you work hard at basketball, then I would be able to help you as far as going to college. . . . I'm makin' a commitment to you if you make a commitment to being a part of this kind of program."

—Coach Pingatore, to Arthur Agee

ARTHUR

· · · · · · · · · · ·

Big Earl Smith, the **super scout of** the playground basketball courts, had been watching Arthur Agee for a day, maybe two, before he made his move and asked Arthur if he would take him home to meet his parents.

It was mid-July 1987, and Arthur was all of fourteen years old, 5'6" and 125 pounds. Big Earl tracked him down at the Delano school's **scruffy**, two-court playground over on Wilcox near the Expressway on Chicago's West Side. The air was filled with the **buzz of cars whirring** past the West Side toward the suburbs; mothers calling their children; and a half-dozen young kids, **all elbows and bones** and dressed in cut-offs and sweaty tanktops, shouting and playing between banged-up cars, in the streets and all around the tenements. Hovering high to the east were the skyscrapers of the business district, walls of steel and glass. Some of the players on the Delano courts could live and die in Chicago and never see the other side of that wall. But they had been playing basketball practically noon till night almost from the day they were born.

Recently Big Earl had been having doubts about scouting playground talent. He was starting to think these boys should search out other dreams. But he was in no mood to challenge the status quo, at least not today. It was dreadfully hot. And he still had some faith in the dream, and he still had dreams of his own.

Arthur was playing against guys two or three years older, and at least six inches taller. They called him "runt." In defiance, Arthur

---

super scout of person who looked for talented players at
scruffy old; worn down
buzz of cars whirring sound of cars speeding
all elbows and bones who were small and skinny

dribbled the ball from one end of the court to the other—coast to coast, as they say—through his legs, around his back, and straight up the middle. He didn't **dunk**—he was too short for that—but he charged strong, drawing cheers from the kids on the edge of the court waiting for their chance to play.

Big Earl liked to be pragmatic, and **had a built-in immunity against inflating talent**. He could see right away, though, that Arthur Agee was special. He had speed and he could jump, but it was a combination of talents and traits that caught Earl's trained eye. Arthur had long, sinewy arms that swept along the ground and spidery fingers that iron-gripped the ball. He probably had another six or so inches to grow. He was quick with the first step and watched the court as he ran. He **had a head**, too—he knew when to pass and when to drive, and he controlled the flow of the game. He had this little spin move, not unlike Isiah Thomas's, and he could bring the ball behind his back or between his legs. When he got hot the shot fell, and he wouldn't miss. He wasn't afraid to shoot, even with the older, taller guys in his face.

This kid was born to play the point, born to run the show, and true point guards are hard to find. You can't hide talent like this, Big Earl thought. *He's going to be discovered sooner or later. Might as well be by me.*

"Hey, son," Big Earl called out to Arthur. "Come over here for a minute."

Arthur strolled over, sweat dripping from his brow. He had, in fact, been watching Big Earl while Big Earl had been watching him. He figured that Big Earl had to be a scout, why else would he come

....

dunk jump up and put the ball through the basket
had a built-in immunity against inflating talent did not
allow players to think they are better than they are
had a head was smart

18

to the West Side on a hot, sticky day to watch a bunch of kids scramble after a ball.

They stood face to face by the fence. Big Earl, well over six feet tall and closing in on three hundred pounds, towered over Arthur. He extended his hand, swallowing Arthur's in a grip. In his **meandering, amiable** way, he introduced himself. "I'm Earl Smith, and I do some high school scouting," he said as he handed Arthur his business card. Arthur slipped the card into his pocket with barely a glance. It was the first business card Arthur had ever seen.

"What's your name, son?" Big Earl asked.

"Arthur Agee."

Big Earl drew a handkerchief from his pocket to wipe his forehead.

"Uh-huh. And what high school are you planning to attend?"

Arthur shrugged. He hadn't **given it much thought**. The closest school was Marshall over on West Adams, where the neighborhood kids went. "Marshall," he said.

"What about St. Joe's?"

Arthur gave him a blank look. St. Joe's meant nothing to him.

"That's where Isiah went," Big Earl said.

That made **Arthur's face brighten**.

"I can arrange a visit, if you're interested. I scout for St. Joe. I know the coach, Gene Pingatore. He coached Isiah, and there isn't a finer high school coach in the suburbs or city."

Arthur had long ago learned from his father that the first rule in negotiations—and that's what this was—was never to show **your hand**. But when Big Earl mentioned Isiah's name all rules were forgotten. Isiah Thomas was Arthur's idol: a six-foot tall point guard,

---

meandering, amiable slow and friendly
given it much thought thought about it very much
Arthur's face brighten Arthur smile
your hand the other person what you are thinking about

another West Side kid who **against all odds climbed his way out of poverty and into** the NBA. Arthur had Isiah's picture on his wall. He had even adopted Isiah's old playground nickname, Tuss, as his own.

"Yeah," said Arthur a little too eagerly. "I'm interested."

Big Earl smiled and wiped his brow again. "I tell you what, Arthur. Let's not get ahead of ourself. This is a very important decision in your life. I should meet your momma . . . does your daddy live at home?"

Arthur nodded.

"Then I should meet him, too. And let's take it from there."

They shook hands again and then Arthur took off. He was too excited to play any more basketball that day. He **darted** home to tell his parents, taking a shortcut through a vacant, weed-filled lot to their six-room apartment on the top floor of a two-story walk-up near Madison and Pulaski. His mother, Sheila, was ironing in the living room and listening to the Temptations on the radio when he flew through the door.

"Momma, Momma, this big fat **dude over** the playground wants me to play basketball where Isiah played," the words came pouring out.

"Slow down, slow down," Sheila said.

Bit by bit the story came out.

Sheila gasped when Arthur had finished. "I can't believe it!"

"It's true, Momma."

Sheila appeared worried. She didn't trust bursts of good luck. It had been a miserable summer, hotter than usual. She, her husband, Bo, and the kids had recently moved from the North Side, and she

....

against all odds climbed his way out of poverty and into got out of poverty and became successful in

darted quickly ran

dude over man at

wasn't settled yet. She missed her friends and she didn't like the new neighborhood. There were too many **gangbangers openly dealing** their drugs. She had left her last job, and Bo couldn't hold on to any work. She was thirty-three years old with three children, and she **was broke**.

Sheila gave her son a questioning look. "You mean to tell me out of all those boys, he picked you?"

"He did, Momma. It's true. Look, he gave me his card."

Arthur showed Sheila Big Earl's card, now sweat stained and crumpled along the edges. Sheila ran her fingers over the card's embossed black lettering. It felt real, but surfaces were deceiving. She had known so many **con men** and had seen so many scams. Her life had been filled with so many disappointments, and she wondered whether anything good would ever happen to her again. Still, maybe this card and its owner, the big man who so excited her son, were signs of good things to come. She decided to have hope.

"Lord, Lord, I've been looking for a break," she said quietly as she gave Arthur a hug. "I'm so proud of you, son."

Big Earl came by the next day. Sheila had put on a flowered white dress; Bo was dressed in a rumpled white shirt, torn jeans, and worn-out sneakers. It was noon and he was just out of bed. His hair hung in greasy curly waves, and his face was stubbled with several days of growth.

The three **exchanged pleasantries**, quickly moving past the awkward introduction largely because Big Earl, also an insurance salesman, rarely had a hard time finding something to say.

....

gangbangers openly dealing people in gangs selling
was broke had no money
con men men who lied to get other people's money
exchanged pleasantries greeted one another

"I played basketball myself," Bo said.

"I'm not surprised," said Big Earl. "I could see by just looking at you that you were an athlete."

"I played back in Birmingham, Alabama—my hometown."

"You kidding, that's where you from?"

"Uh-huh."

"I was just down there myself on business. You go by there much?"

Bo and Sheila looked at each other. "I be by there some," Bo said cautiously.

"I played basketball, too," said Big Earl. "Back at Hyde Park High School on the South Side, though you wouldn't know from **this stomach I'm carrying**. But, listen, I've come here to talk about your son."

The Agees sat in the living room, eager to hear what Big Earl had to say, knowing full well that they had something he wanted, and he had something they needed. Big Earl stood against the window, his huge body blocking the sun, and **launched into** what he called his preamble. "I'm sure you're wondering why I'm here," he said. "Everybody wonders that. I don't do it for the money; they don't pay me a thing. I don't get the recognition or the fame. I do it because it's the right thing to do, helping black kids get a good education."

Big Earl began to pace the room. "I've scouted playgrounds for a long time. I've seen every great player to come out of the city in the last twenty years. And I saw your son do some truly impressive things out on that court."

While he was talking, Big Earl was also watching, because that's what scouts do, looking for **telltale** signs of trouble. Did the Agees

....

this stomach I'm carrying the way I look

launched into began

telltale clear, obvious

22

seem on the brink of poverty? Would they **be able to keep up with** tuition payments? Were there blaring radios or yelling kids shattering the peace and quiet Arthur would need to do his homework? Was there evidence of drugs, or kids in gang colors, or any signs of lawlessness or family disorder?

No, there didn't seem to be anything ominous in sight. The house was neat. Arthur's younger brother and older sister, Sweetie and Tomekia, wandered in quietly. No radio blared. The walls were lined with grammar school graduation photos of the children.

"You want some coffee?" asked Bo.

"No, don't bother," said Big Earl.

He paused, as if what came next would be difficult to say. And then he just **plowed straight ahead**. "Family background is important," he told them. "I don't want to bring trouble into a school."

"I understand that," said Bo.

Big Earl could see there would be no trouble with Arthur. He could see he came from a good family, that he'd been raised right, that one day he would develop into a fine, young man. Big Earl told Bo and Sheila that Arthur would succeed at basketball no matter where he went to school, even if he went to Marshall. Not that he **had anything against** Marshall. Luther Bedford coached Marshall, and Coach Bedford was his friend. And even if he wasn't his friend, he'd have to admit that Coach Bedford was one of the finest high school basketball coaches in the city, maybe even the state. It's just that Marshall was an inner-city school with nasty inner-city problems like gangs and drugs, and, well, the Agees understood. "I never lie to people," said Big Earl. "I never **talk down** a school. My role is to

---

be able to keep up with have enough money for the
plowed straight ahead said what he was thinking
had anything against did not like
talk down say anything bad about

expose you to what you can have for him. Your role is to make the decision as to what you want."

"Oh, yeah," said Bo. "I appreciate that. We got nothing against the public school. Tomekia is a senior at a fine public school."

Big Earl **cut to the point**. He was recommending two high schools: Collins and St. Joseph. They were both outstanding. The principal at Collins, which was a public school not far from their home, was a good friend of his. "It's a great school, but the outside area is kind of rough."

St. Joseph, on the other hand, was in one of those high-income, all-white western suburbs, and though anything can happen anywhere, and there are no guarantees, obviously there would be fewer problems with gangs and drugs. In fact, his own son attended St. Joseph.

"St. Joseph will be a challenge," he continued. "It's tougher academically than any West Side school. Arthur would be a black boy in a mostly white environment. There would be no girls. It would be hard to survive, let alone prosper. But other West Side boys have done it," and he **rattled off** their names: "Carl Hayes, Tony Freeman, Deryl Cunningham, and, of course, Isiah—and Arthur could do it, too."

The more he talked, the straighter Bo and Sheila sat, **radiating** pride. Of course they were flattered. Anyone would be. Big Earl was telling them that of all the boys he had seen on all the courts of this great city—and he had been everywhere: North, South, and West— only one boy, their son, had the talent, toughness, and **tenacity** to qualify for greatness.

Big Earl went on and on about the hardships Arthur would

....

cut to the point spoke directly; didn't waste time
rattled off listed; quickly said
radiating filled with
tenacity persistence

endure at St. Joseph. **"It's a long commute** every morning."

"Hear that, son?" said Bo.

"He'll have to get up early every morning."

"We don't mind that," said Bo.

"They make you work hard. There are no easy grades. It's not easy. But life's not easy."

"That's right," said Bo.

"If you **pay your dues**, there's something at the end of the rainbow. If your child works hard, there's a college scholarship at the end of the rainbow." Big Earl stopped talking and let the image of the rainbow linger.

"It's really up to Arthur," said Sheila. "I won't force him."

"To go to a university today . . . it's an easy $40,000," Big Earl said.

"And the tuition for St. Joseph?" asked Bo.

"About $2,000. You don't have to pay all of it, though. The more need you show, the more money you get. But you gotta pay something to go to Catholic school."

"Not that we're looking for money," said Bo.

"I know that."

"But we don't have a phone. Though it's coming."

"Don't worry about that."

By now it was clear they had forgotten all about Marshall or Collins, and that all their focus was on St. Joseph. Bo turned to Arthur and, as if to demonstrate his stern parenting style for Big Earl, recited all the rules he'd been preaching to his children since they were born.

....

It's a long commute It takes a long time to travel to St. Joseph

pay your dues work hard

"Hear that, son, you're gonna have to work hard."

Arthur said nothing.

"And don't touch nothin' if it don't belong to you."

Arthur **flashed** his father a cold stare.

Bo was on a run. "What I'm saying, son," he continued, "is . . . opportunity's **at hand**. You have to take advantage of it."

"You have to stay in the house more than the average kid," added Sheila. "No playing around after school. You'll have to come straight home. Just homework and studies."

Big Earl made an offer. He lived, he said, in a suburb not far from Westchester, the town that was home to St. Joe. Arthur would always be welcome to stay there with him and his wife on those cold, snowy nights when he was too tired to make the long trip home, just like Carl Hayes, the starting center, does. "I never forget a boy I bring to St. Joseph."

Now it was Arthur's turn, and Big Earl asked if he had anything to say. Arthur opened his mouth, but the words **stuck in his throat**, and the best he could offer was something that sounded like a gurgle, which made the others laugh. Clearly, this was a dazzling moment. He was mesmerized by this big man and the opportunities he offered. His head was flying miles away, new horizons rapidly approaching. This huge mysterious stranger had showed up out of nowhere, and now it was as though his front door opened on to a freshly paved road to fame and fortune.

Big Earl stood to leave.

"You can come back anytime," Sheila said. "I apologize for not being more hospitable. Next time I'll **fix** you something to eat."

....

flashed gave
at hand near, close
stuck in his throat would not come out of his mouth
fix make, prepare

Big Earl patted his stomach. "I'd like that."

"I'll fix you some corn bread," Sheila said.

"Corn bread?" said Big Earl.

"I make it from scratch."

Big Earl laughed. "If you can make scratch corn bread, for sure I'm coming back."

He was halfway out the door, when Tomekia, who had been watching and listening for almost ten minutes, spoke up. "Personally, I don't think there's nothin' that special about Catholic schools."

One or two seconds passed before Big Earl responded with a laugh, as if to say: Well, well, looks like big sister's got an opinion on everything. Bo also laughed and shook Big Earl's hand. They all knew that **the line had been cast, the bait had been grabbed, and the hook had held.**

Later that night, as Arthur sat in the bedroom he shared with Sweetie and the sounds of the street slipped through his open window, he stared dreamily at Isiah's poster on the walls and calculated the cost of the cars and comforts he'd buy his father and mother once he **made his mark in the pros.**

A few days later Big Earl drove Arthur, Sheila, and Bo to St. Joseph for a summer basketball camp and a meeting with Coach Pingatore. They drove down Pulaski past boarded-up storefronts, the Korean-owned fruit and vegetable stores, and the currency exchange, whose operator sat behind bulletproof glass. They sped along the expressway past the outer ring of inner-city Chicago into all-white, suburban communities, gliding by strip malls, discount chains,

....

the line had been cast, the bait had been grabbed, and the hook had held Bo and Sheila were very interested in sending Arthur to St. Joseph

made his mark in the pros became successful playing professional basketball

convenience stores, and expansive gas stations.

"Your role today, Arthur, is to impress the coaches," said Big Earl as he drove. "Try not to be too fancy."

Arthur nodded, his eyes glued to the passing scenery.

"Take the open shot when you have it. Play good defense and make good passes. The rest of it just play natural. I'll come out to watch you when I can, but my time's limited because of my job," Big Earl explained.

Arthur looked surprised to hear that Big Earl couldn't come and go as he pleased. "I thought you were the president of that company?" he asked.

"What?" Big Earl exclaimed. "Where did you get that information?"

"I looked at the card."

"And did it say president?"

Arthur **sheepishly grinned**.

Big Earl shook his head. The boy must have figured that anyone with a business card must be important enough to run a company. The kid had a lot to learn. "Where did you get that idea from?" asked Big Earl, trying to sound very serious. "We better turn around now if you can't read a card."

They drove into Westchester, a middle-class suburb of split-level ranch homes that sold for around $200,000 and up. Arthur tried not to stare or gawk or reveal any of his uneasiness. It was a little scary for him. It was a new world, a white world. The silence **struck** him. There were no kids on the sidewalks, no cars, trucks, or buses rumbling down the streets. It was quiet.

....

sheepishly grinned smiled and was a little bit embarrassed
struck surprised

The school itself was unpretentious, a low-running brick building facing a grassy athletic field. Arthur had seen bigger, more impressive high schools back in Chicago. But this one seemed clean and well ordered. The grass was trimmed, the hallways free of dust or graffiti. The floor of the gym was so shiny it squeaked. Banners, red and white, hung on the wall, signifying champion teams from the past. This **was a basketball powerhouse,** the St. Joseph Chargers, winner of six consecutive conference titles. Out in the hallways were row after row of shiny trophy cases—and a special case for Isiah, with his poster and his **retired jersey** on display.

"Isiah's supposed to show up today," Big Earl said.

Arthur dismissed that idea with a grunt. *Isiah's got no reason to come here*, he thought.

Before attending the camp, the Agees had **their one-on-one** with Pingatore. He was sitting behind his desk in a big swivel chair when they entered his office. His wide bespectacled face was sallow, untouched by the sun during all those days spent indoors at the camp. He had a husky voice that droned as he spoke. He began matter of factly with a warning and ended with a promise: "If you don't get grades, you're not going to play. If you work hard at the grades and if you work hard at basketball, then I would be able to help you as far as going to college. I can't promise you where you're goin' to go and if you're goin' to be a star, but I can guarantee that I'll help you to get into the school that would be best for you. I'm makin' a commitment to you if you make a commitment to being a part of this kind of program."

Arthur nodded but he wasn't listening. He was daydreaming

....

was a basketball powerhouse school was known for their great basketball team

retired jersey old basketball uniform

their one-on-one a meeting

about his future, and wondering if Isiah was really going to come.

After meeting with Pingatore, Arthur went to the locker room. The sign above the entrance read, He Conquers Who Labors. He **slipped into his flowered Bermudas**, went to the court and scrimmaged with the campers, and then took a seat in the bleachers. There was only one kid he recognized among the two hundred or so in the stands: William Gates. The two used to live near each other on the North Side.

I wonder how he got here? Arthur thought. He waved at William, and William waved back. William seemed to have grown. He looked strong for a freshman, almost six feet with steely legs and broad shoulders.

Arthur turned his attention to the front of the gym and what he saw **made his jaw drop**. There, next to Pingatore, wearing a St. Joseph T-shirt and blue shorts, was Isiah Thomas. He was listening to something Pingatore was saying. Arthur couldn't talk; he couldn't listen; he couldn't keep his eyes on anyone or anything else. He was too far away to hear what Isiah was saying, but he **soaked up** Isiah's every move: Isiah laughed, bent down to pick up a basketball, nodded, bit his lips, nodded again, laughed. He moved with an effortless grace. Arthur knew almost every detail of Isiah's life, but he never dreamed he'd ever see him up close. **A rising buzz** began to fill the gym as word spread of Isiah's presence—hundreds of arms pointing all at once: Look, there he is!

"When he came to school he could shoot, but he couldn't dribble," said Pingatore by way of an introduction. By the time he left, Isiah Thomas was among the greatest dribblers in the history of

....

slipped into his flowered Bermudas put on his shorts
made his jaw drop surprised him
soaked up carefully watched
A rising buzz People's excited voices

the game. For the kids in the bleachers, it was their first lesson of the day: The key to success is to confront and conquer your weaknesses.

"In everybody's neighborhood there's a guy who can really play," Thomas told the campers. "He can **shoot the lights out**. Every time **down court**—*swish, swish, swish*. Then he goes to St. Joseph High School, and the guy **gets cut**. And you say, 'Tom was real good. Why did he get cut?' See, Tom didn't learn the fundamentals of team basketball, which is what you're learning to play."

Isiah surveyed the crowded bleachers and asked if anyone wanted to play one-on-one. From all the eager hands waving for attention, he picked Arthur's. Arthur walked to center court with the brightest, widest smile possible.

"Nice shorts," Isiah whispered.

"What?"

"I said, nice shorts."

Arthur looked down at his Bermudas and looked up just in time to see Isiah skip past **for a layup**. When Arthur got the ball, Isiah blocked his shot. Then he blocked his second shot, and his third, flashing Arthur a warm mischievous smile.

The next one-on-one with Isiah was with William Gates. Pingatore introduced them, and Isiah allowed William to sit by his side while he signed autographs.

"I hear Coach Pingatore speaks highly of you," Isiah told William.

William swallowed hard. "Yes, sir."

Isiah smiled. "You don't have to call me sir."

"Okay."

....

shoot the lights out make every basket

down court—*swish, swish, swish* he makes the basket

gets cut does not get on the team

for a layup to shoot the ball into the basket

"I got to tell you, there are great kids in gyms all over the country. Kids like you, just starting out. If you want to make it to the next level, you'll have to work hard and listen to your coach."

"I will."

"Everything you're gonna do, I had to do too—don't feel you're alone," Isiah said. "I came from a poor family. For a long time we didn't know if we would have food to eat. I had to travel a long way to get to St. Joseph. But that never bothered me. If you feel traveling far out here is hard, you ain't going to make it. If you know you can do it, it's going to be **a breeze**."

William didn't know what to say, so he said nothing. He was in a dream sitting so close to Isiah. He didn't dare say what Isiah probably already knew—that more than anything else he wanted to be like Isiah. As did Arthur. As did all the kids in the gym. Isiah's life was their dream. More than anything they wanted to play in the NBA.

It was a special moment for William. William had been leaning toward St. Joseph ever since one of Pingatore's assistants, Michael O'Brien, discovered him playing in an eighth-grade game. Under the bizarre and **byzantine** rules that govern Chicago's high school enrollment eligibility, Arthur and William could have attended virtually any high school they wanted, public or private. Any school would almost certainly have taken them, unable to resist such basketball brilliance. That moment with Isiah though **cemented William's** decision. He was going to St. Joseph.

Back on the bleachers, Arthur and William watched Pingatore on the court, but they were lost in their dreams of Isiah, and of greatness. They thought about their friends and classmates, brothers

....

a breeze very easy
byzantine confusing, complex
cemented William's helped William make his

and sisters, filing into their old, rundown schools, so **decrepit** and dark, back home in the inner city. They felt enormously grateful. They were the lucky ones with the **ticket in their hands**, their dreams within reach.

....

decrepit in need of repair
ticket in their hands chance to be successful

BEFORE YOU MOVE ON...

1. **Inference** Arthur gave himself the same nickname as Isiah Thomas. What does this tell you about Arthur?

2. **Conclusions** Coach Pingatore and Isiah Thomas kept saying that it is important to work hard and get good grades. Why?

LOOK AHEAD Read pages 34–51 to see how Arthur and William were treated at St. Joseph.

WILLIAM

The alarm rang at dawn as it did every school day. Even **from the fog of sleep** William managed to quickly roll over and swat the alarm clock to stop the ringing before it woke the baby in the crib at the foot of his bed. His two-year-old nephew, Cartel, slept so lightly that it seemed as if a dropped pin would wake him. Despite William's efforts Cartel began to cry, waking William's brother-in-law, Alvin Bibbs. William felt uncomfortable living with Peggy, his twenty-four-year-old sister, and her family, like an intruder disturbing the peace, an unwelcome guest. He was frustrated living away from home.

It was a burden for all of them. William couldn't complain, though, because as bad as it was for him, he knew it was worse for them. He did appreciate that they had welcomed him to their home, a bungalow on the city's West Side, but he wanted to stay with his mother in the apartment where he was born and raised. That was in the Cabrini-Green housing project, more than seven miles and at least another hour away. So everyone—meaning his mother, Emma, and his older brother, Curtis, whose opinion on all things related to basketball William valued most—agreed that this arrangement was best because it saved him at least two hours on his daily commute to St. Joe.

He slipped on his clothes in the dark, the standard St. Joseph attire—slacks, tie, shirt, sweater—and **crept out the door** without breakfast, not even a glass of juice. He never had time to eat in the morning. The first thing he saw as he stepped out the door was the

---

from the fog of sleep though he was still sleepy
crept out the door quietly left the house

rickety wood-frame flats and squat brick bungalows that made up his sister's working-class neighborhood. He walked east to the bus stop on Pulaski and waited on the corner next to a bent and mangled sign. The bus rolled in at 6:20. William climbed aboard, slipped his coins through the slot, grunted a hello to the driver, and headed to the back, passing the cleaning ladies with their work clothes packed in paper bags and a factory worker studying the racing sheet.

They all rode in silence, barely awake, to the Congress Expressway, already **a bumper-to-bumper mess**. There William changed to the commuter train that rumbled down the center of the expressway. The train left him off somewhere in suburban Maywood. He never knew exactly where because no matter how many times he made the trip, he still felt **disoriented** outside of Chicago. At the Maywood station he met Arthur Agee, and together they rode the Roosevelt bus deep into Westchester.

He loved that ride with Arthur. Arthur brought him to life. Arthur Agee was the funniest kid he knew—a wiry little guy **sizzling with** energy. The kind of kid who couldn't sit still. He jumped from one seat to the next, commenting on the passing scenery one minute, mimicking the cackle of the bus driver the next.

The time flew when he was with Arthur; it was the best part of the day. They bragged about girls, made fun of the coaches, and shook their heads in wonder over the brazen arrogance and ignorance of some of their white classmates.

"First thing they say when they meet me is, 'What sport **you out for?**'" said William. "Like no black boy ever come to St. Joe unless he's playin' sports."

....

a bumper-to-bumper mess filled with traffic
disoriented lost
sizzling with full of
you out for are you going to play

"I don't worry about them," said Arthur.

"Some of them don't even look at me," said William. "It's like I'm not there. They're waiting for basketball season to see if I'm good enough to talk to. Then it will be, 'Oh, hi, William, how are you today?'"

Invariably the talk led to basketball. Arthur had a **bold vision**. They would be backcourt mates, with Arthur **running the point**, on a state championship team—a triumph not even Isiah had achieved.

"Can't nobody stop us," said Arthur.

"Pingatore gonna invite us to his summer camp."

They **got a big kick out of** that, imagining Pingatore praising them as he had praised Isiah in his opening remarks to the crowd of starstruck campers.

The bus left them at Roosevelt and Orchard, still a half mile from the school. The sun was still low as they hiked through Oakridge Cemetery and across wide streets and fields. In the winter it would be like crossing Alaska, the snow would be so expansive and deep.

At the end of the cemetery, its entrance guarded by a tall, shining cross, stood St. Joseph High School. If all went well, if the trains and buses ran on time, William stashed his coat in his locker by eight, five minutes before the day's first class, and two and a half hours after his alarm clock rang.

His first class was religion. The students sat in perfectly arranged rows of chairs beneath a sign that read, If You Were Accused of Being a Christian, Would There Be Any Evidence to Prove It? The teacher roamed around the room choosing students to recite passages

....

bold vision plan
running the point leading his teammates
got a big kick out of really enjoyed

from the Bible. Each recital lasted for three or four **agonizing minutes as a self-conscious** teenager stumbled over the ancient prose. Most of the other students also fought to stay awake.

"What kind of story is this?" asked the teacher.

No one said a word.

"Is it a parable?"

Silence.

"William."

William cleared his throat. "Uh, yeah, it's a parable."

"That's right. And what is a parable?"

"Uh, it's a story."

"That's right. But it's a story that has a special message and meaning, and which we can apply to our everyday trials and tribulations."

William took it all down, writing his notes neatly in his notebook. It was a routine that developed his soul the way weight lifting built his body, he told himself. It was all part of the St. Joseph program—the St. Joseph system—which William was determined to master because he believed it was the key to his personal success.

By noon he'd been through two other classes, and it was time for lunch. He went to the cafeteria, where he sat with Arthur and fourteen other black freshmen and ate his first meal of the day, usually a hamburger, spaghetti, or meat loaf. Arthur was the star of the table, keeping his friends **roaring** with jokes, **anecdotes**, and impressions.

"Man, you wouldn't believe what happened in my religion class this mornin'," said Arthur.

"Aw, Arthur, don't start," said William.

....

agonizing minutes as a self-conscious long minutes as an embarrassed

roaring laughing

anecdotes stories

"This kid threw the teacher out the window."

The others hooted. "Aw, man, you're lyin'," said William.

Arthur **had a knack for weaving tall tales**.

"I ain't. He did, too. Listen here. The teacher had hit him in the head for talkin' in class. And he said, 'Man, I'm sick of this.' And he just threw him out of the window."

"Man, Arthur, I don't believe you."

"You don't? Well, screw you then."

Occasionally a white kid joined them, but only once in a while. Whites and blacks lived in peace at St. Joseph. Open displays of bigotry were not tolerated, but, as is the case with most schools, **the races rarely mixed**. They stuck to their own and asked no questions about it.

In the afternoon William went to Sister Marilyn's English class. She was his favorite teacher: a black woman, who stood straight and dignified, with big, piercing brown eyes that seemed to read William's inner thoughts. "Where's your homework?" she asked each day.

If he didn't have it he mumbled an excuse, but she knew better. "William, there are no easy routes."

"Yes, ma'am."

"You can't **coast** on the basketball court, can you?"

"No, ma'am."

"Do you coast there?"

"No."

"Well, you can't coast here either. I want to talk to you for a minute after class."

....

had a knack for weaving tall tales was great at telling unbelievable stories

the races rarely mixed students of different races did not interact

coast do well without working hard

They sat at the front of the classroom after the other kids had departed. Her voice was soft but stern, and her "esses" hissed with emphasis. William knew what was coming, they'd been here before: a bunch of wise, **bite-size aphorisms and mottos.**

"You have to keep your eyes and ears open to reach your potential, William," she said. "If you listen, you'll learn."

"Yes ma'am."

"You should be the best. You should tell yourself you can be the best."

"Yes, ma'am."

She sighed, unfolded her hands, rose, and walked to the blackboard. In neat, precise strokes she wrote the word "Best." She turned to William. You've got to be the *best* you can be. That's what the B and E in best stands for. You have to motivate yourself. Stay motivated and you'll **take off.**"

"But I'm not good at English," he protested.

"We are not learning English," she countered.

"What?"

"I said, I do not teach English, I teach the person. I am teaching you. And you can learn English. If you have the desire and motivation you can learn anything you want."

He had been placed in a class **of low achievers, filled with students** unprepared for a rigorous college-bound curriculum. And this class was still further divided by ability, so actually William began with the lowest of the low achievers. When he started high school he was reading on a fourth-grade level.

....

bite-size aphorisms and mottos short sayings that were supposed to teach William lessons

take off do well in school

of low achievers, filled with students with students who did not do well in school and who were

"You must be a pretty good basketball player to get in here with these grades," Sister Marilyn told him.

It wasn't the first time she had said that to him. She **sifted** through a pile of papers on her desk and found his most recent composition. "Why I love the game of basketball." She had him write a composition every day. "This is very good, William. A great improvement."

"Thank you."

"I believe in you," she told him.

"Yes, ma'am."

"The key is getting you to believe in yourself."

"Yes, ma'am."

"If you believe in yourself there's nothing you can't do."

St. Joseph allowed **needy students to work off** a portion of their yearly tuition, and William was assigned janitorial duties to offset his financial obligation. After school he mopped and scrubbed the hallways and cafeteria. The other kids scurried past him as he scrubbed. He thought they **sneered**. They whisked out of the school's doors without even one goodbye. He felt insignificant in this privileged environment and saw himself as they saw him, or how he imagined they saw him: a black boy from the ghetto mopping their floor.

He watched his white classmates congregate on the front lawn and wondered where they went, where they lived, and what life must be like for someone who didn't have to work after school or ride a train and two buses to and from school. He recognized their faces and knew their names, and they knew his. But they didn't really know

....

sifted looked

needy students to work off students without money to work in order to pay

sneered were making mean faces at him because he had to work

each other. They might as well have been going to different schools.

William's great release came at practice. He was the best of the underclassmen. He could jump higher and hang longer than any of the others. He had brilliant moves and **bullet bursts of speed**. He could drive the middle, **hit the three**, dribble through his legs, and dunk. At age fourteen, he could already dunk.

Pingatore and his assistants, John Hornacek, Dennis Doyle, and Michael O'Brien, stood on the sidelines **all but frothing at the mouth** as William froze his man with a fake, exploded down the middle, and rocked the rim with a dunk.

"Guys like Gates come around once in a lifetime," said Pingatore. "I always say there will never be another Isiah. And yet . . . I think I see it in Gates. You never know how they're going to continue to develop, but he seems to be special. He flows with a smoothness and confidence and strength that you don't see in every kid. I think that potentially he can be a great player."

The 1987 varsity team had several promising players: Carl Hayes, a 6'8" center, Deryl Cunningham, a 6'7" inside scorer, and Chuckie Murphy, a perky little point guard. But were they good enough to dominate Marist or Holy Cross, their leading competitors for the East Suburban Catholic Conference championship? Pingatore didn't know. Six consecutive conference titles were on the line. Adding William could put them over the top.

"I think I may bring him up to varsity," Pingatore confided. There had never been a four-year starter at St. Joseph, though, and it wasn't his style to force things. Push too fast and you **set a kid up for a fall**. Then again, allow them to linger too long without strong

....

bullet bursts of speed was very fast
hit the three make a long shot for 3 points
all but frothing at the mouth amazed
set a kid up for a fall could cause the player to fail one day

competition, and they grow lazy and complacent. "I could have brought up Isiah, but I didn't," he said. "He could have played. He would have helped our team. I just didn't do it."

After practice Pingatore called William over and patted him on the back.

"You're doin' a great job, William," he said.

"Yes, coach."

"But you ain't gettin' any better lookin'." William smiled and looked at the floor. He didn't know what to do with his hands so he put them behind his back. Pingatore playfully slapped his arm; William's smile remained frozen. He knew it was coming, that punch. Pingatore usually punched his players when he was happy. It was a playful punch—**a sign of affection for all** his players, black or white. The first time he did it, though, William was shocked; he had never been hit by a white man before.

On the train going home after practice, William told Arthur that Pingatore had punched him again. Arthur nodded. "Yeah, you must be doin' good, man, cause that's like his way of huggin'."

"But, man, did you see that ring on his finger?" said William. "That thing hurts, man."

"Hey, it's just one of them things white people do."

When William got back home, Peggy and Alvin had already finished dinner, so he ate what Peggy had left for him. He took out the garbage, cleaned his dishes, and sat at his desk and opened his math book. **The words blurred, his eyes flickered**—it was no use. He snapped the book shut. The day was long and he was tired; he was lucky if he lasted past 9:30. He missed his mother, and his

....

a sign of affection for all something Pingatore did to show he liked

The words blurred, his eyes flickered He could not see the words clearly, his eyes were tired and started to close

girlfriend, Catherine Mines, and his two best friends, Cleve Lester and Theo Johnson. He wondered what they were doing. Catherine was probably hanging at home, listening to music or reading. Cleve and Theo were probably playing ball at the local playground they called The Avenue.

He quietly went to the living room to call his mother.

She **shrieked** with happiness at the sound of his voice. "Baby, I miss you so much," she said. "Just come home."

"I wish I could, Momma, but I can't. I got to do this," whispered William.

He went back to his bedroom and got into bed feeling alone and depressed. He was too young to be so isolated, **living the life of a monk**. He ached with loneliness.

On weekends William returned home to Cabrini-Green. His mother cooked him his favorite meal of roast beef, mashed potatoes, and string beans; and he slept in his own bed, in his own room, where the walls were covered with posters of Michael Jordan. There was a time when Emma Gates's four boys and two girls were crammed into this bedroom; they had two sets of bunk beds and two cots. But now William's older brothers and sisters had families of their own. His room seemed large and empty. *All these years I wanted this room to myself,* he thought. *And now that I got it I can't even use it 'cause I don't even live here.*

It was funny the way William rushed back to Cabrini-Green. The projects were so dreary. Twenty-three **squalid high-rises**, nineteen stories tall, contained three thousand apartments piled one

....

shrieked screamed

living the life of a monk and doing nothing else besides working and sleeping

squalid high-rises dirty apartment buildings

on top of the other like boxes. The complex was surrounded by rows of drab brick townhouses. In all, Cabrini-Green covered nearly eight square blocks. It was a world of its own, set off from the rest of the city by a boundary of factories and rusty elevated train tracks, home to nearly ten thousand people, all of them poor. William's family lived in the townhouses, which were more pleasant than the high-rises, many of which were controlled by gangs. Their bullets could be heard ricocheting off the concrete walls and courtyards.

Real-estate developers dreamed of demolishing Cabrini. **It occupied a choice parcel of land** a few blocks from Lake Michigan, just east of the Gold Coast and three or four elevated stops from the Loop, the city's central business district. **Gentrification was overtaking** the North Side and hordes of young professionals living in the graystones, limestones, and brick bungalows could be seen each morning streaking past Cabrini in their sports cars on their way to their offices downtown. Sometimes they had to stop outside Cabrini's main gate, where they waited nervously for the light to change. William knew these rich folks in their sports cars feared Cabrini. He heard the clicking of their locks as they drove by, and he understood why. The gangs and the bullets frightened him, too, and he wished his family could get away. Yet, this was home, and he and his brothers were those young guys the rich folks saw on the street.

"If only they can get rid of Cabrini," he'd heard that before. *What they really mean is, If only they can get rid of me*, thought William. He sat upright in bed and looked to the east where the bright lights from the Gold Coast high-rises dazzled the night sky. Over the **el's** distant rumble he thought he heard the faint echoes of Rush Street. He and

....

It occupied a choice parcel of land It was on valuable land

Gentrification was overtaking People with money were moving to and changing the poor neighborhoods on

el's train's

his friends walked through Rush Street during the summers, wandering past night clubs and pickup bars blaring rock 'n roll, and sailors, tourists, and hookers. They could go to the beach only a few blocks away, or for one or two dollars they could see three or four kung fu epics at the downtown movie palaces, where their feet crunched on popcorn stuck to the floor and no one cared if they hooted and laughed real loud. He had memories here, and roots. He wanted to be loyal; he wanted to remain the same, but he knew he was changing. *One day I'm gonna be rich and famous*, he thought. *One day, I'm gonna play in the NBA. But no matter how rich or famous I get, this will always be my home.*

On Saturday, William and his brothers Curtis and David went to The Avenue, where they played one-on-one.

"**Come at** me," said Curtis. "Take it to me."

William drove to the basket, but Curtis cut him off and pushed him back.

"Come at me hard, boy. Don't come weak."

The court was stubbled with grass and bits of shattered glass. The rims tilted and the nets were ripped. Car horns honked and voices rang out from the other end of the court.

William **faked** left and swiveled right, darting down the baseline. He had Curtis beat, but his older brother grabbed him from behind and threw him out of bounds.

William sprang to his feet. His fists were **clenched**, his lips tight.

"Oh, you're a big boy now," Curtis sneered. "Ready to beat up your older brother."

....

Come at Run toward
faked pretended to move to the
clenched closed tightly

William **seethed and** raised his fists.

"You know what your problem is? You're lazy," Curtis said. "You don't want to work. I know what it means to work. That's why I gotta bang you and bruise you. The only thing you can't take is being hit. You're going to be hit. You're going to get banged. So you better get used to it."

There was an edge of **fury to Curtis's taunts** and David was concerned. He was the middle brother—two years younger than Curtis, four years older than William—and he frequently stepped between them.

"Cut it out, Curtis," David said. "Why you have to be so **hard on the guy**?"

"How else he gonna learn?"

"No one did that to you," David said.

Curtis glared at David; he was undermining his lesson. "They didn't have to, 'cause I had it in here," he said, jabbing at his heart.

Curtis picked up the loose basketball and handed it to William.

"Come on, man, come at me again."

William's leg ached from where he had hit the ground, and there were bits of gravel embedded in his knee. He wanted to pick away the gravel, to rub away the pain, but he didn't want to concede that Curtis could make him hurt. He dribbled the ball, releasing his anger with each bounce and keeping his eyes on Curtis.

"Now, you're thinkin'," Curtis said. "Ooh, my big brother's so mean. He pushed me down and it hurts. And you're wonderin', 'What's gonna happen if I go inside? Is my big brother gonna hit me again? Maybe I'll take a outside shot.' And with all that thinkin', you

....

seethed and angrily
fury to Curtis's taunts anger to the way Curtis was teasing
hard on the guy tough with William

ain't concentratin' on the game and that means I can steal the ball."

Curtis swiped the ball away from William. He **had at least fifty pounds on** William, a mix of muscle and flab, yet he was agile for his girth. He **tracked down the loose ball and rammed it home** with a dunk.

On the way back to their mother's house, Curtis kept lecturing William on what he had done wrong.

"You're not in my face. You're not playing defense. You scared to get hit. Can't be scared."

"Curtis, **let up**," said David.

Curtis ignored the interruption. "A good man will see that and take advantage of you," he continued, "Hell, I could see it in your eyes."

They passed two hooded gangbangers. They nodded at Curtis and Curtis nodded back. The gangs never hassled William because he was Curtis's baby brother, and Curtis was a local legend—the finest basketball player to emerge from Cabrini's courts.

They stopped at the corner to let a truck pass. William kicked a soda can. He decided many years ago that getting abused by Curtis was part of what it took to be great. There was a lot he could learn about basketball, and life, from his older, wiser brother. As good as William was, and he knew he was very good, Curtis was the best.

"Who was the greatest basketball player you ever saw?" Curtis asked him. He knew the answer because he had asked the same question many times before.

"You were."

"Who could have gone to any college in the country?"

....

had at least fifty pounds on weighed fifty pounds more than

tracked down the loose ball and rammed it home grabbed the loose ball and shot it through the net

let up stop yelling at William

"You, Curtis."

"If I went to a high school like St. Joseph there's no tellin' where I'd be right now," he told William. "If I had that kind of exposure, that kind of coaching, that kind of competition, I coulda been Michael Jordan."

They crossed the street and stood outside their mother's townhouse. Curtis dribbled the ball.

"I'm tellin' you, I ain't goin' to no more of your games."

William looked **pained**. "Why, man?"

"'Cause I ain't wastin' my time watchin' **biddy ball**. Call me back when you make the varsity."

William looked down at the ground. For a moment, Curtis felt sorry for him, then the moment passed. "You better not **screw up**."

"I'm not, Curtis."

"Are you studying?"

"Yeah."

"Boy, you better study harder than that."

In late November, right after Thanksgiving, Pingatore told William he wanted to give him a ride home. It was unseasonably cold, actually frigid, and the windows were caked with ice. They rode in silence for several minutes before Pingatore **played his hand** without warning.

"Did anybody tell you about the varsity?" Coach Pingatore asked.

"No, sir."

"Well, I think you're ready."

"Yes, sir."

"Do you think you're ready?"

....

pained hurt, saddened
biddy ball boys without experience play basketball
screw up make a mistake
played his hand started to lecture William

"Well, yeah. I guess."

"I believe in you, William. I know you have the capacity to be great. I know this will be hard work. But I think you're ready for this challenge."

William stammered and stuttered, unsure of what to say and unsure of what he thought. He wasn't prepared for this promotion, didn't even know it had been on Pingatore's mind. He didn't know if he wanted to be promoted. The varsity ran according to Coach Pingatore's precise and rigid system, which he was only starting to understand. They took you in slow at St. Joseph. You learned one **play** and then went on to the next. William liked it that way. He needed time to prepare. The demands were great on varsity. Pingatore expected his players to run the plays when he called them. You couldn't stop the play and say, "Sorry coach, but I wasn't listening," or, "I didn't learn that play yet." Pingatore had no patience for such foolishness. For a few days William was too nervous to tell his family of the news. He was afraid they would come to the games and witness his humiliation. Finally he **worked up the nerve** to call Curtis.

"I made the varsity, Curtis," William said.

"You didn't."

"Yeah, man, I did."

"Are you **startin**'?"

"I don't know."

"Well, you better find out 'cause I ain't goin' out there unless you're startin'. I'm not goin' out there to see the team. I'm goin' out there to see you."

William's first game as a varsity player was on a Friday night

....

play strategy for playing the game
worked up the nerve felt brave enough
startin' in the group that plays first in the game

against Holy Cross. William wanted jersey number 22 (as close as he dared to Michael Jordan's 23), but some other player already claimed it. So he settled for 13. His hands trembled as he dressed in the locker room; he could barely tie his shoes. The St. Joseph Chargers ran on the court. They circled the gym. The band played the theme from *Rocky*. But none of it registered. William was in a daze and **butterflies fluttered hard in his belly**.

His eyes raced round the gym looking for familiar faces. Up in the stands he saw his brothers Curtis and David, Peggy, Alvin, Emma, and his girlfriend, Catherine. He smiled at Catherine and she waved back.

"Hey, boy. Boy." It was Arthur, yelling from behind the bench. William walked over and they embraced. "You nervous?" Arthur asked.

"Yeah."

"Man, don't worry about these clowns—none of them can play."

William's first score came on a layup, an easy breakaway basket. **His first jumper came off a screen on** a play called by Coach Pingatore. It felt good when it rolled in. He was playing off guard so he didn't have to call the plays. He just stayed out of the point guard's way, set screens, took the open jumpers, and **played his man tight**. After awhile it flowed smooth, no different than playing back home at The Avenue.

Curtis sat up in the stands, high above the court, never cheering, sometimes frowning. Memories of his own basketball career clashed with his hopes for William. Five years ago he had been an all-star

....

butterflies fluttered hard in his belly felt very nervous

His first jumper came off a screen on William's first successful jump shot was because of

played his man tight closely guarded his opponent

guard at Wells High School, scoring forty, even fifty points a game, with dreams of his own. Now he was living his dreams through William.

As he watched the game, **voices** filled his head with conflicts and contradictions. *Am I happy or disappointed? I'm happy my playing days are over. I wish they were still here. I should have done things differently. I did the best that I could. I was better than any of these **flunkies***. *I hope to hell it doesn't end for William like it did for me.*

....

voices thoughts
flunkies fools

BEFORE YOU MOVE ON...

1. **Conclusions** How do you know that Arthur and William were not fully accepted at St. Joseph's in the beginning?

2. **Cause and Effect** Reread pages 43–44. William grew up in a dangerous neighborhood in Chicago. How did this affect him?

LOOK AHEAD Read pages 52–79 to find out the real reason Arthur became the class clown.

ARTHUR

When the weather was right, Arthur rode his bike to school. It was a dangerous journey through ten miles of treacherous traffic. He pedaled with a book-filled knapsack on his back along Roosevelt Road, pumping hard to make the lights, crossing complicated intersections, dodging buses, cars, and trucks.

Sheila gave him bus tokens, but if he rode his bike he could sell those tokens to other kids and **pocket** the change for lunch. In that way, his family noted, he was his daddy's son, never without a trick or a scheme, always a boy with larger ambitions.

One morning when he got to school, he marched into the hallway and up to six white freshmen standing outside the main office.

"Hey, what's happening?" he said.

Their faces lit up when they saw him. Arthur was one of the school's most popular kids, with a growing reputation as a class clown who was always getting marched down to the principal's office for this or that offense. Just the other day he had ignited a stink bomb in the lunchroom.

He **exchanged high fives with** the boys. The happiest to see him was a pudgy, pimple-faced kid called Bull. "Hey, man," said Bull, "tell these guys what you did in religion class yesterday."

"Wha'd I do?" said Arthur.

"You know, with Dick."

"Oh, that."

The boys gathered in a tighter circle with expectant smiles on

---

pocket keep
Their faces lit up They smiled
exchanged high fives with greeted

their faces because they knew it had to be good. Arthur was always poking fun at the religion teacher, poor guy. He was a short, chubby, bald man with **rancid** breath and tangled tufts of black hair on his neck. Arthur called him Mr. Alfalfa, and used him **as his straight man**.

"Well, ol' Mr. Alfalfa was standin' up there talkin' about some dude name Richard," Arthur began.

"Who?" asked one of the kids.

Arthur frowned. "I don't know, man. Forget that, it ain't important. Some guy in the Bible or somethin'. Anyway, I raise my hand and go, . . ." Arthur started talking with a **bit of an effeminate lisp** and an English accent, the way Eddie Murphy imitates a white boy, "'I was wondering, did you say the man's name was Richard?'"

"And Alfalfa goes, 'yes.'"

"'Well, did people ever call him Dick?'"

"'No, Arthur.'"

"'Well, does Richard have a dick?'"

All six of the boys roared with laughter, like it was the funniest joke they had ever heard, Bull howling loudest.

"Man, Tuss, you crazy," said Bull.

"Boy, that wasn't nothin'," said Arthur. "But, listen here, man, come on, man, lend me some money."

Bull looked at his friends. They shrugged. So he reached into his pocket and pulled out several bills.

"I'll lend you five bucks."

"I'll pay you back."

Of course, Bull knew he never would because he never did, even

---

rancid horrible

as his straight man to make jokes

bit of an effeminate lisp voice that sounded like a woman

though he borrowed money nearly every day.

"Just make sure you come to religion class today," said Bull. "We need you, man, to get through that stuff."

William, who watched the exchange, was amazed. "How can you do that?" he asked Arthur as they hustled to their lockers.

"They got it, don't they? You see **that big fat wad of dough** he's got? Ain't none of them carryin' less than seventy-five dollars in their pocket. They can't spend it all if they tried. Folks rich like that ain't gonna miss five dollars they give to me. You can't let them think you're scared. You gotta walk in here like you own this place."

In homeroom, Arthur's teacher announced that each student would have to sell ten St. Joseph calendars at twenty dollars apiece to raise money for the school. Arthur **eyed** the calendars featuring out-of-focus snapshots of school scenes and shook his head in disbelief. *Where in hell am I gonna find someone dumb enough to buy this?* he thought. His hand went up.

"Yes, Arthur."

"You mean to tell me, I gotta sell these calendars?"

"That's right, Arthur."

"Man, you could go to Joe's Fish Market in the city and get a better calendar than this for free."

"Well, maybe you can go to a bank and sell them."

"A bank. A *bank!* Man, what bank gonna buy this calendar from a black boy?" He rolled his eyes and shook his head as if to say, How can any teacher be so stupid. His classmates **busted up and Arthur bathed in** the satisfying waves of their laughter.

....

that big fat wad of dough how much money

eyed looked at

busted up and Arthur bathed in laughed and Arthur enjoyed

In the hallway after class, the kids **fawned over him**. Some even dragged over a few upperclassmen and begged Arthur to repeat for them what he had said and exactly how he had said it, which Arthur did. Why not? These students were more naive and easier to please than the teachers. They knew nothing about the real world.

There was one white kid named Mark, though, who Arthur liked more than all the others. Mark had gotten in trouble with school officials back in his hometown in California. His parents had **packed him off** to live with an uncle in Bellwood who believed a little St. Joseph–style discipline would knock some sense into him. But you couldn't bulldoze sense into Mark. He was as rebellious as Arthur. He didn't fit into any group or clique. Sometimes he invited Arthur to his uncle's house. Mark was the only white kid who ever invited Arthur home. They'd raid his uncle's well-stocked kitchen, eating salami, ham, cheese, cookies, cake, and Cokes.

In return Mark got to sit with the black freshmen in the cafeteria, the only white boy in their **ranks**. He heard them talk the way black boys talk to each other—nigger this and nigger that—and he made the big mistake of joining in.

"What's up, nigger?" he said to a barrel-chested football player.

All tabletop conversation stopped. The football player glared at Mark and said, "Better **chill out**, white boy."

Then he turned to Arthur. "Hey, man, get your white friend out of here."

"Aw, man he didn't mean nothin'," Arthur said.

"Hey, man, wha'd I do?" asked Mark.

"You can't call him nigger," said Arthur.

....

fawned over him gave him a lot of attention
packed him off sent him away
ranks group
chill out be careful; watch what you say

"But *you* did."

"But you ain't black."

Mark still didn't get it, and even Arthur had to admit none of it really made sense. If blacks could call blacks niggers, why couldn't whites do the same thing? Arthur knew all about racism. But Mark wasn't a racist, he was cool. He just wanted to be one of the guys. Arthur knew it hurt Mark when the black kids ostracized him—no one wants to be a racial outcast. Arthur felt for Mark; he figured Mark tried too hard to fit in with the black guys because he couldn't fit in with anyone else. And he understood what it meant to feel lost and alienated and dreadfully out of place. Arthur sometimes felt that way, though he admitted it to no one.

Mark was a **straight-up** guy. You could trust him; he wouldn't **rat**. They were accomplices in so many pranks. Mark was with him the day he set off the stink bomb. Another time they left a slimy black glob, the remains of a piece of chewing gum, on a lunchroom tray. Then they watched the other students wretch at its sight.

Then one day Mark was suddenly gone from St. Joseph. Arthur was profoundly disappointed when he heard that Mark had returned to California.

After school, Arthur joined William on the mop brigade. William scrubbed hard, convinced that his future **lay in the balance**, but Arthur barely tickled the floor with his mop.

Then he stopped pretending to work when a devilish idea came to him.

"Hey, William, wanna see me do Eddie Murphy?"

....

straight-up good

rat tell the teachers if you did a bad thing

lay in the balance depended on it

William pursed his lips. Of course he wanted to see it. Arthur **had an absorbing ear and an artful tongue.** He was **a wicked mimic.**

But William shook his head. "No, man. We gotta finish this floor."

Arthur scoffed. "Come on. How about Pingatore?"

That was irresistible. William loved it when Arthur did the coach.

"Come on, look, man." And Arthur spread his legs, stuck out his stomach, and squinted his eyes. William started laughing at the sight.

"Hey, William," Arthur bellowed, adopting a growling, raspy voice a little like Marlon Brando's in *The Godfather*. "I went and saw room 234. And it didn't look good, buddy. The floor, you can do a better cleaning job than that."

"Man, you gotta cut that stuff before Pingatore hears you."

"Hey, man, check this out. Is this Ping or what?" And Arthur stuck his belly out even farther and began **waddling about.** "Hey, William, I told you to clean that floor."

Arthur walked up to William and slugged him in the arm. "Huh, buddy, huh?"

All of a sudden from around the corner strode the coach. Pingatore called out a greeting.

Arthur and William almost fell over each other grabbing for their mops to hustle back to the floor.

"Watch it, man," Arthur whispered to William. "He gonna punch yo' ass."

"How ya' doin', coach?" called out Arthur.

"Workin' hard?" said Pingatore.

"Sure am, coach," said Arthur.

....

had an absorbing ear and an artful tongue was a good listener and talker

a wicked mimic very good at imitating other people

waddling about walking around, his body moving from side to side

"Yes, coach," said William.

"**Atta boy**," Pingatore said as he slapped William on the back.

William tried to grin.

Pingatore walked a little closer and stopped to watch them scrub. "You know, Agee, you don't seem to be gettin' any better lookin'."

"Aw, coach," said Arthur.

Pingatore looked him over. "Are you gettin' any taller?"

"I be tryin', coach," Arthur said.

Pingatore laughed. "Probably gonna be six foot two when it's all over." As he walked away, Arthur followed several feet behind, imitating the **coach's swagger**.

William laughed so hard he dropped his mop.

"Do I got him?" Arthur asked.

"Yeah, man, you do."

"Well, all right. Now tell me this—who plays the point?"

"You do."

"And who plays two?"

"Me."

"And who's the best guards in the state?"

"We are."

"Well, all right then," Arthur said as they slapped hands. "And remember this—we're gonna win old Pingatore a championship. Even Isiah didn't do that."

At first Arthur envied William's promotion to varsity. He was happy for his friend, but he feared his own talents were wasted on freshman competition. He felt he didn't have to listen to John Hornacek, the

....

Atta boy That's the way to play, boy; Good job
coach's swagger way the coach walked

freshman team coach. He didn't think Hornacek had anything new to teach him. Arthur stared into the stands during some time-outs, barely **feigning interest**. "Agee," Hornacek barked, "get your head in the game."

The coaches didn't know what to make of Arthur. He **was raw and** undisciplined; he dribbled too much and forced too many shots. To Pingatore, the kid was intriguing. "Arthur has all the **intangibles** you can't teach a kid," Pingatore said. "At times he's almost poetry in motion; then all of a sudden he'll do something crazy."

It was difficult for Pingatore to predict how great Arthur would be; so much depended on his growth. Pingatore had several theories on growth projection. "You look at a player's legs, you look at his feet, you look at the size of his hands," Pingatore said. "You look at his parents, especially the mother. I have a theory that the mother's side of the family determines size. If you see a 6'9" father and 5'2" mother, chances are the kid's not going to be as big as the father. But if you see a 6'3" mother, there's a good chance the kid's going to be that big. If a kid's six feet as a freshman, muscular, with hairy legs and he has to shave, more than likely that kid's not going to grow anymore. On the other hand, if he's six-two, gangly, doesn't shave, baby faced, he's probably going to have some growth spurts left in him."

Well, Arthur was a gangly, baby-faced freshman. And above all, he was unafraid down the stretch. Against Weber, in the season's final freshman game with the score tied and a few seconds left, Hornacek called a time-out and told Arthur to pass the ball to the center. But the center was covered, so Arthur drove the lane and **banked in** the winning shot. Arthur thought he might be chastised

....

feigning interest pretending to be interested
was raw and had no experience and was
intangibles natural skills
banked in shot the ball to make

for not following the play. But the coaches congratulated him—even Pingatore, who had been watching in the stands. That's when Arthur decided he knew the secret to success at St. Joseph: Win for the coaches and they'll let you get away with almost anything.

When he didn't have after-school practice, Arthur would rush home and bolt to the nearest park fieldhouse. Arthur thought the kids at school probably assumed he came from a TV-perfect family, with a Bill Cosby kind of dad. But Bo wasn't Doctor Huxtable, he **was a junkie**. If Arthur saw Bo on the street, they'd pass without a word, not even hello. Bo was so **strung out** he probably didn't even recognize his son. It made Arthur's eyes burn with shame, and he didn't want to acknowledge this man as his father.

Usually a dozen or so guys were hanging around the local court when he got there. They'd shoot for teams, losers sitting out. Arthur never lost. They played five-on-five full court. Often he was up against taller, stronger men. But they couldn't keep pace with Arthur. In the end their only weapon was to taunt Arthur.

"Hey, boy, I saw your daddy this mornin'."

Don't listen, Arthur told himself as he dribbled up the court.

"I sold him some **dope**."

Arthur moved toward the corner.

"Your daddy's a dope head."

Arthur slipped toward the key.

"Nigger, you can't hit that shot. I just sold your daddy some dope."

Arthur **drained a twenty-footer**.

He punished them for their talk, gaining vengeance the only way

....

was a junkie used illegal drugs

strung out sick from the drugs

dope drugs

drained a twenty-footer made a great shot from far away

he could—on the court and with the ball. He stayed at the park until long after dark. He hated going home.

One night when Arthur was nine or ten, the police came to his house. It was after midnight and they were banging at the door, rousing everyone from bed.

"Where is it?" the cops yelled.

"Get out of my house," screamed Sheila.

"Where's your man?"

"He ain't here."

"We know he's got it **stashed** here. Where is it?"

They overturned beds; they cleaned out the cabinets; they ripped through flower pots; they dropped dirt on the floor; they **tracked up** the kitchen, which Sheila scrubbed hard to keep spotlessly clean. Neighbors in their robes watched from the hallway. Arthur's little brother howled; his sister cried. In the midst of it all Bo walked in, cool and calm, as though nothing were happening. He was wearing a wide-brimmed hat, full-length rabbit-fur coat, polyester pants of flaming orange, and platform shoes.

"Officers, officers," Bo declared. "What's going on?"

The police threw Bo against the wall and **cuffed** his hands behind his back.

All they found were two pistols.

"Where's your license for these guns?"

"They ain't mine. They're my wife's."

"If you don't tell us where your drugs are, we're gonna throw her ass in jail."

Bo leaned over his left shoulder. "Look, man, I saw you guys up

....

stashed hidden

tracked up walked all over and messed up

cuffed put handcuffs on

here. If I wanted to I could of got away. I came here on my own. If I had any drugs would I just come walkin' in here? Would I?"

The police took Bo to jail and charged him with having unregistered firearms, but the case collapsed and the charges were dropped. A few days later Arthur saw his father sitting around the kitchen table with friends. They were drinking whiskey from a bottle, and the table was cluttered with stacks of **fives, tens, and twenties**.

"The cocaine was in the shower curtain rod," Bo told his buddies. "And some of it was in the butter case."

Everyone cackled.

"Those cops are so stupid," Bo continued, "they couldn't find a thing."

After awhile the police didn't come around looking for Bo anymore. His dealing days ended when he **got hooked on** his own drugs. He couldn't keep track of who he owed and who owed him. He failed even at dealing, and he did whatever it took to **feed his habit**, including stealing tools and tires and selling them at flea markets where no questions were asked.

The drug money had vanished. It was all spent. At night Arthur lay awake listening to his parents warring over nickels and dimes.

"How I'm gonna pay these bills without money?" his mother yelled. "We owe that school over one thousand dollars."

"Shut up."

"You can't hold a job."

Arthur wished he had a friend to talk to, but he kept these late-night arguments to himself. He didn't tell anyone at St. Joseph, not even William. If he told his friends they might realize that his

....

fives, tens, and twenties money
got hooked on started to use
feed his habit continue using drugs

clowning was a mask. That he **strutted the school stage**, innocent and carefree, because inside he hurt. He made them laugh with him because he feared they might laugh at him. If you believe in nothing, he thought, you'll never get hurt. And he believed in nothing except the game.

As jaded as he was, he still believed the game was real. You either could play or couldn't.

Arthur left his room to get a glass of water and saw his mother and father leaving their bedroom. His father staggered as he walked, and his mother **was glassy eyed**.

Arthur knew what they had been doing in there, and he hated his father for having made his mother do drugs. He didn't blame Sheila. What she did in that room was only her foolish attempt to hold on to Bo and keep the family together. Arthur vowed that if he ever made it at the game and he planned to make it big—he would buy his mother a nice house with a big yard and set her up so she would never have to work again.

Bo and Sheila returned to the bedroom and started fighting again. "I can't even give my boy decent money for lunch," she said.

"Shut up," he screamed.

"He had to walk home from school. Did you know that?"

They were still **going at it when Arthur drifted off to sleep**.

The next morning Bo came stumbling into the apartment just as Arthur was getting ready to leave for school.

"Boy, how you doin' in that school?" Bo said.

Arthur moved around the kitchen heading for the door.

"Boy, I'm talkin' to you."

....

strutted the school stage acted like he was fine

was glassy eyed looked lifeless

going at it when Arthur drifted off to sleep fighting when Arthur fell asleep

Arthur stopped. "I'm doin' fine."

"Are you **bucklin' down**, like I told you?"

Arthur nodded. "'Cause I told you," Bo continued, "you ain't gonna get ahead unless you do that there homework and listen to them nuns."

It sickened Arthur to hear such hypocrisy. He had heard it all his life. Old Bo, the con man with the easy answers and his prison past. Bo fooled everyone, but he couldn't fool Arthur. Arthur knew that Bo was high on drugs or coming down, even as he stood there telling him how he should live the straight life. He was high the day Big Earl showed up, and the night after, Bo **prowled** the streets and alleys, rummaging through cars, pawing through garbage cans, looking for things to steal to buy **another binge**.

"Don't forget what I told you, son."

But Arthur darted out the doorway, down the steps, and into the streets. Unlike William he couldn't get to school fast enough. In a strange way he enjoyed St. Joseph. It was there that he got to be good old Arthur, **the life of the party**.

"Man, they love you here," William told him. "You could be class president."

"Maybe I will," Arthur boasted.

And no one suspected a thing.

....

bucklin' down studying hard
prowled walked through
another binge more drugs
the life of the party the funniest kid in school

WILLIAM

· · · · · · · · · · ·

The first few days following William's promotion to varsity were particularly frustrating because it seemed that the distance between where he was and where he wanted to be was widening. He had always effortlessly merged into the flow of the game, but now he found himself stumbling over the basics, **befuddled by the fundamentals** of St. Joseph basketball, and questioning, for the first time, his ability to achieve his dreams of glory.

"On offense, we run a motion," William repeated to himself. "On defense man to man."

Actually, the motion offense was brilliant in its simplicity: five men rotating around the perimeter, darting through the paint, passing, setting picks, cutting toward the basket, the open man taking the shot. The key was movement, forcing the opposition to **buckle under the strain** of keeping pace.

But sometimes William forgot to keep moving, or he moved to the wrong place and collided with a teammate, and it was the offense that backfired, each player skidding out of control like a car sliding on a slippery, wet street. Pingatore, his face blood red, halted the scrimmage with an angry toot on his whistle.

"Listen, William, what do I always tell you about offense?" The gym **fell stone** quiet. "You have to keep movin'," William whispered.

"What's that?" Coach Pingatore barked.

"You have to move, coach."

"That's right. Keep moving—*move, move, move, move*. You have

---

befuddled by the fundamentals confused by the basic rules
buckle under the strain get tired
fell stone became very

to concentrate."

"Yes, coach."

He blew his whistle. "Now, try it again."

The older players, accustomed to the coach's tirades, snickered **at the dressing down**. "Play time's over, rookie," they teased him. "You're in the big leagues now."

William felt that some of the starters resented him. They seemed to take his presence as a threat, and it wasn't much fun playing with these guys. They didn't include him in their jokes, invite him to their parties, or introduce him to their friends. They never took him aside and welcomed him to the team. Some days came and went and they didn't even say hello.

What bothered him most was that **in crunch time** they didn't pass him the ball. Or if he got hot, and hit two or three in a row, they **froze him out**. It was as though they didn't want him to get the winning shot or score the most points. At first he thought it was his imagination, but there were games when he was wide open, waving his arms, and the player with the ball turned the other way.

At times like that, when he trotted up court, **ears burning**, all he wanted was the season to end.

Pingatore worked them hard. He made them run wind sprints, lift weights, and endlessly repeat the same tedious half-court drills. He started and closed practice with free throws. If you missed the final two free throws of practice, he made you run the stairs, twenty-five of them. Even after practice Pingatore did not let up. He made William work on his jumper.

....

at the dressing down when the coach yelled at William
in crunch time when the score was very close
froze him out stopped passing to him
ears burning extremely angry

"Step left, cut right, receive the ball, square up, shoot. Atta, boy. Again.

"And again.

"And again."

Sometimes Pingatore brought out the old tapes and he replayed the great games against the great teams. "You are part of a great tradition," he told William. "It began before you got here and will continue after you have gone: the St. Joseph tradition."

The fact is St. Joseph, founded not long before by the Christian Brothers, wasn't always a basketball powerhouse. It was one of the worst teams in the league when Pingatore took over in 1970. But Pingatore had a vision. He saw himself as a teacher, **stitching together a squad** of shooters and drivers—some black, some white— teaching them to play as a team. It took five years for him to win his first conference championship, a momentous accomplishment which, nonetheless, wasn't completely fulfilling. The truer test came from **besting** the public schools, city or suburban, where the best black kids played: Proviso East and Proviso West, as well as Westinghouse, King, Simeon, Marshall and all the other basketball titans.

At first some rival coaches privately mocked St. Joseph, patronizing Pingatore's early efforts. But their derision turned to envy as his losses turned to wins, and they devised excuses to explain **the turn of events**. They said his recruits were plundered from the inner city; that he was stealing the best Chicago and Maywood had to offer, and that he used high-schoolers to **indulge his Bobby Knight fantasies**.

Pingatore ignored the barbs. He had nothing to be ashamed of.

....

stitching together a squad creating a team
besting playing better than; beating
the turn of events St. Joseph's success
indulge his Bobby Knight fantasies fulfill his own dreams

He had built a serious, college-like program on the high school level. He broke no rules. He raided no schools. He didn't take transfer students. He didn't woo freshmen with sneakers, girls, or phony promises. His kids graduated on time. Yes, it was true that public schools all around him teetered on the edge of bankruptcy; ravaged from within by the realities of inner-city life, but was that his fault? He did what he could, which was better than most. Each year he sheltered more kids from the inner city. He could name their names and see their faces. Isiah was not the only one. If he and his colleagues at St. Joseph had constructed a home away from home, where teenage boys could grow and learn in peace and stability, well, what was wrong with that?

As Pingatore saw it, William was about to enter a magical world of high school basketball, and he did his best to make him appreciate it. He told him about the Christmas tournament at Proviso West, which featured dozens of schools, public and private, from city and suburb, playing before a gym **rocking from the din** of 5,000 fans. "It's unbelievable, William. On one side you got our fans, on the other side their fans. And the noise, you never heard so much noise."

He told him of the statewide, postseason tournament, from regional to sectionals to super-sectionals; and then, "If you're lucky and good—no, not good, but great—the Elite Eight. You get to board the bus for the three-hour drive downstate to Champaign-Urbana, home of the University of Illinois." It was there, in Assembly Hall, a 16,000-seat arena, where the eight surviving teams played for the state title. What an exhilarating and nerve-wracking climb that was, each step **fraught with** uncertainty—one loss meant

....

rocking from the din filled with the noises
fraught with full of

elimination—each team determined to win it all.

Only once had St. Joseph even made it to the final game. That was back in 1978, a particularly good year for high school basketball unbelievably rich in local talent. There was Mark Aguirre and Doc Rivers and Craig Hodges and, of course, Isiah—all of them future pros.

"Ours was a special team," Pingatore told William. "George Johnson, Tyrone Brewer, Ray Clark—"

"And Isiah?"

"And Isiah."

He showed William articles, yellowed with age, from the local paper. "If many people in Illinois were unaware of the town of Westchester before," the lead story began, "St. Joseph's basketball team not only **put it on the map, but circled it in red**."

"We rallied the whole school and the whole community behind us," Pingatore continued. "We broke down all the barriers. It wasn't whites here and blacks there—it was white and black together. After that, St. Joseph had a reputation. The coaches came from all over the country wanting to recruit our kids. And kids started wanting to come here."

Together they watched tapes from that glorious season. They saw Isiah dribbling out the clock in the 63 to 60 win over Mark Aguirre and Westinghouse; Isiah drilling shot after shot to beat Rockford East: and then finally, Isiah, **dog** tired, in the finals against Lockport. St. Joseph probably should have won that game. They were the better team, but the season was long and in the end they tired, even Isiah, and their shots fell short. "You can't dwell on these things," said Pingatore, though William suspected he did.

....

put it on the map, but circled it in red made the town known, it made the town famous

dog very, extremely

Early in the season, in a game against Fenwick, Pingatore called for a full-court press, but William backed off for fear of **drawing a foul**.

"William," Pingatore yelled from the bench, "keep the press."

"I can't," William replied, approaching the bench. "I got two fouls." Meanwhile, the man he was supposed to be covering scored an easy basket.

Pingatore quivered, his cheeks darkened, and his jet-black hair swirled madly across his forehead. He **yanked William from** the game. "You want to talk over plays," he roared. "Well, think about it from the bench."

William sat with his head in his hands. Feeling disgraced by Pingatore's public denunciations, he seethed with anger and resentment.

In the locker room, Pingatore stopped by as William dressed.

"Do you think I'm too hard on you?" he asked, his voice lower, almost sweet.

William said nothing.

"Son, there's a reason I do this. I want you to be great. I see in you great talent, but you're going to have to work hard to **have it blossom**. Do you hear what I'm saying?"

Pingatore spoke quietly, in a soft, **sudsy** voice that dissolved William's anger and soothed his inner aches. Tears stung William's eyes.

"There's a difference between a great playground player and a great team player," Pingatore continued. "The ones that have the talent and that are willing to listen—they're going to be great players. Some will rebel. Some will think they know more than the coach."

....

drawing a foul getting a penalty
yanked William from took William out of
have it blossom make it happen
sudsy gentle

He paused for a moment. "I know what you're going through, William. You think I don't, but I do. I know you're getting up early and traveling a long way and putting up with a lot. I know you're working a lot harder than if you had stayed at home. But there's a reason. Don't lose sight of that. You're developing character, William. You're learning responsibility, and that's a **plus**. That will get you farther in life than basketball can."

Pingatore went on to predict **a big breakthrough for William**. And a few days later, at the end of a game in the Proviso West Tournament, that big breakthrough came. Coincidentally it was December 28, William's fifteenth birthday. They were down by one to Collins High School when Carl Hayes passed to William and William launched his shot. What followed was the crystallization of every schoolboy's dream: a few seconds on the clock, the fans on their feet, the ball in the air. A perfect shot. The ball sailed through the net, and St. Joseph won the game. A mob of students **flocked on** the court to embrace William. He looked up to see Catherine, Emma, Curtis, and David jumping up and down in the stands. His jubilant teammates all but carried William, sticky with sweat, to the locker room, where a pack of reporters asked him how he felt.

Off in the back William could see Arthur standing by the locker, watching with a smile on his face. William winked. He knew what to say; he'd seen the pros answer that question many times before. "It felt good," he said, as if reciting the words from a page. "It felt good right away."

The next day on a subway heading downtown, he saw his name beneath his picture in the sports pages of a newspaper. He read the

....

plus good thing

a big breakthrough for William the moment when William would see that he has become a better player

flocked on ran onto

caption once, then twice, and then a third time, and a big smile filled his face. *The amazing thing is that it happened on my fifteenth birthday*, he thought.

In the seat across the aisle sat a man and a woman with book bags in their laps. William caught them looking his way and wondered if they had been staring at him and talking about him, if they recognized him. If one told the other, "Hey, there's that basketball player who's in the paper." But they never looked his way again and left the train at the next stop. William shrugged and thought, *One day, they'll all know who I am.*

Someone did hang the photograph in the St. Joseph cafeteria, and kids stopped him in the hall to marvel over his **poise in those closing seconds**. The team **was 11 and 1 and gaining momentum**. They won the Christmas tournament and were ranked number one in the area. Just before a practice, Pingatore called William into his office and shut the door.

"I want to show you something," he said, pulling a piece of paper from a folder on his desk.

He looked at William and smiled. "I don't know if I should show you this."

William shuffled in his seat. Was Pingatore joking? He wasn't sure. And if he was, was he supposed to joke back? "Aw, come on, coach."

"You're gonna get **bigheaded**. I know you're gonna get bigheaded. But, well, ever since that Collins game, I've gotten some letters for you."

....

poise in those closing seconds calm and confidence towards the end of the game

was 11 and 1 and gaining momentum had won 11 out of 12 games and was playing better

bigheaded too confident; arrogant

"Letters?"

"From college coaches. Eight of them."

And he lifted them from the folder and handed them to William. They were neatly typed letters of introduction from coaches at various colleges.

"They're watching you, William. You're only a freshman, but they're watching you already. They saw what you did against Collins and they liked what they saw. But you can't rest on that. You can't get bigheaded. Do you hear what I'm saying?"

"Yes, coach."

"If you get bigheaded, you'll stop learning, and if you stop learning, you'll stop developing. And if that happens, you won't get any letters again."

That night William **crept** into his bedroom, shut the door, and read the letters two or three times. They were formal and determinedly cheerful, and all remarkably similar in substance and tone. "We are very proud of you for having played such an outstanding game in the Proviso West Christmas Tournament," was a sample opening.

It slowly started to dawn on William that he was part of a pack running a long-distance race, and that as they finished the first lap, he was in the lead, or among the leaders—the special ones, the gifted ones, for whom the world awaits. From here on out he was no longer William Gates, son of Emma, brother of Curtis, but William Gates, basketball star. From here on out that identity would be the ruler by which all his achievements were measured. It was a bold and

---

crept quietly walked

frightening prospect.

He began to read the sports pages more carefully, looking for the names of the competition, the other **front-runners** in the race, the guys who would be running at his side—moving forward, falling back—for the rest of his life. They were his competitors, there being only so many winners in any race. So far there were only two other freshmen getting significant notice: Tom Kleinschmidt and Sean Pearson. William **made a point of keeping his eye on** them.

He was playing well, though not brilliantly, averaging about ten points a game. What was so amazing is that he played at all—very few freshmen ever do. The *Sun-Times* mentioned him in a story about St. Joseph, and he had the **sweeping gratification** of knowing that the boys back home in Cabrini might see his name in print. A few days later, while watching a sports talk show, he heard his name emerge from the gravelly voice of Bill Gleason, a veteran Chicago sportswriter.

"I think I may have seen the next Isiah Thomas," Gleason said. "St. Joe of Westchester has a kid named William Gates who is starting as a freshman."

"Remember you heard it first from Bill Gleason," cracked another writer on the show. "Put it in your memory banks—William Gates."

He sat stunned, Gleason's words bouncing around his head. A sportswriter on TV had compared him to Isiah! The words casually **popped off of Gleason's tongue**, but they stuck with William. His heart raced faster, and his imagination soared as he pictured himself in the white and red of the hometown Bulls, playing at the Chicago Stadium in the backcourt with Jordan. He caught a hold of himself

....

front-runners leaders
made a point of keeping his eye on started to pay attention to
sweeping gratification great feeling
popped off of Gleason's tongue came out of Gleason's mouth

and remembered Coach Pingatore's advice: "Don't get a big head." He didn't know if he was scared or excited. *I don't want to be Isiah*, he thought. *I'm William Gates.*

As the season advanced some of William's white classmates showed a new appreciation for the freshman star. Two of them approached him outside his locker as the hallways filled with students hustling to class. They were upperclassmen, one short and dumpy, the other gangly and tall. William had never met them before and didn't know their names.

"Hey, William. What's happenin'?" said the short guy.

William nodded his head.

"Man, you were **bad**, brother," the short guy continued. "Your shot against Collins was awesome, man."

William sighed. *How come white guys don't realize how silly they sound when they try to talk black? What makes them think that black guys want them to talk black?*

"Yeah, it was cool," said the tall guy.

"I'm glad you liked it," said William. He shut his locker and **fiddled** with his notebook. *What do they want from me? They have to **have something up their sleeves**, or are they just making conversation?*

"Man, when you kicked Proviso East's ass, you showed them," said the fat one.

"Yeah," the skinny student agreed. "You think you're gonna go downstate?"

How the hell do I know? William thought. He supposed they were trying to be friendly, but they made him feel uncomfortable. He felt

....

bad amazing, great

fiddled played

have something up their sleeves want something

they were looking him over.

The bell sounded. "Gotta go," William said. "I'll be late for class."

The two kids looked at each other as if to say, What's the matter with him?

Arthur laughed when William told him about the exchange. "Man, you gotta talk to these guys. It's no big deal. Some of these **cats** are so stupid, they don't know nothin'."

"I got nothin' to say to them," said William. "They're only talkin' to me 'cause I'm on the varsity. When I was on the freshman team they didn't know I was alive."

William and Arthur were standing in the parking lot, waiting for Pingatore, who had promised them a ride home. When Pingatore pulled up, Arthur **scrambled** in the front and William settled in the back seat. These moments alone with the coach were always a little awkward. They never had regular conversations; they didn't talk about what was in the paper or what happened in school. Mostly Coach Pingatore gave them advice.

"William, you have to work on going to your left," Pingatore told him, as they headed for the expressway. "We know you can go right."

William nodded and stared out the window. He had learned to stay silent when the coach gave advice.

"And Arthur," Pingatore added, "you've made advances, but you have to learn to pace yourself more. You're the fastest guy on the team, but you have to slow down some and **let the team catch up to you**."

William saw Arthur **fidgeting** and wanted to warn him to keep quiet, but Arthur was talking almost before Pingatore finished his advice. "See, coach, thing is—"

....

cats guys, boys
scrambled moved quickly to sit
let the team catch up to you play with the team
fidgeting moving nervously; getting restless

76

"Arthur, I'm trying to tell you something. You have to learn to listen."

Arthur slouched and became sullen.

When they left the car Arthur was upset. "Pingatore's the guy who don't listen."

William shook his head. "That ain't how it works. I don't care if he asks you a question. No matter what he says, or how he says it, all you do is say, 'Yes, coach' or 'No, coach.'"

"Man, I ain't talkin' to him like that."

"You better learn then."

As the regular season came to a conclusion, St. Joseph was **on a roll**. They were conference champions with an overall record of twenty-four wins and two defeats. Every day Pingatore prepared them for the play-offs. He warned them against cockiness by telling the painful tale of his '79 team. Isiah was a senior, and they had advanced to the sectionals to play De La Salle, a team they had defeated earlier that season. The game was closer than it should have been and, with one second left, a **little-used reserve** named Albert Williams came off the bench to **hit a thirty-foot desperation jumper**, and De La Salle won by a point. "Isiah still talks about that game as a major disappointment," Pingatore told them. "The moral, fellas, is that nothing comes free. You can't take tomorrow for granted. The other guy wants to win, too."

At the season's final play-offs, St. Joseph ran past their first opponents, Proviso East and Proviso West, and advanced to the super-sectionals against St. Francis de Sales—the winner to go downstate.

....

on a roll winning almost every game

little-used reserve guy who did not play often

hit a thirty-foot desperation jumper throw the ball in the basket from thirty feet away

St. Joseph was the favorite. St. Francis, a Catholic school from Chicago's far South Side, had only one notable player, Eric Anderson, a 6'9" center.

The game was played in a western suburb, and the biggest cheers were for St. Joseph. But despite the crowd's exuberance, St. Joseph **came out flat**. Maybe they were nervous or maybe they were looking ahead or maybe they were tired. Whatever, they didn't block out on rebounds. They let John Simmons, **an unheralded forward**, score sixteen points. They let Anderson and his long arms intimidate them; they didn't drive the lane.

St. Joe was down fourteen points late in the third quarter when William took charge. He nailed a three, dunked, hit a jumper, and almost single-handedly cut the lead to three. But the ball stopped coming after that. He was spinning off of picks, bursting wide open, and Chuckie Murphy was going inside to the big men—Carl Hayes and Deryl Cunningham. He didn't know why, he didn't ask. He didn't think the time was right to raise a fuss or cause a commotion. "Shoot, William, shoot," Curtis yelled from the stands. But William didn't think it was his place to go after the ball; he was only a freshman.

St. Francis got tough, the whiff of victory inspired them. They sagged low, hands quick as pistons, darting in and out, slapping, tapping, knocking loose the ball. Pingatore was **beside himself**, yelling, tugging his hair, stomping his feet; another season was slipping away and he knew it.

In the final quarter Anderson **caught fire**, scoring sixteen of his thirty-three points, and William really wasn't a factor at all down the stretch. He didn't shoot; he had lost his surge. He passed off to the

....

came out flat did not play well

an unheralded forward a player who was not well known

beside himself very angry

caught fire started to play very well

seniors. He wasn't the leader. This was their moment and he couldn't win it for them. St. Francis won 67 to 58. As William walked off the court, he turned to watch the fans **swarm over** Anderson.

Some of the seniors were **shedding tears**, but William felt no sorrow. Only weariness. The last six weeks had been all basketball. What was he supposed to do now?

The sky was dark, a heavy snow on its way. He walked carefully over the icy sidewalk and was the first to **board** the bus. He sat near the front and closed his eyes. It was the fourth of March. Three more months before summer vacation. He had survived the worst of it. His first season was done. Next year he would be a sophomore—he would take those shots at the end. Next year he and Arthur would take the team downstate.

....

swarm over run toward; surround
shedding tears crying
board get on

BEFORE YOU MOVE ON...

1. **Paraphrase** On page 62, what did Arthur mean when he said that his clowning around was a mask?

2. **Comparisons** How were Arthur and William different when working with Coach Pingatore?

LOOK AHEAD Read pages 80–103 to find out how Arthur felt when he was kicked out of school.

SOPHOMORE YEAR
1988

"Man, let me tell you about coaches. Coaches want to win. . . . If the coach don't like you shootin', it's 'cause you're missin', not 'cause you're shootin'. If you miss three in a row, he'll holler at you. But as soon as you hit three in a row, you're his newfound friend."
— *Curtis Gates, to his brother William*

ARTHUR

· · · · · · · · · · · ·

The call from the office came on a quiet October day, while Arthur **slumbered through religion**. The official in charge of student finances wanted to see him right away. Relieved to be free of class, Arthur **waltzed** into the tiny office and got the news straight, without softeners.

"Your family has fallen several hundred dollars behind on tuition payments. You'll have to leave school until **the obligation is retired**."

Arthur leaned forward. "Say what?"

"You'll have to go home, Arthur, unless your family can come up with a $500 down payment on that debt."

They're kicking me out of school, he thought. *Where we gonna get that kind of money?*

The official said he was sorry but that there was nothing he could do.

"I thought these things would be taken care of if I played basketball," Arthur said, finally.

The official shook his head and explained that there were no athletic scholarships at St. Joseph; that the school kept tuition as affordably low as it could; that Arthur's tuition had already been reduced significantly in recognition of his after-school duties; that St. Joseph wasn't a public institution, it didn't receive state aid, it couldn't continue without tuition; and that his parents had undoubtedly been **apprised of** their obligations before he enrolled. "I'm sorry," he concluded. "I hope something can be worked out."

....

slumbered through religion almost fell asleep in class
waltzed went, walked
the obligation is retired your family pays the full amount due
apprised of told about

Arthur left in a daze and sat against the wall outside the office. He couldn't believe it. *This wasn't supposed to happen to guys who followed the St. Joseph system. I obeyed their rules. I got up early, I rode that train, I got to school on time, and I hit the game-winning shot. What the hell am I supposed to do now? I gotta think. What am I gonna tell Momma? She'll be so disappointed. She'll think I'm just like Bo.*

The official's words **rang in his head and rocked him with rage**. *Damn their financial obligations! This dump isn't good enough for Arthur Agee. They were lucky to have me. They should pay me to come here.*

But **his anger diminished as his humiliation rose**. From around the bend came voices. A group of white freshmen approached. Arthur staggered to his feet. He had to leave before they saw him. One must always be ready to raise the mask, to fool the world and hide the truth—his father had taught him that. But no mask could shield his shame. They were kicking him out. *They might as well come out and say it: Get out! You ain't good enough for St. Joseph.*

He knew his family was poor, but he didn't know they **were falling so far behind on** their bills. Why was there always so much about his family he didn't know?

The first time Sheila Gaye Goldthwaite met Arthur "Bo" Agee was in 1969. She was walking through the halls of A. H. Parker High School in her hometown of Birmingham, Alabama, and Bo came up to her from behind.

"Hello, Miss Pretty."

She giggled and blushed.

Bo was wearing alligator shoes and a white dress shirt buttoned

....

rang in his head and rocked him with rage made him very angry

his anger diminished as his humiliation rose he became less angry and more embarrassed

were falling so far behind on could not pay

at the collar, neatly tucked into his khakis, "Can I carry your books?"

He held out his arms, and she deposited her books in his hands. She was a sixteen-year-old junior—shy and petite with beautiful, soft brown eyes. He was a seventeen-year-old senior, a **dashing, charismatic** young man who starred on the basketball team and sang in the choir. He was goodtime Bo, a **devilish mimic** full of jokes and laughter. Wherever he wandered, it seemed a party **broke out**.

Sheila had never dated until Bo came along. Most of her free time was spent with her older sister, Cookie, and a few girlfriends. They formed a make-believe singing group they called the Pepperettes. They dressed in fishnet stockings and green-and-black miniskirts, puffed up their hair, slathered on lipstick, and disappeared into their bedrooms to stand before the mirror and lip-sync to the Supremes, played from singles on a tinny sounding record player.

Bo **courted** Sheila in the proper ways. He made dates days in advance, and when he picked her up he went to the door. He didn't honk the horn and wait for her to come to his car like other boys did. Bo parked his car and walked to the porch, knocked on the door and took off his hat when he greeted her parents, Marshall and Georgia Goldthwaite. He made a point of asking for a piece of Mrs. Goldthwaite's prized sweet potato pie. He complimented Cookie on her dresses and hair. He talked basketball with Sheila's younger brothers, who idolized him, and discussed baseball with her father.

Her family liked his manners because good manners were important in the Goldthwaite house. The Goldthwaites ran a neighborhood grocery store and were gone most of the day, so each of their ten children had his or her chores: make the bed, clean the

....

dashing, charismatic handsome, popular
devilish mimic fun guy who was
broke out began; got started
courted showed that he liked

kitchen, wash the dishes. They had to follow family rules and obligations. Dinner was served promptly at six; no one ate until Mr. Goldthwaite was seated; they attended church on Sunday; the children called their elders sir or ma'am. They rarely disobeyed. Mrs. Goldthwaite **ruled like a despot**, punishing rebels and halting rebellions with the crack of an electric cord she wielded like a whip.

Bo and Sheila became one of Parker High's most popular couples. They got invited to all the parties. Sometimes they played records; other times they listened to the radio turned to Tall Paul, the **hippest** deejay of the day. All the parties were well chaperoned, parents **standing sentry** along the walls and in the corners. There was no bumping and grinding; the best any boy could hope for was to dance close on the slow songs. Sheila reserved such moments of delight for Bo. They slow danced to the Temptations, Al Green, Sam Cooke. And Bo could sing like Sam Cooke; he had the voice of a sweet, soaring tenor. At the senior-year Halloween talent show, Bo took the stage in the Parker gym and sang Garland Grey's bluesy song of love: "If You Were My Woman." When he reached the chorus, his eyes found Sheila's. **She was the envy of every girl** because Bo was singing to her.

Bo walked her home that night, and they planned their future. They would get married. She would go to college and become a nurse; and he would sing. Eventually they would raise enough money to buy their own business, maybe a grocery store. They would have at least three or four children. The first boy would be named Arthur Junior, because it was important to show respect for the father. They would live in a big house with a wide lawn where the children, and then

....

ruled like a despot was like a tough ruler
hippest coolest, best
standing sentry watching closely as they stood
She was the envy of every girl All the girls were jealous

grandchildren and then maybe even great-grandchildren could play.

They walked along a **tree-lined boulevard** and stopped to sit on a bench in a little park not far from Sheila's house. It was a quiet, peaceful night. The stars were shining, and the tips of the trees glowed in the moonlight.

Bo took off his gold sweater and laid it across Sheila's bare arms. Her skin tingled as he brushed back her hair.

"I love you, Sheila Gaye," he told her.

When they got to Sheila's house, he gave her one last good-night kiss. "I'll see you tomorrow."

"I love you, baby."

As she opened the screen door, Bo began singing Sam Cooke's "You Send Me." Sheila turned to him. "I wish I could stay out all night with you," she said.

Bo laughed. "You know your mamma wouldn't like that."

The screen door slipped shut behind her and Sheila ran upstairs to the bedroom she shared with Cookie.

And Bo? Well, you could fill a book with all the secrets he kept from Sheila. While Sheila and Cookie **snuggled beneath their covers and chattered** about romance and marriage, Bo went to the other side of town where his secret girlfriend lived, a girl whose parents didn't care if she stayed out all night. They drove to **a deserted** field and lay in the back of his car until the sun was up, and Sheila and her family were on their way to church.

Without school Arthur had no reason to get up at five in the morning anymore. He didn't have to get up at all—he had nowhere

....

tree-lined boulevard street with many trees

snuggled beneath their covers and chattered lay close to each other under their blankets and talked

a deserted an empty

85

to go and nothing to do. His friends weren't around, they were in school, but he didn't want to talk to anyone anyway. In the morning he watched TV and in the afternoon he went to the gym to shoot baskets. He walked around with his head down, his shoulders **slumped**, and his hands in his pockets. He had planned on being the next Isiah, but now he was just another loser.

The school said the **issue** was tuition, but Arthur saw it differently. As he saw it, had he been a better player, St. Joseph would have found a way to pay his tuition, like they did for William, who was attending the school **on a partial** scholarship. *They don't think I'm worth the money. When they recruited me, they told me I was special.*

"You can't sit in your room all day," Sheila told him softly.

"I don't want to talk about it, Momma," he said.

"You got to get out."

"Where am I supposed to go?"

"You gotta get on with your life, Man. We all **suffer little setbacks**."

"They think I'm a loser, Momma."

"Don't say that."

"Coach Pingatore, he be sayin' all the time, 'When you gonna grow, Arthur?' He kicked me out 'cause he didn't think I was gonna grow tall enough."

Sheila sat on the bed and stroked his head. "It's not how tall you are, Man, it's what you got inside."

"No, no, no," said Arthur. "That ain't it. They don't know nothin' 'bout what you got inside. They only think about how good you play right now. That's why they found the money for William

---

slumped pulled down; slouched
issue reason he could not stay in school
on a partial by receiving some of a
suffer little setbacks go through some difficult times

but couldn't find it for me."

Two weeks went by and the Agees still didn't have the money for Arthur's tuition.

"I'll find somethin'," Bo had promised when he learned of the family's **predicament**. Then he disappeared.

"Did you hear from daddy?" Arthur asked every morning.

Sheila shook her head.

Several days later Arthur heard Bo's voice rising out of the kitchen. He was telling the Alabama story while Sheila washed the dishes. Arthur crept into the kitchen and took a seat at the table next to his father. It was an old story, one he'd heard many times before, about the time Bo **bumped into the white warden of the jail where Bo did time**.

"I see this white guy and he says, 'How you doin', Mr. Agee?' I said, 'Man, get out of my face. Last year when you had me locked up you weren't talkin' to me like that.' He was just kissin' my ass 'cause I was suin' the state. It felt good talkin' to a white man like that."

Arthur waited for Bo to say something about the tuition. But one story led to another and the topic never came up. Old Bo always had a good story to tell. Arthur chewed his fingers: *Yeah, big tough Bo. Well, a big tough man would pay his son's tuition so his son wouldn't get kicked out of school.*

"Stop tellin' lies," Arthur said.

There was silence. Bo turned to Sheila. "Sheila Gaye, what you been tellin' this boy?"

"Nothin' he don't already know," she replied.

"You got to tell this boy to respect his father," Bo said. "He

....

predicament problem, trouble

bumped into the white warden of the jail where Bo did time saw the supervisor of the jail where he had been imprisoned

gonna respect me, dammit. I'll make him respect me." Bo whacked the table so hard it shook. Arthur returned to his bedroom.

Bo was raised in the Jim Crow South, where **segregation** was law. At a young age he learned the limitations of the land—where he could go, what he could say, what he could expect of life. He had to sit **in the Colored section of** the movie theaters, and drink from the water fountains and relieve himself in the restrooms for Coloreds. He was barred from the white lunchrooms and the downtown department stores. He had to call white men Sir and white women Ma'am, and listen to whites, young and old, call his stepfather Boy.

Birmingham was run by police commissioner Eugene "Bull" Connor, a blowsy, thick-bodied man easily led by temptation. When he was caught in a motel room with his secretary it became quite a scandal, being that he was a married man with children. The voters ousted him from office, and the only way he **slithered back into their good graces** was to fuel the worst fears whites had about blacks. He positioned himself as the white man's best defender against **integration**, as though any defense was needed.

In the spring of 1961, a bus filled with white and black students calling themselves Freedom Riders arrived in Birmingham, determined to free the South from segregation's chains. When the bus rolled into the Birmingham station, Bull Connor's police were nowhere in sight when a venomous white mob kicked, clubbed, and gouged the two Freedom Riders, Chuck Person and Jim Peck, who dared to use the station's restroom.

Bull Connor blamed the violence on the victims. "I have said for

---

segregation the separation of people based on their race
in the Colored section of where African Americans had to sit in
slithered back into their good graces got back into office
integration making black and white people equal in society

the last twenty years that these out-of-town meddlers were going to cause bloodshed if they keep meddling in the South's business," he told reporters. No one was arrested for the beatings.

Within a year, Martin Luther King Jr., and his allies—Ralph David Abernathy, Andy Young, Bernard Lee, James Bevel, and Diane Nash—decided to make Birmingham the focus of a national desegregation campaign.

King led a series of marches in downtown Birmingham, and Bull Connor had him arrested and thrown into **solitary confinement**. It was from one of Bull Connor's cells that King wrote his famous "Letter from Birmingham Jail," a stirring appeal to white clergymen and other white liberals.

"We have waited for more than three hundred and forty years for our constitutional and God-given rights," King wrote in his letter. "The Negro has **many pent-up resentments and latent frustrations**, and he must release **them**. So let him march; let him make prayer pilgrimages to the city hall; let him go on freedom rides—and try to understand why he must do so. If his repressed emotions are not released in nonviolent ways, they will seek expression through violence; this is not a threat but a fact of history."

Reverend Bevel, using King's imprisonment as a source of inspiration, organized children's marches from the Sixteenth Street Baptist Church in downtown. Birmingham children and other marchers would sit in the all-white eateries and shop in the all-white department stores to protest segregation laws. Bull Connor started arresting children before they left the black neighborhood. When more children marched he had them shot with water from

....

solitary confinement a jail cell by himself

many pent-up resentments and latent frustrations been angry for a long time

them his emotions

high-pressured hoses and attacked by German Shepherd police dogs. And still the children marched. Connor's jails overflowed with children; at least 3,000 had been arrested with as many as seventy-five crammed into cells built for eight. Governor George Wallace, **pledging allegiance to** segregation, called out the state militia, but the marchers didn't stop.

In desperation, Birmingham's most savage bigots bombed black-owned hotels, houses, and churches. On Sunday, September 15, 1963, they bombed the Sixteenth Street Baptist Church. The broken bodies of four little girls, none older than ten, were found in the rubble of that blast.

Birmingham hovered on the edge of chaos. As the marches and arrests continued, black children committed the unthinkable. They rioted, pelting Bull Connor's police with rocks, overturning cars, and burning storefronts. They rampaged through Kelly Ingram Park, which was just down the street from the Sixteenth Street Baptist Church.

Images of snarling dogs and sobbing mothers and fathers burying their young daughters flashed round the world and helped to **bring down** the racist Jim Crow segregation laws. By the time Bo got to high school, Bull Connor was virtually powerless and segregation was outlawed. There was even a black clerk or two in the downtown department stores. The Birmingham crusade inspired freedom movements in Africa, Asia, and Europe, but the **triumphs were hard won**, and the black boys and girls who **came of age** at that time never forgot the violence, hatred, and degradation they saw there.

So it was with Bo. He knew the girls who died in the Sixteenth

....

pledging allegiance to promising to keep
bring down end, destroy
triumphs were hard won victories did not happen easily
came of age became adults; grew up

Baptist Street Church—Denise McNair, Addie Mae Collins, Carole Robertson, and Cynthia Wesley. His family attended the church and was related to Reverend Abernathy. He could not escape the thought that it might have been his sisters killed by the bombs. It might have been his flesh ripped by those dogs. It might have been him knocked senseless. That might have been him at the forefront of the marches. Reverend Bevel had preached a complicated **form of civil disobedience**, but it required more discipline than Bo could sustain. As it was, he took a different route. Bo was tired of being called Boy. He didn't want to **turn the other cheek**. He wanted to strike back. He stayed away from marches and ran with the mob. On the night of the riots he was there in Kelly Ingram Park throwing rocks and taunting the police. And when they charged he scampered away, quick as a rabbit, into the night.

A response that would remain characteristic for many years to come took root. When society pushed Bo, Bo pushed back, usually in indirect ways. He was brilliant at masquerades and deception. These were skills he mastered at an early age, not only to survive Jim Crow, but to conceal his shame and anger over the impoverished circumstances of his upbringing.

He was the first of six children born to Claudia Agee. He never met his father, Roosevelt Blunt, a serviceman passing through Birmingham. His mother cooked and waited tables in a cafe on the edge of town. She married a truck driver named Willie Lee Nelson, who lost most of whatever he made betting on the Georgia Skins and had to **pawn off family possessions to make ends meet**.

Claudia Agee was a heavy drinker who died of cirrhosis of the

....

form of civil disobedience way of protesting peacefully
turn the other cheek ignore the way black people were treated
pawn off family possessions to make ends meet sell his family's things to earn enough money

liver when Bo was sixteen. There had been times when she staggered home so drunk she collapsed on the front steps. Bo had to suffer the snickers and sneers from neighborhood children. He wanted to defend his mother's honor, but he usually **held back**. He was not a fighter. There was no percentage in it; the risks outweighed the rewards. He learned to fool people by smiling or acting dumb or talking sweet, whatever the moment required. He delighted in his ability to manipulate and to con, but his hurt and anger never disappeared. It just receded somewhere deep inside, rising to the surface in violent self-destructive outbursts, which even Bo knew were pointless.

His first arrest came when he was fifteen. He was sentenced to several days in the juvenile detention center for breaking the windows in a local grammar school. His second arrest was for shoplifting. His third arrest was for breaking into a house. Almost a year after he and Sheila began dating, Bo and a friend named James were caught stealing pants from a mall. They were sent to jail. Almost from the moment of his capture he plotted escape. *You don't let things happen to you*, he thought. *I **ain't no cork bobbin'** in the ocean. You gotta grab your chances when they come or you might never get them again.*

While waiting to **be processed**, James and Bo escaped from a holding cell, slipped out a side door, and Bo caught the first bus leaving Birmingham for Chicago.

When he got to Chicago, Bo moved in with his grandfather, Cleveland, on Felton Court, a tiny street around the corner from Cabrini-Green. It was **a fertile little acre** of Chicago, a loud and funky place to be. Bo worked days in a factory and spent his nights

---

held back did not say anything
ain't no cork bobbin' *am not just floating directionless*
be processed be put into jail
a fertile little acre an exciting part

in dark, smoky lounges crowded with hookers and pimps and off-duty cops.

It was a time of tumult and change. **Chicago swelled with a mighty wave of black migration.** There was no future in the South where mechanization had squeezed jobs from the farms. It was either move to the cities in the north, or join the army and go to Vietnam. Each day brought new busloads of young men and women from Itta Bena, Tupelo, Clarksdale, Indianola, Moundville, and the other little Delta towns of Mississippi and farm towns of Alabama.

To the east of Felton Court was Old Town, the neighborhood where the hippies lived. It amazed Bo to watch long-haired white boys and girls in tattered army coats, bell-bottomed jeans, and leather vests parade up and down Wells or LaSalle streets. They'd smile at him and flash him the peace sign and ask him to join their revolution.

Bo might have made thousands of dollars selling **grass** to these kids, but Bo wanted nothing to do with white folks, no matter how much they smiled or called him a soul brother. "Ain't no future in sellin' drugs to white folks," he said. He hadn't gotten this far trusting white people and he wasn't going to start now. "A hippie can cut his hair and be any old white guy, but a black guy will always be black."

Instead he started selling marijuana to the factory workers, garbage haulers, bus drivers, mailmen, and laborers who lived in and around Cabrini. Before long Bo was making several hundred dollars a week. And with all that money he lived a wild time, up day and night, no time to sleep, enjoying the sweetness of women of all ages—single, widowed, divorced, married. The women up north, like the ones back home, **fell for** his sweet talk and believed in his lies.

....

Chicago swelled with a mighty wave of black migration. A lot of people from the South moved to Chicago.

grass drugs, marijuana

fell for believed

People have so little to believe in, might as well tell them what they want to hear, he thought. *It ain't my fault if they believe this crap.*

In letters to Sheila he still **professed his love** and expressed his yearning for the kids, the store, the house, the sweeping lawn. He sent her brooches, rings, bracelets, and other symbols of his affection. "I'm ready to settle down," he wrote her. "I want you to come to Chicago. I want to marry you."

Bo's letters only confused Sheila. She was still a high school junior, still living with her parents. She spent many nights with Cookie in their bedroom, reviewing Bo's **merits and faults**.

"Bo's a con man," Cookie told her. "Forget about him."

"No, Bo's a good man; he just hasn't been the same since his mamma died," Sheila told Cookie.

"Girl, this has nothin' to do with his mamma," Cookie said.

"You're just jealous 'cause Bo's nice to me and he buys me little things, and your boyfriend don't buy you nothin'."

"Those little presents don't mean nothin' 'cause he probably stole them."

In the winter Bo returned to Birmingham. He showed up unannounced, not the least bit concerned about being **apprehended** by the police. He had, he said, come home to marry Sheila and take her back to Chicago as soon as she graduated. "I'm makin' good money workin' in a factory," he told her. "I'm gonna give you a good life—movies, records, jewelry, clothes." A few weeks later, Sheila discovered she was pregnant. Bo had lain with her those first nights and talked nice, but she never dreamed she would get pregnant. She didn't think a woman could get pregnant if she loved the man and

---

professed his love told her how much he loved her
merits and faults strengths and weaknesses
apprehended caught; taken in

the man loved her.

Foolishly, she hoped the pregnancy might magically vanish, but her belly continued to swell. Cookie tried to talk her into an abortion, but Sheila refused for fear that her mother might find out. At night she lay in bed and anguished over her fate. At school she was withdrawn and depressed. *This don't happen to good girls like me. I'm* **college bound**. *I'm on the honor roll. I eat lunch with the principal. My God, the principal. He's gonna expel me; then what am I gonna do?* For months she hid her belly by wearing baggy shirts and loose-fitting dresses. Only her dad—Mr. Nosey, she called him—seemed suspicious. "Sheila, girl," he said, "you don't look right."

"I'm okay, Daddy."

Mr. Goldthwaite shook his head. "Georgia, I think you should take Sheila to a doctor."

After six months of deception, Sheila told her parents. Mrs. Goldthwaite fainted, just **keeled** over, off her chair and onto the floor. When her mother **came to**, she wasn't nearly as upset as Sheila had feared. The family decided to keep Sheila's pregnancy a secret. She spent most of the summer in her bedroom, staying away from church and parties.

Cookie gently teased her, calling her a princess locked away in her castle. "Lord, Lord," Sheila said, "the things we do to get by."

On September 8, 1970, Sheila gave birth at the University Hospital in Birmingham, with her mother at her side and her father and Bo in the waiting room. It was a girl; they called her Tomekia. One of Bo's sisters came up with the name. It had a lovely **ring**.

A few days later Sheila started her senior year. When the

....

college bound *supposed to go to college*
keeled *fell*
came to *felt better; awoke*
ring *sound*

principal asked, she said her summer had been uneventful.

Sheila agreed to marry Bo after her high school graduation, and a date was set for the summer of 1971. Bo bought a tuxedo. Invitations were ordered. Bo was on his way to get those invitations when two police officers recognized him and cornered him in a parking lot.

"You ain't runnin' away this time, boy," the arresting officer said as he slammed Bo against the van and slapped on the handcuffs.

They took Bo to jail, stripped him, and threw him on a metal cot in a cramped cell where he lay in darkness for hours. The bare metal sliced into his back, and he shivered in the cold. No one knew he had been arrested. No one knew where he had gone.

He finally drifted off to sleep and woke **with a start** to see a stick above his head. He began to rise from the cot as the stick cracked against his jaw. Blood trickled down his chin.

"Hey, man, what the—"

He was **hammered senseless**, pounded with blow after blow after blow. His nose and lips split open and his teeth shattered. When he woke he was strapped to a white bed in a white room with white nurses **scurrying** around and two white cops, carrying guns, standing guard. From this blizzard of white came one black face, barely in focus.

"Bo-Bo? Bo-Bo?"

It was his aunt. He recognized her voice. Behind her stood his grandmother, Ethel Mae. Their eyes were **raw** from crying.

"Bo-Bo, are you all right?"

He opened his mouth, but no words came out.

"What did they do to you, child?"

....

with a start suddenly
hammered senseless hit very hard; badly beat up
scurrying running
raw red, sore

From behind his grandmother stepped Sheila. "Bo, it's me, Sheila Gaye."

He tried to lift his head but couldn't raise it from the pillow.

Sheila cringed at the sight of him. His lips were **caked** with blood, the skin around his eyes was purple. His head was wrapped in bandages. She stroked his cheek and then the guard led her from the room and into the hallway.

"He tried to hang himself," one cop told her.

"That's a lie," Sheila said.

"We were lucky to save him."

"That was no hangin'," said the grandmother. "How's a boy gonna do that to himself by hangin'?"

The cop shrugged. "I said it was a hangin'. You folks are lucky that boy's alive."

Two weeks later Bo was transferred from the hospital back to jail. Sheila visited him. She dabbed on his favorite perfume, but he couldn't smell the fragrance—they sat on opposite sides of a window and talked through a telephone. He wore **prison grays**, his hair was uncombed, his lips were still swollen, and his eyes oozed puss. She started crying.

"Bo, why?"

"I didn't hang myself."

"I know that. We called a lawyer. We're gonna sue the police."

Bo shook his head. "Forget that."

"You can't let them **do you** this way."

"Forget it, I say. If you **mess with them**, they'll find a way to keep me in jail until I die. You gotta leave these people alone,

----

caked covered

prison grays the gray prison uniform

do you treat you

mess with them give them trouble

they play rough."

Sheila's tears flowed harder. "This is killing me, Bo," she said. "I can't stand to see you in jail." They raised their hands to touch, but all they felt was the cold pane of glass between them.

"I've done wrong, Sheila Gaye. I know that."

Sheila shook her head. "I'm not gonna leave you, Bo."

Bo started to cry. "I can do right, Sheila Gaye. I can do better."

In late spring they moved Bo to Draper Penitentiary, a prison work farm just outside of Montgomery. He worked in the prison farmyard digging dirt under the **sweltering** sun, supervised by rifle-bearing white prison guards on horses.

He slept in a large, long room filled with sixty cots neatly aligned in rows of ten. The prisoners segregated themselves by race and hometown. Bo stayed with the black men from Birmingham. There were more than he expected and many that he knew. He put together a little gospel group, and they sang on breaks and at Sunday service. After lights out he lay in his cot and sang solo. The other prisoners found solace in his mournful ballads and spirituals.

In June he was brought back to court and sentenced to seven years for a variety of robberies, thefts, and break-ins that **had accumulated on his rap sheet** over the years. The judge's **pronouncement** left Bo trembling with fear. He couldn't imagine surviving seven years in prison. He felt trapped.

On the Fourth of July, the prison held a picnic for prisoners and their families. Bo was joined by Sheila, his stepfather, and his grandmother. They sat in the prison courtyard, eating chicken and corn bread, **washing it down with** ice tea. Bo held Sheila's hand, and

....

sweltering hot, burning
had accumulated on his rap sheet he had done
pronouncement statement, decision
washing it down with and drinking

the walls of the prison almost disappeared. All too soon the picnic was over and Bo was returned to his dormitory. Then a guard came to his cell. "You're being released," he told Bo. And he led Bo through the gates and into the parking lot.

Bo asked no questions; he simply followed the process, assuming that he was **the beneficiary of some bizarre bureaucratic** mistake. He reeled with joy as the gates shut behind him. He was in the parking lot. *Look calm. Look relaxed—you're just a normal guy walking to his car. Don't draw attention to yourself.* It all happened so fast. His family had just approached their car. His grandmother slowly opened the front door on the passenger's side, Sheila got into the back, his stepfather was behind the wheel. Bo half ran and half walked, fearing that the guards along the watchtower might recognize him and realize the wrong prisoner had been released. Sheila stretched to shut the door just as Bo slipped beneath her arm and dove to the floor of the car.

Sheila looked **aghast**. He put his finger to his lips and lay on the floor until the car slid out of the parking lot. Then he popped his head over the seat. His stepfather saw him in the rearview mirror.

"Oh, man," he exclaimed.

"What's that, son?" asked Bo's grandmother.

His stepfather shook his head. "Miss Ethel, you ain't ready for this."

"What's that, Willie."

"Bo-Bo's in the back seat of this car."

Bo never saw his grandmother move so quickly. She **wheeled** her head, peered into the back, and screamed. "Bo-Bo. What you doin' here?" She turned to Bo's stepfather. "Willie, stop this car."

....

the beneficiary of some bizarre bureaucratic lucky because of a strange

aghast shocked and afraid

wheeled turned

"But, Ma," Bo pleaded. "They let me go."

"Boy, you crazy. Them white folks gonna kill us all," she said.

"Don't scream, Ma."

"You can't be doin' this to white folks." She turned back to his stepfather. "I said, 'Willie, stop this car.'"

"On the highway?" Willie said.

Sheila screamed. "No, let's just keep goin'!"

Bo crept around Birmingham for a month, constantly looking over his shoulder, watching for police, afraid that at any minute the prison would discover its mistake. But the police never called or came, and Bo decided to head back to Chicago.

His stepfather and Sheila drove him to the station. At the top of the bus's steps, Bo waved one last good-bye and then, **as an afterthought**, took off his cap and tossed it in the air. He was ridding himself of all his burdens and entering a new future, freed of the past. It was a miracle the way the hat hung in the air, and it was still blowing in the breeze as Bo turned toward his seat. He felt just like that hat, **in defiance of** all the laws, as the bus crossed the Alabama line and into Tennessee. From here on out there was no heading back. **For better or worse**, Chicago would be his home.

St. Joseph wanted five hundred dollars as a down payment before they would let Arthur back into school, but Sheila didn't have that kind of money. She didn't have any money at all. She had no job. Bo was in and out of the house. They were living on her monthly $386 **welfare check**, and whatever money Bo could scratch up. After spending $300 for rent, there was barely enough money for gas, light,

---

as an afterthought before he got on the bus

in defiance of going against

For better or worse No matter what

welfare check check from the government

heat, water, and food, let alone tuition.

Each morning Arthur looked at her with longing, hoping for good news. Each morning he **was crushed**. "I'm tryin', honey," she told him.

One day she saw him in his room, face down on his pillow, crying. It was too much for her to bear.

"I'll call St. Joseph again."

As she walked to the pay phone on Pulaski, she cursed herself for having let St. Joseph into her life. *I should have known they were up to no good,* she thought. *I should have known they wouldn't want my child. What's a Catholic school from the suburbs want with a black boy from the ghetto anyway? They sold me something I don't need, stuck me with a bill I can't afford, and now they want* **to repossess** *my son's education.*

After several rings, she found herself talking to an assistant in the finance office. "You know my situation," she said. "I can't pay that kind of money."

"You knew about our tuition requirements **up front**."

"I thought the school would be payin' most of that. I didn't know he'd have to mop the floors and sell calendars."

"Consider our perspective. Your debt is **compounding**. You fell behind last year, and you've been falling behind ever since. We warned you about this. We can't let it continue. I'm sorry."

"You're sorry! My son can't go to school and you're sorry. You sent your people to *my* house to tell *my* son to come to St. Joseph. I didn't even want him to go to there. And now you say I owe you five hundred dollars?"

"You're shouting."

....

was crushed was disappointed and upset
to repossess to take away
up front before he started school; from the beginning
compounding adding up; increasing

"Where's he supposed to go? It's the middle of the year. What kind of coldhearted school just throws a child into the street? That ain't no kind of Christian way to act."

"I said, you're shouting."

"I'm sorry," said Sheila. And she was. She didn't mean to lose her temper—they would be more forgiving if she were humble. She asked to speak to Pingatore, and when he came on the phone she **poured out her heart**. "Why tear down Arthur's hopes because I can't pay the money?" she said. "It ain't Arthur's fault."

Pingatore told her that **it was out of his hands** but he would do what he could do.

She wanted to lash out. You found the money for William! But she held back. *If I scream, he'll think I'm a troublemaker, and he won't want to help me. But if I'm meek—if I act like a stupid old nobody, he may take pity.* "Oh, thank you, coach," she said. "God bless you, coach."

Eventually Sheila was able to borrow enough money from her landlord to retire a small portion of the debt. Three weeks after they told him to leave, St. Joseph let Arthur come back.

Returning to St. Joseph was the toughest thing Arthur ever had to do. **It took every ounce of** composure and courage he could muster to walk through those front doors. But that's what he did. He strolled in, head high and shoulders back, with the casual indifference of a man **unencumbered by** any care in the world. The white students in the hallways almost cheered when they saw him. "We missed you, Tuss," they said. "Where you been?"

Arthur had devised an excuse on the train coming out. "I had to

....

poured out her heart was emotional

it was out of his hands he could not help

It took every ounce of Arthur used all of the

unencumbered by who did not have

help my mamma," he said. "She was sick."

"With what?"

Arthur frowned. "Damn, man, you some kind of lawyer or what?"

They reassigned him to the mop brigade, and he and William resumed their routine, cleaning the halls. "I'm sick of this," Arthur said one day, throwing down his mop.

William leaned against his mop and sighed. William was one of the few students who knew Arthur's secret. "I talked to Pingatore and he said there was nothin' he could do."

"Yeah, right," said Arthur.

Suddenly William realized that the money that might have paid Arthur's tuition was being spent on him.

"Man, Tuss, how am I gonna survive this place without you?" William asked.

"Aw, man, I ain't goin' nowhere."

"If I could, Tuss, I'd give half my scholarship to you."

Arthur saw William's eyes **start to water**. "Don't worry about it, William," he said, and he gave his friend a hug. "I told you, we're gonna take these **chumps** downstate."

But Arthur's family was unable to make any more payments. A few days later, in mid-November, St. Joseph asked Arthur to leave. This time he was **gone for good**.

....

start to water fill with tears

chumps fools, troublemakers

gone for good not going to come back

BEFORE YOU MOVE ON...

1. **Cause and Effect** Arthur was depressed when he was kicked out of school for not paying his tuition. What caused him to feel this way?

2. **Inference** Why did St. Joseph decide to keep William but not Arthur?

LOOK AHEAD Read pages 104–130 to find out why Curtis never made it as a professional basketball player.

WILLIAM

· · · · · · · · · · ·

William stood at the baseline, hands on knees, **sucking wind**, sweat dripping from his chin and puddling on the door. It was day one of practice, and Pingatore had them running sprints. William felt great, side aches and all.

"Run," Pingatore **barked**, and the players sprinted to the other end of the gym. As he ran, William felt stronger: *This is my season, my team, this year I control the ball.*

"Hmm," said Pingatore with mock concern, as his gasping players reached the other end of the gym. "Maybe I'm not running you guys hard enough—you don't look **in shape**."

The players groaned good-naturedly. William laughed along with them. He appreciated the good things happening to him. He had recently been introduced to Patricia Weir, president of Encyclopedia Britannica and a member of the Christian Brothers Adopt-a-Student Program, who had decided to pay for part of William's tuition. She had come to school to meet him, and William gave her a tour of the school while he told her about his plans. "I want to attend Georgetown University and play for Coach John Thompson," he said.

She looked surprised: "I would think a young man like you would want to play for Bobby Knight at Indiana," she said.

William smiled. It seemed that everyone at St. Joseph wanted him to follow Isiah's path to Indiana. But William's brothers had warned him against that. "You don't want to play for **a tyrant** who's

··

sucking wind breathing very hard

barked shouted

in shape very strong; healthy

a tyrant a coach who is strong and controlling

always yellin' at his players," they told him. Besides, John Thompson's Georgetown Hoyas were **the rage of** Cabrini. He was a black coach and Georgetown was an all-black team that had its own sneaker brand, which all the kids wanted to wear. William knew next to nothing about the university except that's where he wanted to go.

"Coach Thompson's an excellent coach," he said, attempting to **sidestep** another discussion about Bobby Knight.

They wound up in the gymnasium, where they sat in the bleachers and she told him how important it was to her to help students like him. She could see he was a quiet, earnest, hard-working young man, unlike so many students today who wanted something for nothing.

The aid helped. *Without Mrs. Weir, I'm in the same **boat** as Arthur 'cause my family's no richer than his.* But one problem still loomed above all others for William. It had to do with Catherine, and he thought of her as he took a seat in the bleachers. Pingatore paced before the team, launching into his annual opening-day remarks, striking familiar themes: duty, dedication, determination; one team with one goal, to march together downstate.

William heard it all, though he wasn't listening. There was something he had to tell Pingatore, something that might make Pingatore feel differently about him, something that the coach might not like at all. And what would Mrs. Weir think?

After practice, William knocked on Pingatore's office door and the coach called him in. He sat in silence while Pingatore fiddled with his pipe. "This is your year to shine," Pingatore told William. "But you have to—have to—**have the eye of the tiger.** You have to

....

the rage of very popular in

sidestep avoid

boat *situation*

have the eye of the tiger be focused; be aggressive

be like Isiah. Did you see how Isiah came out and played one-on-one against the little kids at camp? He let the little kids score, but when the game was on the line, he refused to lose, even against sixth graders." William nodded. Pingatore stared at him.

"Is there something you want to tell me?"

William opened his mouth but couldn't speak. "Nothin', coach."

"Fine, I'll see you tomorrow."

All the way to Peggy's, William **dreaded** the phone call. He didn't want to dial her number. As it was, Catherine called him first.

"Did you tell him?" she asked.

"No, I couldn't do it. I—"

"William, this is important."

"I'm gonna tell him—"

"'Cause, William, the baby's comin' whether you tell Pingatore or not."

Catherine Mines was the youngest of eight children and was raised in the townhouses of Cabrini-Green, not far from where William grew up. Her father, Roy, was a packer at a local fish market; her mother, Eula, was a nurse's assistant. At an early age, Catherine had **high aspirations**: college, graduate school, then a career—in fashion, medicine, or law.

In the summer she attended a day camp sponsored by Cycle, a local social service organization. They took her on three- and four-day **outings** to Wisconsin, Michigan, and even West Virginia. It was soothing to escape the city and sleep in solitude undisturbed by sirens, screams, or gunshots. *There's more to the world than*

....

dreaded did not want to make

high aspirations big dreams

outings trips

Cabrini-Green, she thought. *And I aim to see it all.*

By seventh grade, William was the basketball star of Jenner grade school, and most of the girls had a crush on him. But not Catherine. "Basketball players are jocks with empty heads," she told her friends. "I rather be jumpin' rope or listenin' to music or readin' than hangin' 'round with boys."

Her indifference drew William closer. He visited her house, **allegedly** to lift weights with her older brother, Gary. But eventually he made no pretense about who he was visiting. They spent their time on the back porch teasing each other and chatting, and by the start of eighth grade William and Catherine were **going steady**. Their romance was hot news among the eighth-grade crowd at Jenner. The girls couldn't believe William had fallen for a bookworm, and the boys couldn't believe a school star like William would waste his time with just one girl.

As the **class salutatorian**, Catherine was required to give a speech at her junior high school graduation luncheon. She wanted to write an unforgettable address, about acting honestly and honorably and overcoming peer pressure. She worked on that speech for hours, trying to make each word sound right. On the day of the luncheon she wore a special pink dress, and William wore a gray suit handed down from his brothers. When the principal called her to the podium, William smiled and squeezed her hand.

"There were times that I felt I had no one to lean on," she began. "Believe me there were times when I wanted to cheat for a grade or a classmate asked me to help them cheat. But I said no. I must admit that some people didn't like me for this, but I was developing into an

....

allegedly acting as if he was there

going steady dating

class salutatorian student with the second highest rank in the graduating class

honest person. I tried to be fair minded. I don't prejudge individuals. I don't make fun of their shortcomings. I had to learn to sacrifice certain pleasures. I had to be fiercely determined to reach my goals. I also had to have discipline. We are tomorrow's future. We must learn to be leaders as well as followers."

The audience **gave her a rousing ovation**, and she returned to the table radiant with ambitions. She truly wanted to lead and not follow.

Her grades were high enough for the most selective high schools in the city: Lane Tech, Whitney Young, and Lincoln Park. But she was intimidated by the prospect of competing with dozens of students as hardworking and academically ambitious as herself. So she settled on Westinghouse, a West Side **vocational school**. It was well run—at least more orderly than some of the North Side schools—and she knew she'd be among the highest achievers.

"Don't go to Westinghouse," William advised her. "It's not good enough for you."

"Who are you to tell me where to go," she countered, "when you're going all the way out to **la-la land**?"

But after a few months she realized William was right. Westinghouse wasn't for her. Many of the other girls acted **frivolous**. They were dull. They lacked her drive. They wasted their free time hanging out in the washrooms, smoking cigarettes, adjusting their hair, plastering on makeup, and gossiping about boys. They mocked the way she talked—so precise, clear, and grammatically correct, the way her mother had taught her. "Catherine talks white," they said behind her back.

She lived with her parents on the West Side, but on the weekends

....

gave her a rousing ovation clapped loudly for her
vocational school school that taught basic job skills
la-la land the suburbs
frivolous silly and childish

she went to the North Side to stay with her sister in Cabrini-Green and be with William. Their time together was so short, and the hours passed quickly. They ordered pizza and rented movies or watched TV. William never had the time to come to Westinghouse; she didn't feel a part of his world at St. Joseph, but she dutifully attended his games, passionately **rooting him on** though she didn't really love the game and could never understand why the fans got so **carried away with** it.

When the summer came she moved in with her sister in Cabrini and spent almost all of her free time with William. They strolled along Lake Michigan and bicycled through the lakeside parks. She was happier than she'd ever been—until a few days after her fifteenth birthday, when she discovered she was pregnant.

These things aren't supposed to happen to me. I'm too smart. I'm too young. **I'm going down.** *How could I have been so dumb?*

Reflecting on her situation, she began to understand what had happened. She knew nothing about birth control. She never discussed the issue with her mother, and the health classes at Jenner had been no help. The teacher used a baseball bat and a catcher's mitt to illustrate the act of intercourse, and the kids tried not to laugh.

"I should have researched these things on my own," she told William. "I should have had some idea of what we were doing. I don't blame you."

William had the opposite reaction: instantaneous joy. He had intentionally stopped using condoms because he wanted to make Catherine pregnant. He *wanted* to create life. William knew so many young people who had been murdered. Death was becoming routine as gang wars **erupted** again around Cabrini-Green. He had

....

rooting him on supporting him; cheering for him
carried away with excited about
I'm going down. My life is not going well.
erupted started

nightmares of his own death—another innocent victim **caught in the line of fire**. "If I die without leaving behind a baby, it's like I never existed," he told Catherine.

No one but William approved of Catherine's pregnancy. Catherine's parents worried that William would ignore his parental responsibilities and **desert** their daughter. William's family thought Catherine was a devilish spider who had trapped him in her web. "Don't tell me she didn't know what she was doing," Peggy said at the time. "In this day and age with sex education in schools, these girls have to know what's going on." Curtis's grades had suffered after his girlfriend, Beatrice, got pregnant. They cautioned William to **keep his distance**: "You can't go to school, study, play basketball, *and* raise a baby," they told him.

Catherine was facing sudden adjustments and new pressures. She left Westinghouse and enrolled in a private school for pregnant teenagers. Her pregnancy changed everyone's image of her. Other girls stared at her growing belly in awe, almost as if they wanted to touch it.

"Girl, is it true you're carrying William's baby?" they asked. "I got to see this baby."

They envied her because they wanted to carry a basketball star's child. Catherine wanted none of their envy. "They're acting ignorant and dumb," she told William. "They don't understand what a baby can do to your life." But she understood. She saw the teenage mothers at Cabrini, deserted by the fathers of their children, trapped on welfare, wasting their lives. That would never happen to her.

"I'm going to love this baby," she told William. "But we're going

....

caught in the line of fire accidentally killed
desert leave, abandon
keep his distance stay away from Catherine

110

to have to raise him or her together."

"Catherine, I want this baby," he said.

"You better not leave me."

"I'll be there."

They figured out that the baby was due at the end of February or in early March.

"You're going to be there when the baby's born," Catherine said.

"I'll be there. But if I have to I'll come after the game."

"No, I need you in the hospital when the baby's being born. Don't desert me, William. I mean, I'm scared. I don't know what to expect. I've never done this before. I hear it hurts. You can't leave your girl alone—not at a time like this."

William nodded. He wanted to be there with all of his heart. But early March was play-off time. What if his child were born the day of a decisive play-off game that determined whether St. Joseph went downstate, and he had to choose between being there for Catherine or his team? He was only sixteen years old; it would be the biggest decision of his life.

In the opening moments of the season's first game, William twisted his ankle and **had to sit out** the rest of the three-game Thanksgiving Tournament. This was **his first taste of vulnerability**. Until his injury sidelined him, William didn't **appreciate that no man is irreplaceable**, and that players come and go, but the game goes on.

The Chargers won nine of their first eleven games, but Pingatore wasn't pleased. The games, he said, were too close. They were inconsistent, they played to the level of their competition. They were

....

had to sit out could not play

his first taste of vulnerability the first time he felt weak

appreciate that no man is irreplaceable understand that every player can be replaced

missing too many free throws, making too many mistakes. "You're too laid back," he told William. "You don't get up against bad teams. You have to take control."

William felt Deryl Cunningham was hogging the ball. It seemed to William that once he passed the ball inside to Deryl, the ball rarely came back.

One day in practice, Deryl overlooked him when he was wide open and William lost his temper. "Look, man, you ain't what you think you are," William said, as he stepped right up against Cunningham. "I **done put up with your B.S.** all last year and I ain't gonna put up with it again."

Cunningham towered over William. He **didn't back down**. "It's my team," he said. "I'm a senior. I run the show."

Two other players came between them and **no punches were thrown**. But the pattern continued, and William didn't know what to do.

Curtis was unsympathetic—in fact, the conflict made him even more critical of William's performance. After one game, Curtis confronted William in the locker room and **berated him** for not shooting enough.

"But, Curtis, coach doesn't want me shootin' the ball like that," William responded.

"Man, let me tell you about coaches. Coaches want to win, and no coach gonna win with his shootin' guard takin' five shots or whatever. If the coach don't like you shootin', it's 'cause you're missin', not cause you're shootin'. If you miss three in a row, he'll holler at you. But as soon as you hit three in a row, you're his

....

done put up with your B.S. accepted your bad behavior

didn't back down was not scared

no punches were thrown they did not fight

berated him yelled at him; made William feel bad

newfound friend."

"But, how can I shoot if the man ain't passin' me the ball?"

"He ain't passin' you the ball?" asked Curtis **with mock concern**.

"That's what I'm tellin you."

"Oh, I'm gonna start cryin'. Boo, hoo, hoo. I'm cryin' 'cause Deryl ain't passin' you the ball. Listen here, William, of course he ain't passin' to you. It's not in his interest to pass to you. If I'm Deryl Cunningham I don't want you to get that ball. 'Cause if you get that ball I don't have it, and if I don't have it I can't shoot, and if I can't shoot I can't score, and if I don't score ain't no coach in no college gonna want me on his team."

William shook his head. "Curtis, look, there are other things a guy should do to help his team," he said.

"Aw, man, don't talk to me about doing the little things, 'cause that's a bunch of crap, too. I don't want a guy who **does the little bitty things**—I want a guy who does things big. Look, who gets the big money, John Paxson or Michael Jordan?"

"Jordan."

"That's right. And who do you want first on your team, Paxson or Jordan?"

"Jordan."

"Right again. See, your problem, William, is you too much of a nice guy. You got to go out there and demand that ball. And if Cunningham won't give it to you, then you jump up and down and wave your arms and start screamin', 'Hey, man, pass me the goddamn ball.' Do it in front of everybody—do it in front of the whole gym. If it was me, I'd holler like a wild man and make sure everyone knew

....

with mock concern rudely, jokingly

does the little bitty things is an average player like everybody else

that he refused to pass me the ball. He'll remember to pass to you the next time."

In a critical moment of the very next game William dribbled down court, passed to Cunningham, and lost his defender on a pick. William was wide open, fifteen feet from the basket, but Cunningham spun toward the hoop and **forced a bad shot over two defenders**. William looked at Curtis, shook his head, and trotted back up court. Curtis was incensed. "Pass William the ball," he yelled, leaping to his feet, "Coach, coach, you gotta get William the ball."

Pingatore sat hunched over in his chair, eyes locked in on the game as though he hadn't heard Curtis. Curtis slammed his foot and slumped back in his seat. *It's insane, this strategy. This is no way to run a team.* "You got a shooter and he ain't shootin' the ball," Curtis said to the man sitting to his left. The man, the parent of one of the **benchwarmers**, offered a forced smile but said nothing. So Curtis turned to his right where Catherine sat, squirming uncomfortably. The bench was hard; the baby was due in a month.

"Can you believe William just runnin' up the court?" Curtis said to her.

"Curtis, I don't know what you're talking about."

"Pingatore **shoulda put Cunningham on the bench**," bellowed Curtis.

"Curtis, I think the baby's moving."

"If I was coachin' this team, I'd put that boy on the bench."

"Curtis, I can't believe you're making such a big deal over a game."

At their mother's house, Curtis hammered at his shoot-more theme, and played videos of Jordan to illustrate his point. On

....

forced a bad shot over two defenders tried to shoot the ball

benchwarmers players who did not play much

shoulda put Cunningham on the bench should have taken
Cunningham out of the game

Monday, Pingatore took over, making the same point with Isiah's highlights as illustrations. After practice William called Catherine.

"I just can't tell him—at least not now. Maybe after the baby's born," William said. "He's too preoccupied with the team."

That night William was unable to sleep. His head ached, and even aspirin couldn't dull the pain. He lay awake for hours as **a cacophony of strident, maddening** voices played in his head. The loudest one of all belonged to Curtis.

The older guys at The Avenue had been the first to discover Curtis's ability. They were astute judges of talent, with personal motivations for finding the best. You played until your team lost, but any team with Curtis **held the court** for hours.

By the time he was thirteen, Curtis was six-foot-one and strong, but height and heft were almost irrelevant because it was his heart and soul that made him great. He played with passion. He played into the night, in the snow, sleet, or rain. He had rock-solid shoulders and springboard legs, and when he drove for the basket, the opposition cleared out. There was a fearlessness to his drive, a hunger to his dunks.

People gathered along the fence that lined The Avenue to watch him jump. He **had a diverse repertoire** of dunks: turnarounds, tomahawks, and baseline jams. The higher he jumped the louder they cheered, and the louder they cheered the harder he played. Basketball was his life. Not once did he doubt that one day he would play in the NBA.

In the future, scouts would roam playgrounds **wooing blue-chip**

....

a cacophony of strident, maddening the sound of many loud
held the court continued playing
had a diverse repertoire could do many different kinds
wooing blue-chip trying to recruit talented

eighth graders. Every powerhouse school in Chicago would have recruited Curtis, but high school coaches were less predatory back in 1979—they hadn't refined the art of recruitment. Kids remained in their neighborhoods and attended the schools closest to home. Curtis went to Wells High School, an old **soot-stained fortress** on Ashland Avenue, as his older siblings, Randy and Peggy, had done before him.

Wells had a **mediocre** team in a mediocre division. Many of the students were Mexican immigrants who knew nothing of basketball. The coach was a well-meaning gym teacher who understood the game, but he was no Pingatore. He didn't build a college-type system like Pingatore did. What was the use? The team was lucky to find twelve guys to fill the roster, let alone guards who could dribble and forwards who could shoot. If the coach had a strategy, it was to get the ball to Gates and get out of his way.

Curtis played as he pleased. He defended the middle—blocking the shots of centers six inches taller—and then brought the ball up court like a guard. "If the coach don't like what I do, let him put me on the bench and see what happens to the team," Curtis said. He played from start to finish and averaged thirty-nine points a game.

In the summer before his sophomore year, some friends from the playground suggested he transfer to Corliss, a South Side school. Curtis thought about it. The days were gone when players stayed at the school where they started. It was not uncommon for players to **crisscross** the city, searching for the best deals they could find. In Curtis's case, he wanted more exposure and tougher competition. So at the start of the school year he hopped a bus for Corliss, where he **lasted for all of** one day—about as long as it took the coach to tell

....

soot-stained fortress dirty building
mediocre below average
crisscross travel across
lasted for all of stayed only

him that transfer students were ineligible to play until the second half of the season.

"You mean I got to wait until January to play basketball?" Curtis asked.

"That's right," the coach said. "But you can participate in our practices."

Curtis laughed in the coach's face. He wasn't traveling two hours a day to practice.

Back he went to Wells, where he closed out his high school career as the greatest player the school had ever seen. In his senior year he **teamed up** with his younger brother David, then a sophomore, and they dominated their division. Their strongest competition came from Roosevelt High School, which featured Chuck Taylor, one of the great shooting guards of his time. They had some incredible scoring duels—Curtis and Chuck—racing across the court, dunking and shooting until each had scored forty, fifty, even sixty points. After his last game against Roosevelt, Curtis exchanged hugs with Roosevelt's coach, Manny Weincord. "Son, I want to tell you, you're one of the greatest players I've ever seen," Weincord said. "It was an honor and a privilege to have coached against you. I wish you all the luck in the world. But I have to tell you somethin', you won't get anywhere with this game unless you **hit the books** and have the grades."

It was a refrain endlessly repeated and advice endlessly ignored. Books and classes **left Curtis cold**—basketball would take him far enough.

Dozens of colleges **courted him**. He accepted a four-year

....

teamed up played on the team
hit the books study hard
left Curtis cold did not interest Curtis
courted him wanted Curtis to come and play at their schools

scholarship from Marquette. But under new **mandates** adopted by the National Collegiate Athletic Association, high school students had to have at least a 2.0 grade point average to play as college freshmen. Curtis's average was lower than that. Marquette had one scholarship for an inactive player, which they wanted to reserve for someone else. So they withdrew their scholarship from Curtis only a few weeks after they had offered it.

Curtis wasn't too upset. His attitude was the same as it had been with Corliss. He wouldn't go where he couldn't play. He wasn't going to college to sit on the bench.

Instead he went to Colby, a two-year college in western Kansas. As a junior college, Colby was not governed by the same stringent NCAA rules as Marquette. Any student, even a **high school dropout**, could obtain a scholarship to play at a junior college. Curtis moved to Kansas, lived in a dormitory, passed his courses, graduated with an associate degree in psychology, and was the king of the court. It wasn't much different from Wells: If he didn't want to practice, he didn't practice. If he wanted to shoot a jumper, he shot the jumper. If the coach called a play he didn't like, he ran the one he did like. The play that mattered most to Curtis was the one where he took the ball to the hole and dunked. He was rarely, if ever, **reprimanded or held accountable for** his behavior. He played almost every minute of every game for two straight seasons, dominating the league, rewriting the school's scoring records. He was selected as Colby's player of the decade. Once again the major colleges came calling; this time he settled on Central Florida, which offered **him a full ride**.

In the fall of 1986 Curtis, Beatrice, and Sparkiesha, their four-

....

mandates rules
high school dropout student who did not finish high school
reprimanded or held accountable for questioned about
him a full ride to let him attend their college for free

year-old daughter, moved to Orlando. From the outset their stay was difficult. They lived in a cramped, one-room dormitory apartment. They knew no one and had no social life. Worst of all, Curtis **rode the bench**. It was the coach's decision. He apparently believed the other guards were better. "Just keep **plugging**," he told Curtis. "Your chance will come."

Those who knew Curtis could only shake their heads. In some ways, he was a victim of his own success. He had always been allowed to slide, to do exactly what he wanted. This was the first time he had ever been seriously challenged, and he didn't know how to handle himself. David, Peggy, and Alvin advised Curtis to be more compromising. They urged him to work on his jump shots and to learn the coach's half-court system. It wasn't like Wells or Colby. This was a big league—Division One basketball. "You can't be a six-foot-one center anymore," they said. "You have to play guard, you have to learn the program, you have to play within the system. You can't just dunk when you want to dunk, you have to do what the coach tells you."

"I'm adapting," Curtis insisted, "But the **coach's got something against** me. I'm working hard, I'm practicing my shot. In practice I'm the hottest guy out there. But he won't give me a chance."

As the season wore on he was continually embarrassed. The coach kept him on the bench, even during a game for which Emma and Peggy had flown down from Chicago. One midseason game Curtis suffered the most painful **indignation** of all: The coach asked him to lend his shorts and jersey to another player who had forgotten his uniform. *You can't take a player's uniform*, Curtis thought as he

....

rode the bench did not get to play

plugging practicing

coach's got something against coach does not like

indignation embarassment, shame

119

watched the game from the bench in his street clothes. *I don't care how bad he is, you can't take his stuff and give it to someone else. You got to be responsible for your own stuff. If you leave your uniform or your gym shoes, you don't play. You can't take another player's.*

He decided to quit. He didn't show up for the next game against Jacksonville. The coach tried to **track him down**. He went to Curtis's apartment and knocked on the door. "Curtis," the coach said, "are you in there? We have to talk." Curtis lay on his bed and didn't reply. From his perspective they had nothing to talk about. He had no patience for the bench. He refused to concede that he wasn't the best. He still felt the same: He wouldn't stay if he couldn't play.

In the morning he and Beatrice packed the bags. Curtis hailed a cab to the airport and flew himself and his family home to Chicago. Until the moment he stepped on the plane, he didn't fully comprehend the enormity of his expectations or **the elusiveness of** his dream. It took more than talent to reach the top. It also took **resiliency** and luck. If you fell to the bottom, you had to **bounce back**. But when Curtis fell, it was with a thud and there was no bouncing back.

It was tough, going home. People wanted to know what he was doing back at Cabrini, and why he wasn't playing ball in college. He didn't run from what had happened, and he didn't lie or make excuses. He hated excuses. He never dodged the truth.

"I still have one year of eligibility left but I might as well give it up because nobody's going to give a senior in college no athletic scholarship," he told those who asked. "I just decided to quit school, period, and go to work. I've got a wife and daughter. I got to think about them now. As far as basketball goes, I don't have any regrets.

....

track him down look for him; find him

the elusiveness of how hard it would be to achieve

resiliency strength and dedication

bounce back try again

That coach broke my heart, but I don't hate him. The coach didn't play me. That's his job. That's his life. He got to take care of his family, he got to do what he sees best for his team. And that's what he saw best, so I can't **downgrade** him for that. But, yeah, well, it just crushed me."

He moved in with his **in-laws** and got a job working as a watchman for a local hospital. He rarely played basketball anymore, he didn't see the point. Alvin tried to convince him to enroll at a small state school, but Curtis didn't see the point of going to college if he couldn't play big-time basketball.

Instead he became William's unofficial coach, attending his games, critiquing his plays.

"You're too hard on him," David told Curtis.

But Curtis disagreed. "I love William. He means so much to me in so many ways. I mean, of course we fight and argue all the time, but deep down, I'm just so proud of him. I mean, I don't want him to not make it for the same reasons I didn't make it. If he don't make it, I want it to be because of his ability, not because some coach said this or that. I want to do something to assure that nothing like that is going to happen. All those basketball dreams he has, I had them once, and now they're gone. All my dreams are in him now. I want him to make it so bad, I don't know what to do. If he don't make it, I'll sit and cry."

The birth of William's baby and the start of the play-offs were like two trains on one track heading for a crash.

On February 23, the Chargers began their play-off march,

....

downgrade say bad things about

in-laws wife's family

You're too hard on him You are too critical of William

whipping Willowbrook High School, 77-54; on March 2, the baby was due.

Pingatore could see that something was bothering William, but he didn't know what. "Stay focused," he told William. "Keep your concentration."

"If you **got it**," Curtis said, "now's the time to show it."

March 2 came and went and Catherine didn't feel **one contraction**. On March 3, the Chargers took on Proviso West. The Chargers ran off to a big lead, but Cunningham picked up his fourth foul early in the fourth quarter, and when he retreated to the bench Proviso clawed back. Pingatore brought in Mark Layton, a 5'11" junior, and Layton shackled Cedrick Hodges, a taller and talented forward. Then Pingatore had them run the stall. They spread over the floor and passed the ball back and forth, always just beyond the reach of an outstretched defender. It was a masterful demonstration of a precise, well-orchestrated team, and Pingatore, his face flushed red with excitement, directed the rotation like a conductor from the bench.

"I can't ask more of them," Pingatore told reporters after the victory. "We had a great effort from nine guys. I'm very pleased. That's what it takes to win."

The next day at practice Pingatore ran his team hard and had them shoot free throws for an hour. When they missed he made them run laps. "You have to focus," barked Pingatore. "This is your great moment; the chance might not come again."

The next game was March 8 against the Fenwick Friars, a tough division rival. Interest was **peaking** as each team inched closer to the finals. The crowd packed the stadium, and TV crews came from

....

whipping winning against; beating
got it have talent
one contraction close to giving birth
peaking growing, increasing

several stations. The Chargers **started cold**, so Pingatore, playing a hunch, brought in Frankie Thames, a little-used senior forward. Frankie **knocked down** eighteen points, hitting nine of ten jumpers, and the Chargers' defense **choked Fenwick's late game rally** for a 65 to 49 win.

"It's my job to come off the bench and score," Thames told reporters in the steaming locker room after the game. "I didn't want to come off taking wild shots, but I was going to take shots they gave me."

The next game was set for Friday, March 10, against Tommy Kleinschmidt and his Rams of Gordon Tech, with the winner going downstate.

In the locker room William sat against the wall, his eyes closed. "You okay, man?" asked Mark Layton. This was his best friend on the team, and he didn't know William's girlfriend was expecting a baby. "You look like you're sick."

"I'm okay," William said.

But he wasn't. He had a headache; he and Catherine had been bickering the night before.

"If you aren't with me at that hospital," Catherine warned, **"we're through**."

"Why we makin' this a big thing," he told her. "We don't even know the baby's goin' to be born on the day of a game."

"It's the principle; it's what's right. Your family's got to come first. This baby is your flesh and blood."

"But basketball's our future. It's how I get to college and then to the pros, so I can take care of our baby."

"Plenty of men take care of their babies all the time, William,

....

started cold did not play well in the beginning
knocked down scored
choked Fenwick's late game rally played well against Fenwick
we're through our relationship is over

without playing basketball. Any fool can play basketball. Any fool can make a baby. But only a man can be a father."

William would lie in bed replaying these conversations for hours. As much as he hated to admit it, he knew Catherine was right. There would always be some game to play, some reason to be away from his family. He didn't want to be the kind of father who always had something more important to do. He knew what it was like to be missing a father. His father had never been around, and his absence **haunted** William in ways he could hardly express. Some moments he **craved** a father's attention—a pat on the back, words of comfort or direction—but it was never there. Emma had to be mother and father to him. It broke his heart when he saw her at the end of the day, weary from work, with no one to help **pick up the slack** or bring home a check, change the storm windows or take out the garbage. No, William wasn't going to let his child grow up like he did. He would never be like his father, who left Emma alone to raise six kids in Cabrini-Green.

Emma Gates was a farm girl from Chickasaw County, Mississippi, who got pregnant in her sophomore year, left school, and never went back. By the time she was nineteen, she had two children, Randy and Peggy. That was in 1963, the year she moved to Chicago. The father of her children left to live with someone else. There were no jobs in Mississippi, and she had no reason to stay. A sister of a friend who lived near Chicago was visiting. She asked Emma to drive with her back to Chicago. **On a whim** Emma hopped into the car and made the eleven-hour trip north. A few months later she came back for

....

haunted continued to bother
craved really wanted
pick up the slack take care of things at home
On a whim Without planning

Peggy and Randy.

They settled in Cabrini-Green, moving into a two-bedroom townhouse just north of Chicago Avenue. In those days, the high-rises were only a few years old, and the complex was a clean, **well-regulated model for subsidized** housing. The Chicago Housing Authority **scrutinized** its applicants, and **unruly or rent-delinquent tenants were evicted**. She had hot and cold running water, newly installed plumbing, and freshly painted walls; she grew a garden in the back. *This is a step up from anything back in Mississippi*, thought Emma.

She fell in love with Willie Crawford, a working man who gave her four children: Curtis, David, Latanya, and William. But Willie never married Emma, and he never lived with her for more than a year or two at a time. He played guitar in a local blues band and ran an auto repair shop. The children occasionally visited him at his shop; sometimes he stopped by the townhouse in his flashy red tow truck. William couldn't have been more than five when Willie put him in the driver's seat.

"Go, ahead, you can turn the steering wheel," Willie said.

"Oh, wow," said William, his eyes aglow. He knelt on the seat so he could see above the steering wheel and made revving sounds, pretending he was a race-car driver.

Months passed between Willie's visits. He had other children by different women, who also lived in Cabrini. Whatever hurt Emma felt she kept to herself. Her personal problems were no one's business. She rarely expressed self-pity. She felt she was no better or worse off than other women whose marriages had failed. "I live for my children," she told her friends. "Everything I don't have, they will have."

....

well-regulated model for subsidized good example of inexpensive
scrutinized carefully chose

unruly or rent-delinquent tenants were evicted troublemakers or
people who paid rent late were forced to leave

Emma had her rules, which she enforced with a leather strap. The children had to be home when she called them; they had to clean the house, make their beds, put away their clothes, look after one another, and stay in school. Every now and then Emma called them to the kitchen to settle a crisis or **deliver an ultimatum**. "I can't make one of you go to college, but all of you gonna get me that high school diploma," she told them. "I'm gonna hang your diplomas on the wall. You don't get a diploma, you can't get a job, and you'll be depending on me for the rest of my life. I left school 'cause I didn't know what I was doing. It's not going to be like that with you."

For several years she raised the family on the monthly eighty-five dollars she got from public aid. In the late seventies she got her high school equivalency diploma, graduated from a nurse's aid program, and found work at a local nursing home. She worked two shifts at the nursing home. There were no men in her life. She rarely left town and never went on vacation. She saw a movie now and then. Her family was her life.

She **fervently** preached family loyalty, and it was a doctrine her children understood and believed in. They took care of themselves when Emma was working. The oldest acted as the parents, the youngest **fell into line**. At an age when most adolescent girls want only to cling to one another, Peggy rushed home from school each day to make dinner for her brothers and sisters. They relentlessly teased her. They nicknamed her "Thelma," after the maid in *Good Times*, but she ignored their **barbs** and demanded obedience. She made them wash before dinner and clean the table afterward. She made fried chicken, spaghetti, or hot dogs and french fries. They

......

deliver an ultimatum make a final demand
fervently strongly and passionately
fell into line listened, obeyed
barbs mean comments

lived on french fries when **money was tight**. They would buy fifty-pound bags of potatoes and have peeling parties—the whole family in the kitchen, radio blaring, voices running through the house and into the street.

They were a loud, raucous bunch. They warred over the bathroom in the morning. They fought over cereal at the breakfast table. They **elbowed** for the best position in front of the TV. There was never enough room, never enough privacy. They knew each other's secrets and examined each other's faults: who was too bossy, too grumpy, too gossipy, too shy. They mistrusted almost every boyfriend or girlfriend brought into the house. "He ain't good enough for my sister" or, "she ain't good enough for my brother" was a common refrain. They depended on each other in ways other siblings never had to. They didn't have a father in the house. They didn't have uncles or aunts or cousins. They walked to and from school together. Peggy was a cheerleader when Curtis played on the team. William watched Curtis and David play basketball. David drove William to youth games and to weekend practices.

They needed each other. Cabrini-Green had become such a dangerous place to live. The old townhouses built in the 1940s were still stable and strong, but the twenty-three high-rises, once sparkling with promise, had fallen apart. The Chicago Housing Authority had given up on scrutinizing applicants. Almost anyone could get in, though only the desperate tried. Most tenants wanted to get out. **Strapped for funds**, and wasting what little cash it had, the CHA stopped making repairs. The public grassways went uncut, trash bins unemptied, burned-out hallway bulbs unreplaced. When the

....

money was tight there was not enough money
elbowed pushed each other
Strapped for funds Without much money

elevators shut down, residents had to walk five, ten, fifteen stories to their apartments. When units fell apart, they weren't repaired; when families moved out, they weren't replaced. One by one, apartments were vacated until most units in the top five floors of the high-rises were abandoned, their windows shattered or boarded up. The gangs moved in, ruling from the rooftops.

In an act of defiance, **with an eye toward** the black vote, Mayor Jane Byrne moved into a vacant Cabrini-Green apartment in early 1980, vowing to "clean Cabrini up." For a few weeks the place **crawled** with police and the gangs disappeared. Disbelieving families walked through the courtyards without fear of gunshots. But when Byrne and her extra police left, the gangs came back and the shooting resumed. Cabrini-Green was left with nothing from Byrne's efforts except a nationwide reputation **as the bane of** public housing.

Emma advised her children to **stay clear of** the high-rises. None of the Gates kids ever ran with the gangs or dealt drugs or shot guns. They spent much of their free time at Cycle, the local social center. They were tutored there and played in its recreation leagues. At night they retreated to their home. They witnessed all the great moments of history crowded around the TV set in their cramped living room. They saw Richard Nixon resign, Mayor Richard J. Daley die, the pope visit Chicago, Ronald Reagan get shot, and black candidate Harold Washington get elected mayor of Chicago. That 1983 mayoral election was a great moment for the family. They were not overtly political; they didn't work in campaigns, or solicit favors from precinct captains, or know their alderman. But Washington's triumph over Bernard Epton inspired the Gates family.

....

with an eye toward hoping to get
crawled was filled
as the bane of as a disaster of
stay clear of stay away from

The empowerment of black voters frightened white residents all over Chicago. Washington had to overcome **a scurrilous** campaign marred by evil rumors, malicious lies, and volatile fliers depicting him in cartoons as a baboon or a gorilla **lasciviously drooling over white maidenhood**. Black voters rallied to his side. Peggy hung a campaign poster on her wall and went to hear the candidate speak. All the kids in Cabrini, including Curtis and David and William, were wearing blue-and-white Washington election buttons.

"I never thought I'd see the day a black man would be elected mayor of Chicago," Emma told her children as they watched the votes roll in.

The world was changing. Emma Gates's children were growing up, and Cabrini-Green couldn't contain them any longer. It seemed as if the house got quiet overnight. Curtis and David went to college. Peggy married Alvin Bibbs and moved to the West Side. And, eventually, William went to St. Joseph. Emma had allowed her baby to move out. It made so much sense. Peggy lived closer to St. Joseph.

Peggy had a full-time job, a newborn son, and a husband with his own needs. The last thing in the world she needed was a teenager living in her house, but she never considered turning William away.

It wasn't easy. She was **fastidious** and he was sloppy. She wanted quiet and he wanted to play his music loud. Peggy was her mother's daughter, and when she made rules she enforced them. It was hard for William to obey, and they bickered all the time. He had to be home by ten. He could take or make no phone calls after eleven. She ordered him to clean up his room.

"Why can't I just shut the door?" he demanded.

....

a scurrilous an insulting; an offensive

lasciviously drooling over white maidenhood desiring white women

fastidious difficult to please; very demanding

"'Cause I want it clean," she answered.

"You ain't my mother."

"But you're living in my house."

"You know, I'm glad tomorrow's Friday," he said, "so I won't have to see you till Sunday."

"Well, I can't wait for you to go home," she **retorted**.

On Sunday night, when William returned, Peggy told him, "in this family, all we got is each other. If we go down, we all go down together."

....

retorted answered back angrily

BEFORE YOU MOVE ON...

1. **Paraphrase** Reread page 119. The author wrote that Curtis was a victim of his own success. What does this mean?

2. **Persuasion** How did Catherine persuade William to be at the hospital for the delivery of their baby?

LOOK AHEAD Read pages 131–162 to see what life was like for Arthur at Marshall High School.

ARTHUR

• • • • • • • • • • •

Sheila tried to enroll Arthur at a local vocational high school.

"Let me get this straight," the principal said, cutting her off in the middle of her story. "You can't pay the money for St. Joseph?"

His agitated tone surprised Sheila, who was expecting sympathy. "Well, w–we—" she stammered.

"And now you want to come here?"

"You mean, he can't?"

"It's really kind of late for that," the principal **snapped**.

"But this is a public high school."

"Well you can't just come in here in the middle of the term."

Sheila had to **bite her tongue** to keep from shouting. "I wasn't asking for anything special," she said, rising from her chair. "I only want to send my son to school."

Now she couldn't contain her anger. "You sound too ignorant to be in the educational system," she said as she slammed the door behind her.

The next day she called Marshall High School. A year ago she would have been reluctant to make that call. A year ago she thought only St. Joseph was good enough for her son. *I guess we're not so special after all. I guess **I'm not so picky** anymore.*

The clerk on the phone told Sheila that Arthur would have to wait another two weeks until the start of the second semester. After that, he could enroll.

"Oh, thank you," Sheila said. "It's so good to feel welcome."

....

snapped said angrily

bite her tongue control herself

I'm not so picky *I do not think Arthur is too good for Marshall*

The clerk laughed. "Honey, this is a public school," she said. "Everybody's welcome here."

For his first day at Marshall, Arthur got up at 7:30 and put on ripped blue jeans, a Dominique Wilkins T-shirt, a Detroit Piston warm-up jacket, and Michael Jordan **high-tops** with his nickname, Tuss, written big and bold on the back. He scrubbed his gym shoes with soap and shined them with wax, and checked himself in the mirror to make sure he looked right.

At the breakfast table, Sheila didn't hide her disappointment. "You didn't wear torn jeans at St. Joseph," she said.

"Momma, it's a different school," said Arthur. "If I wear a tie and slacks they'll laugh me out of school."

He didn't carry any books because he didn't have any to carry. He wouldn't have carried them anyway—no one he knew at Marshall was carrying books.

When Arthur got to Marshall, he saw some familiar faces in the groups hanging out in front of the school, waiting for the doors to open. Shannon, a boy Arthur knew from the playgrounds, approached. "How come you ain't at that school where Isiah went?"

Arthur **scoffed** as though the question were silly. "I left 'cause I wanted to. I want to play ball for Marshall." That answer satisfied Shannon, but Arthur had to repeat the routine again and again as the day went on. It seemed everyone wanted to know about St. Joseph.

When the school was opened, a line of students backed up from the front door, where a security guard was searching students for weapons. They had to wait out in the cold as a wet snow fell, and a

....

high-tops gym shoes; sneakers
scoffed laughed

squad car crept up and back along the street in front of the school.

"Can't take no beeper in here," the security guard said to a student ahead of Arthur. "Don't make no scene."

"Y'all can't take my beeper, man."

A second guard approached the student. "I need to see you at the front door."

"I'm gonna go, man," the student said.

The security guard laughed. "I know where you're gonna go," he said. "You're gonna go to jail. No beeper in here. Now don't make no scene."

Arthur walked to the main office along a corridor that bustled with students, teachers, administrators, and security guards. Marshall High was a massive, three-story, limestone building, but it was almost ninety years old and needed **painting and tuck-pointing**. The big sign out front was losing letters, the floor was scuffed, the stairs tread-worn, the lockers dented. The office smelled of new paint, old wood, and burnt coffee. A message coming over the loudspeaker was lost amid crackle and static.

Arthur waited in the central office for his meeting with the school counselor and watched the teachers chattering by the mailbox. It had been a very frustrating year for Chicago public school teachers. The year before, they had **gone on strike** after the superintendent tried to cut their pay. They stayed out for three weeks, and when they returned everything had changed and nothing had changed. A new school reform law was adopted, intended to strip the central office of its power. But **the money lagged behind the reform**. Many schools lacked pencils, paper, or workbooks. The miraculous transformation

....

painting and tuck-pointing to be repaired

gone on strike stopped working to protest

the money lagged behind the reform there was no money to make changes

never occurred. The systemwide dropout rate still neared fifty percent, one-third of the students were absent each day, and only one-third read at or above grade level. Even the business leaders had complained: High school graduates lacked the most elementary reading and writing skills needed for even minimum-wage employment.

Arthur heard his name called and rose to meet his counselor, Marjorie Heard, a tall, black woman, who led him into her office. She opened his file, read it, and shook her head. "You've been out of school for two months, Arthur, and you lost a whole semester credit. Do you understand?"

He nodded. She was telling him that as far as the credits went, he was still a freshman.

"Had you stayed at St. Joseph, you would have been able to receive credit for the first semester." She put down the folder. Arthur was looking at the floor. "Arthur, look at me," she said softly. He looked up. "I know it's unfair, but you have been caught in the middle of two separate school systems."

Arthur looked at the floor. "Yes, ma'am."

Heard wrote him a note of introduction and directed him to algebra, his first class of the day. A bell rang, and hundreds of feet rumbled down the hallways. Arthur **sliced through the sea of** students, looking for his classroom. He was quiet and expressionless like a zombie; he walked with his head down. He wanted to get **the feel of things** before he attracted any attention.

He entered his algebra class, gave his teacher Heard's note, and took a seat as far from the front of the room as he could. The teacher

....

sliced through the sea of moved through all the
the feel of things to know the school

read the note and frowned—kids came and went so quickly, it was hard to **keep track**. They started the year with thirty in this class, but now there were twenty including Arthur. The teacher didn't know what happened to the other eleven students. They simply stopped coming to school. **The truant officers** tried to find them, but they were hard to track. Some of them had no phones or had moved from their last listed address.

Arthur looked at his work sheet. *We did this stuff at St. Joe's last year*, he thought. *I don't even have to worry about this.* He wasn't bad at algebra, sometimes he even enjoyed it. But he wouldn't need math, not to play basketball anyway, which was what he was going to do. He put algebra out of his mind and didn't give it another thought.

His next class was history. They were discussing the Reconstruction. "What kind of techniques were being used to take away the freedoms that had been earned?" the teacher asked.

No one answered.

The teacher looked around the room and then called on a girl in the back. "Jeannette?"

"A poll tax," said Jeannette.

"Right," said the teacher. "Okay, Arthur, what other techniques were used to keep black Americans from voting."

Arthur shrugged. "I dunno."

While the teacher lectured some kids slept. One kid was chewing gum and blowing bubbles. No one listened. *St. Joseph wouldn't put up with this*, Arthur thought. Kids at St. Joseph might fall asleep in class, but they were **discreet about it**. They didn't just put their heads on the desk. In the back of the room two boys were talking. One

---

keep track know where all the students were
The truant officers School workers
discreet about it careful not to let the teacher see

punched the other and they burst out laughing. *Those guys wouldn't last at St. Joseph*, Arthur thought. *Probably would have been kicked out.*

The teacher started talking about the Ku Klux Klan, Dr. King, the Civil Rights Movement, the Birmingham marches. Arthur yawned. He definitely didn't need this stuff to play basketball. He rested his head on the desk and closed his eyes.

Back in 1969, Bo had written letters to Sheila in Birmingham almost every week, **imploring** her to come to Chicago. "I need to see my child," he wrote.

Cookie **reversed her stand**. "I think you should move to Chicago," she told Sheila. "It's better for the baby to have a daddy. Bo can't be all that bad. How many guys ask for their kids?"

"But, I'm scared," pleaded Sheila. "I've never been in a city that big. I'll be alone."

"You gotta go with your husband, Sheila. You've gotta grow up. You can't be daddy's little girl forever."

After months of back and forth, Sheila **made up her mind** to move north. On a cold, rainy night in December her parents, brothers, and sisters accompanied her to the Greyhound station. Her mother packed a basket with chicken, biscuits, and fruit. When the boarding announcement came over the loudspeaker, they all broke down, wailing and weeping. Mr. Goldthwaite took Sheila aside. She was holding Tomekia, wrapped in a pink woolen blanket.

"I know I can't make you stay," he said. But listen here: If you don't like it, you can always come back."

As soon as Sheila boarded the bus, she wanted to get off. But it

....

imploring begging
reversed her stand changed her mind
made up her mind decided

was too late. The doors closed with a hiss and the bus backed out into the rain. It rained all night and well into the morning as the bus hummed along the highway. Cars and trucks splashed past the bus. The highway bustled with determined travelers; only Sheila **was ambivalent**. She drifted off to sleep, awakening when Tomekia dampened her diaper and started to cry. When the bus reached northern Indiana, the rain turned to snow. Sheila's first view of Chicago was of the steel mills with their **smokestacks belching** clouds of smoke. Beyond the highway were rows of houses, TVs glittering in the night.

A **seedy**, desperate bunch lingered around the bus station in downtown Chicago. Sheila drew Tomekia closer to her breast as she waited. Where was Bo? He had promised he would meet her, but all she saw were **winos** and junkies and old beggars holding tin cups. Sheila called Bo's number, and Bo's grandfather, Cleveland, answered the phone. "Bo's at work," he told her. "You better catch a cab."

The howling icy wind cut through her overcoat and froze her blood. She wobbled left and right trying to hail a cab, unsteadied by trying to carry Tomekia and the suitcase. She slipped on the sidewalk and lost her footing in the snow. A black man in a yellow cab pulled over. "I'll take the short cut," he said, and he grinned. She didn't know where she was or where they were going, or how long it would take or how much it would cost to get there. He drove fast, zipping around corners and through red lights, winding along bumpy roads past vast stretches of abandoned factories and empty lots. He looked at her in the rearview mirror.

"You must have never been here before?"

....

was ambivalent didn't care
smokestacks belching tall chimneys sending out
seedy dirty, shabby
winos drunks, alcoholics

She nodded.

They pulled up to a darkened house on a leafy street. He turned and smiled, "Can I help you with your bags?"

"No," she said, almost running to the door.

For an hour she sat in the living room **making small talk with Cleveland, seething with anger** at Bo, and feeling like a fool for having left home for this frosty hell. But when Bo swept through the door, she was so happy to see a familiar face that all was forgiven.

Bo picked her up, twirled her, and gave her a long, lingering kiss. "My family," he cried. He picked up Tomekia, who had been sleeping. Tomekia started wailing, and Bo laughed and pranced her and Sheila around the room in a jubilant dance. "My family," Bo kept crying. "My dream has come true."

During her first year in Chicago, Sheila almost never left the house. Her only friend was Valerie, the landlady's **heavy-set spinster** daughter. When she wasn't cleaning, cooking, or tending to Tomekia, she looked out her window at the strangers walking by.

Bo was gone day and night, working two jobs. Or so he said. Sheila had no doubts. He had to be working: How else could he afford the nice clothes he bought her and the chickens and steaks that stocked their refrigerator?

After a few months they found their own apartment in a recently renovated complex a few blocks from where Cleveland lived. They were married in a simple ceremony, handled like a **clerical transaction** in the basement wedding room at city hall. There was no reason for a big, formal affair; they had few friends or family to invite.

Four weeks later Sheila realized she was pregnant. After visiting

....

making small talk with Cleveland, seething with anger talking to Cleveland, feeling angry

heavy-set spinster overweight and unmarried

clerical transaction business deal

the doctor to confirm the pregnancy, Sheila made the long walk home. She sat in the living room while day turned to night and cried bitter tears of disappointment. Life was going wrong. Time was running too fast. Nursing school and college seemed unreachable dreams. She was nineteen—too young to feel so old. "Am I going to be giving him babies all my life?" she sobbed. "Is that all I'm going to do?"

She decided to get an abortion, but her father, calling from Birmingham, changed her mind. "That's one of God's children," he told her.

"Oh, Daddy, there's no one on my side."

"Now, Sheila, this isn't about you—it's about that baby. If you don't want that baby, send him home to me."

Arthur Jr., was born on October 22, 1972. Cleveland drove her to the hospital, and Valerie led her through admissions. The pain of delivery was excruciating. "Lord, help me," she screamed as Valerie held her hand and whispered comforting words. Bo wasn't there, he had to work. He came by that evening. "Look at how big his hands are," Bo exclaimed as he held and examined Arthur. Bo turned to Sheila and laughed, his eyes watering with tears of pride. "The boy's gonna be a basketball player, Sheila Gaye, just like his daddy." Bo held the baby at arm's length to allow himself a more **exacting examination**. "Lord almighty, we're lookin' at the next Earl 'the Pearl' Monroe. Just look at his hands. This boy's gotta be twenty-nine inches long. I mean, this is a long child. His hands are as big as a man's."

From then on the baby's nickname was Man. Man would **comprise** the better halves of both his parents, Bo predicted. "He's

....

exacting examination careful look
comprise have qualities of

gonna be anything he wants," Bo said. "But I tell you this, a child as long as this is gonna want to play basketball."

Arthur was four when he learned he and Tomekia had other siblings. Tomekia **broke the news** one day after school. "Guess what, Momma? Me and Man have two brothers," she squealed.

Sheila smiled at Tomekia's innocent exuberance. "No, you don't," she said.

"Yes, we do. There's this boy in my school who says Daddy's his daddy, too. He even looks like me. And he's got a younger brother."

When Sheila repeated Tomekia's comments to Bo, he laughed them off. But a few days later Sheila called the principal: "Do you have two other children in the school roughly the same age as Tomekia and Arthur, and their last name is Agee?"

Bo now had to acknowledge the children as his own. Sheila fell into a chair, running over in her mind all the evidence she had previously ignored: the late nights (he said he was working), the **hush-hush** conversations on the telephone (he said it was just some friends). They were lies, all lies. She moved north to live with him; she gave him two children. She sacrificed her life, and he had deceived her. She imagined what the other mothers at school said about her. They probably had it all figured out. Probably **got a good laugh at her expense**, probably thought she was a fool, probably slept with him, too.

"I've always been faithful," Sheila said. "And all this time you've been **carryin' on**."

She pressed him for details—how many women? How many

....

broke the news told her mother
hush-hush quiet, private
got a good laugh at her expense laughed at her
carryin' on acting badly; with other women

other children? But he volunteered nothing and showed neither shame nor remorse but defiance. "I don't owe you nothin'," he declared. "I bring home the money. I pay the rent. My money feeds and clothes you and our children." He **gestured wildly** toward the TV, the records, the furniture, and the drapes. "I bought it all."

"That don't mean nothin', Bo," Sheila screamed. "That petty little stuff don't tell how a man's supposed to live his life."

"You ungrateful bitch," Bo snarled, and he knocked her to the floor with a fist to her face. It was the first time he had hit her, and he wasn't even sorry. He hated when people told him what to do; he was so sick of having to hustle and con and hide his secrets. He wanted to let everything out: "I ain't got nothin' to be ashamed of," he yelled. "You should be kissin' my ass."

She rose to her feet and he kicked her back down. She had pushed him too far, always pressing him to come home early, always begging him to take her out. "You don't appreciate nothin'," he yelled at her. "You were nothin' without me. I got you out of Alabama."

"Got me out of Alabama! You didn't do me no favors, Bo Agee. I should have stayed down there."

After that they fought almost every night: He rose to leave, she demanded to know where he was going and who he was seeing, and he told her what he did was none of her affair. She was too angry to cry anymore, and tears only confused the issue and made her weak. She fought **with unimpeded fury**. When he hit her, she hit back, lunging for his eyes with her fingers, clawing his flesh with her nails.

Their raging voices wakened the children and disturbed the neighbors. Time after time he slammed the door behind him and

---

gestured wildly pointed angrily

with unimpeded fury without hiding her anger

disappeared for days on end, spending nights with his lovers, to whom he confessed all the messy details of his fights with Sheila. Pretty soon Sheila started getting calls at all hours of the night from **anonymous women** telling her to let Bo go. "You ain't doin' it for him," one woman told her. "A man needs a woman, not a girl, to make him feel like a man."

Sheila tried to keep cool. "Don't you dare try to take this man away from his children," she warned.

"I've got his children, too."

"But I have his name," Sheila said. "He married me. Don't that mean nothin' anymore?"

Sometimes the women hammered at her door, leaving only after Sheila threatened to call the police. They were trying to rip Bo away, but in a strange way Sheila pitied them. Their lives must be pretty wretched to want the misery she had.

At times, Sheila plotted vengeance: *Old Bo really thinks he's some hot little rooster, prowling the henhouses and coupling with the hens. Well, how would he like it if this little hen went a prowling and found some roosters of her own?* For a while she went from bar to bar, accepting drinks from strangers. But nothing came of these encounters. She left alone, her drinks half finished. The men never **enticed** her. She was tormented by a cruel paradox. As miserable as she was with Bo, she feared life would be worse without him.

Meanwhile Bo switched from dealing marijuana to cocaine. It was easier to handle. His customers were neighborhood nobodies, junkies **so wasted and helplessly hooked** that they didn't realize he was selling them **coke cut** with baby laxative powder. He bought an

---

anonymous women women she did not know
enticed interested, attracted
so wasted and hopelessly hooked who used so many drugs
coke cut drugs mixed

ounce for $2,000 and sold it for $6,000. He made thousands and thousands of dollars. He bought a Cadillac, a Grand Prix, gold rings, gold chains, rabbit-hair coats, and platform shoes. The coat rack in his closet bowed from the weight of the shirts, suits, and pants. He bought the most expensive toys and tailor-made clothes for his children. Arthur and Tomekia were the best dressed kids in the neighborhood.

Bo was proud of his **business acumen**; he never forgot a debt or fell behind on a payment. But he was also surprisingly unsophisticated about money matters. He made no attempt to save or diversify his drug profits; he either spent the money or stuffed it in a safe deposit box, where it **drew no interest**.

His best friends were two other dealers—one white, one black. They went to Bulls games together, getting in for free by flashing phony police badges and telling the baby-faced ushers at the door that they were undercover cops on a secret mission. This was the pre-Jordan Bulls, an unlikely collection of defensive-minded overachievers. Bo's favorite player was Norm Van Lier, the gutsy little point guard who skinned his knees diving for loose balls and banged elbows with the big men under the boards.

Bo liked to think that he and Van Lier had a lot in common: defiance, fearlessness, tenacity, and smarts. In his own neighborhood Bo was already a star. He entertained the locals with **colorful tall tales in which he always outfoxed** the white man, always stayed a step ahead of the police no matter how hard they ran.

He played basketball every once in awhile over at The Avenue, the playground near Cabrini-Green. He brought Arthur along to watch,

....

business acumen ability to make money
drew no interest did not collect more money
colorful tall tales in which he always outfoxed exciting stories about how he was smarter than

allowing his son to hold his jacket when he played. "I coulda been in the NBA," Bo told Arthur. "If you go back to A. H. Parker High School, you'll see my name on their championship basketball trophy. Yeah, you can learn somethin', son, from watchin' me play ball."

One player at The Avenue who stood out was Curtis Gates, a preteen who could already dunk. Tagging along with Curtis was his four-year-old baby brother, Will, who sat on the side next to Arthur, watching the big guys play.

Bo didn't have the **wind to run full-out** for more than five minutes at a time, and he often played in platform shoes, which were like lead weights on his ankles. But he was more savvy than the younger players, who were easily **psyched out** by his shenanigans. He called himself ol' Bo, as in, "Look out for ol' Bo, he's on the prowl." The kids were amazed to see a man dressed like a peacock crisscross his dribble or spin past the defense to take the baseline. His team always seemed ahead no matter who hit what, mainly because Bo kept track of the score. "Stop whinin'," he scolded complainers. "I can't help it if you ain't payin' attention."

By Christmas of 1977, Sheila, **weary of the ceaseless turmoil**, took Arthur and Tomekia back to Birmingham. "Go live with your girlfriends," she told Bo. "Go beat some other woman up." But Bo flew to Birmingham, determined to bring her back.

"I know married folks go through their **ups and downs**," Mr. Goldthwaite told Bo. "But I can't tolerate you hitting my daughter."

Bo looked at the ground. Tears came to his eyes. He struggled to say what he meant, as though his grief was greater than words. "I'm sorry Mr. Goldthwaite," Bo said. "I promise to be better. I know

---

wind to run full-out ability to run very fast
psyched out fooled, tricked
weary of the ceaseless turmoil tired of the constant fighting
ups and downs problems, difficulties

what a loss it would be if I didn't have Sheila."

Eventually Sheila gave in—for the good of the kids—and moved back to Chicago. For a while things were better. She found herself a job as a housekeeper in a convalescent home for rich white people. It didn't pay much, but the trivial tasks—cleaning toilets, mopping floors—reawakened her ambitions and she decided to take nighttime nursing courses. She and Bo didn't fight as much, and Bo didn't run around at night. As long as she was able to overlook his dealing, Sheila felt some normalcy in her life. She ran the house with her mother's rules and rigidity, demanding cleanliness, order, and family loyalty. They ate together and **said grace** together, went to church together and cleaned together. "We ain't pigs, this ain't no pig sty," she admonished the children. "We got standards." The children moaned and groaned and dragged their feet, but Sheila ignored their grumbling. "The easiest bad habits to break are the ones you never make," she told them.

Not long after Sheila returned from Birmingham, their third child was born. They named him Joe and called him Sweetie. That year Bo celebrated their wedding anniversary by taking Sheila to a **swank** restaurant on the top of the Hancock building, where they ate steak and drank champagne and watched the sun set.

But little by little old habits returned—the late nights, the women, the phone calls, the fights. Many times Sheila went to the hospital for stitches. She **concocted** lies to explain her bruises to her friends: I walked into a door, I slipped on the ice. But they knew better; they knew Bo was beating her again.

One night Sheila came home from the hairdresser to find Bo

....

said grace prayed
swank fancy
concocted made up

on the brink of madness. "Where you been?" he demanded. "Did I say you could go out?"

"I don't need your permission to do anything, Bo."

"The hell you don't."

He knocked her to the ground, grabbed her keys, stormed out of the apartment, and locked the door behind him.

"Bo, let me out," she hollered.

She stomped her feet, rattled the door, batted the walls, and screamed as loud as she could. But no one responded. She felt like a parrot locked in a cage. She paced the living room and pulled at her hair. The kids were out, not due for another hour. In a panic she stripped the sheets from the beds and roped them in one long cord. She tied one end to the refrigerator and dropped the other end through the living room window. It would be like the hair of Rapunzel, lowering her to freedom. She slipped onto the window ledge and sat on the edge, peering down to the sidewalk five stories below. "Lord, give me strength," she whispered, and then she **shimmied** down the sheets.

The knots snapped, and she fell five stories, hitting the ground with a sickening crunch. Three months later the broken bone in her back healed and the hospital released her. The doctors called her the miracle patient because "it's a miracle you're alive."

On December 26, 1978, the police caught up with Bo. He was crossing the Ogden Avenue bridge not far from Cabrini in an unlicensed, rusty heap, its tail pipe dragging. One cop pulled him out of the car and had him spread his hands on the hood, the other cop searched the car.

....

on the brink of madness very angry
shimmied climbed, slid

"Jesus Christ," he said as he pulled a revolver and an ounce of cocaine from the glove compartment. When the cop covering Bo turned to look, Bo **broke for** Cabrini. They sent out four or five squad cars to track him down and caught him cowering in the stairwell of a high-rise. A simple fingerprint search discovered his secret.

"Now I see why you were running," a cop told him. "You're wanted back in Alabama."

They put him in a holding cell in the Cook County jail with about twenty other prisoners, and for the first night in years Bo slept soundly. He felt strangely at peace knowing his adversary was in front of him.

His lawyer got the charges dropped on the grounds that the cocaine and gun were inadmissible without a warrant. "**Hang low**," his lawyer advised him, after Bo was freed on a fugitive warrant bond. "Lead a model life—it will help your case." But Bo didn't listen to his lawyer. It was a matter of survival as well as style. The only way he could contain his fear of being returned to an Alabama work farm was to pretend that fear didn't exist—to live lawlessly, precariously defying reason. For the four years that **his extradition case was pending**, Bo dealt drugs in the open, drove unlicensed cars through red lights, and talked his way out of arrests when the police pulled him over. At one point he flew to Birmingham to visit friends.

I'm bigger than the law, he thought. *I'm smarter than the white man. They can't catch Bo. Bo ain't spendin' no time in no Alabama prison. No, no. They got the rope out ready to hang me, but the catchin' come before the hangin'. They ain't never gonna catch me.*

His status as a fugitive became legendary around Cabrini, and for

....

broke for started to run towards

Hang low Do not cause trouble

his extradition case was pending he waited to find out if he would be sent back to Alabama

anyone who asked he told his story, with little ten-year-old Arthur absorbing each detail and asking for more. "Daddy," he said, "tell me about that time on the expressway."

Bo chuckled. "Again?"

"Please."

"Well," said Bo lowering his voice to add tension to the drama, "The cops had caught me with some stolen checks. They took me to the Kedzie Street station, but I was able to sneak out. Two officers chased me. Two shots rang out. I stumbled like I had been hit, but I kept on running until I was up against the fence that runs along the expressway. And there I was in a terrible **fix**—it was either the Congress Expressway or two cops ready to take me back to Birmingham."

He paused to sip his beer.

"And then?" asked Arthur.

I jumped the fence and ran across four lanes of traffic with cars goin' fifty, sixty miles an hour. I don't know how I survived those cars. Cars were swervin' this way and that to avoid hittin' me, and horns were blarin'. Then I **jumped** the fence that runs along the elevated train and I ran across the railroad tracks, and then I jumped another fence and ran across four more lanes of highway traffic, and then I jumped a final fence and ran up the embankment on the other side."

"Oh, man," said Arthur.

Bo **drained** his beer. "Them police were hoppin' mad. They couldn't believe I got away. They thought they had me trapped. I must have busted my heel on my right foot 'cause it hurt like hell, but I didn't go to no doctor. I just wrapped it up. Ain't no police gonna

....

fix situation

jumped climbed over

drained finished drinking

catch old Bo."

Not long afterwards the police did catch Bo. It was well past midnight and he was standing in the middle of a busy street noisily fighting with another drug dealer. Two squad cars were dispatched to settle their ruckus. "This guy's wanted back in Alabama," his combatant cried, as the police pulled them apart. This time the police **kept Bo under tight wraps** as he was flown back to Alabama and put back in prison.

On the plane to Alabama, with state marshals on either side of him, Bo took stock of his life and experienced a unique twinge of remorse. *What a fool I am. I ain't gonna do no one no good in prison.* He thought about the many talents he squandered—he might have been a preacher or a singer or a basketball player or a coach. *This must be the Lord's message tellin' me to change.*

He thought about his many sins—the lies, the violence, the deception, the dealing, the drugs. "Dear Lord," he prayed. "I will change."

This was perhaps his first moment of self-analysis and would not be his last. He wept convulsively and privately promised God that he would change his ways.

He was called before a judge and sentenced to thirty years for escaping prison. Bo argued that he hadn't escaped, he'd been released. Reluctantly the state dropped the escape charge because they couldn't prove that Bo had not been released. That left Bo with the remaining six years of his original seven-year sentence for robbery.

Bo was determined to **make the most of his stay**. He worked in the prison library, sang gospel on Sunday, stayed to himself and was

....

kept Bo under tight wraps watched Bo closely

make the most of his stay do something useful while he was in prison

neither brash nor a braggart. "You've changed," Sheila told him during a visit.

"It's the Lord's work," said Bo.

He spent hours reading law, building a case for his freedom. It was laborious work, **poring over stilted legalese**. But eventually he discovered what he wanted—a ruling that said prisoners could not be held accountable for the time remaining on their sentence after they were inadvertently released. In other words, his jail sentence ended in 1978 whether he was erroneously released or not.

He filed his own writ of habeas corpus, asking for a hearing. He got his hearing, but a local judge denied his request for immediate release. He appealed that case, drafting his own brief all the way to the highest court in the state. On September 4, 1985, the Alabama Supreme Court unanimously ordered Bo's release. He flew back to Chicago the very next day.

From the day he started at Marshall, Arthur wanted to play on the basketball team. And he had devised an explanation as to how he never really wanted to play for St. Joseph at all. But when he saw Bedford standing under the basket—a basketball in one arm, a whistle around his neck—**the words faded from his mouth**. Bedford wasn't much taller than Arthur, but he had a large head, piercing eyes, and the deepest, most resonating voice Arthur had ever heard.

"What is it, son?" Coach Bedford asked.

Arthur told the truth, even the details about his father and mother being out of work. While he talked, Bedford **scoured** him with a penetrating stare. Bedford was fifty-two years old. He had

....

poring over stilted legalese reading many law books
the words faded from his mouth he could not lie
scoured carefully looked at

been teaching gym since 1961 and coaching boys basketball since 1972. He had heard every story every kid had ever told, and he **could spot a lie** by looking at a kid's eyes.

"You mean to tell me, St. Joseph let you go 'cause your parents couldn't pay the bill?" Bedford asked.

"Yes, sir."

"That was it—you did nothing wrong?"

"Nothin'. I didn't do nothin'."

Bedford pursed his lips and **gave Arthur the once-over** one more time. The kid was just short of six feet tall, still bony and thin. But he had long fingers and long arms, and he might shoot up in a year. *If he was playing like they had predicted him to play, he wouldn't be here. Somebody would have made some arrangement and this kid would still be at St. Joe's*, thought Bedford.

Bedford gave Arthur a ball and watched him dribble behind his back and through his legs. *Flashy kid*, Bedford thought. *But no flashier than all the rest of them.*

Arthur started shooting jumpers. He made more than he missed. *Aw, what the hell*, Bedford thought. *It won't kill me to keep him around.* He called Arthur over. "I'll put you on the **frosh-soph** team." He patted Arthur on the shoulder. "You should have come here in the first place."

Arthur looked at the ground.

"Well, we all make mistakes," said Bedford.

In his first games with the Marshall Commandos, Arthur noticed big differences between city and suburban basketball. Unlike the suburban schools, the public league didn't play at night or on

....

could spot a lie knew when a kid was lying
gave Arthur the once-over looked at Arthur
frosh-soph freshman and sophomore

weekends. They couldn't afford **the overtime janitorial costs**. They played after school on weekday afternoons. The frosh-soph team played in empty gyms. Sheila showed up, but not Bo. There were other parents, but not many. They either worked or didn't care.

Marshall was in the Red West conference—one of the toughest divisions in the public league. There wasn't much money for frills. The floors were slippery and the lighting was dim. Some gyms were like little boxes, the walls flush against the baseline. They went without cheerleaders, mascots, or bands.

The games were faster and tougher. The coaches yelled as much, but they didn't call as many time-outs or plays. They let the kids play; they weren't as controlling.

Out in the suburbs the **refs** arrived at least half an hour before **tip-off** and conducted their own warm-up drills, jogging and stretching alongside the teams. In the city, the refs arrived when they could, usually just before tip-off, knocking the slush from their boots as they rushed through the door, complaining about being tied up in traffic. They let the kids run free, hacking and holding. And the games ran fast, a bunch of scrawny, skinny kids madly chasing the ball until all the seconds on the clock were gone.

Bedford gave Arthur an old uniform that was a size too big and worn along the edges. Arthur didn't complain. He was glad to be back on a team. They had a quick little point guard named Derrick Zinnerman and a dashing, darting small forward named Cesare Christian. Arthur played shooting guard or backed Zinnerman up at point.

The team finished second in their conference and **zipped** all the

....

the overtime janitorial costs to pay the janitors extra money

refs referees; game officials

tip-off the game started

zipped went

152

way to the final game of the frosh-soph play-offs. They were up against Westinghouse, and the game was played at the Pavilion, home court for the University of Illinois at Chicago. There were only about a hundred spectators in an arena that seats 12,000, but Arthur was thrilled. This was where the public league finals were held. This was where the greatest players who ever played in Chicago's public schools—Mark Aguirre, Terry Cummings, Marcus Liberty, Nick Anderson—made their reputations. The public league was the best basketball conference in the country. *I belong here,* Arthur thought, *not in some **snooty suburb**.* He never felt better about leaving St. Joseph. That school never seemed so far away.

As he raced through layup drills, he was loose but not nervous. The game was big, but he felt no pressure. He had been playing basketball all his life. The ball bounced off the floor with an even bounce, his shots fell in. He looked up and saw row after row of empty seats, and he imagined the arena jammed, a band playing, and the fans calling his name. He wished William could see him. Hell, he wished William played here.

Westinghouse led from the outset. With twenty seconds left they had a four-point lead and the ball. But Arthur swiped the ball from a point guard and drove for a layup that cut the lead to two. On the inbounds, Zinnerman stole the ball and shot. The ball rolled around and off the rim. Someone batted it into the air and it fell, almost miraculously, through a **thicket** of longer arms into Arthur's outstretched fingers. He turned, shot, and banked the ball off the backboard and through the net as the buzzer sounded. His teammates hugged him. Sheila, Sweetie, and Tomekia exuberantly

....

snooty suburb *suburb where the people think they are better than us*

thicket lot

clapped and cheered.

Marshall lost in overtime, but the kids were giggling and making jokes in the locker room anyway. Arthur was the center of attention. He was doing an imitation of the referee. "Man, that dude walk like a duck." The other kids roared with laughter. Bedford stood in the back and **cracked a smile**. He liked Agee's exuberance and resiliency. He liked his instincts and daring. He went right for the challenge: he wanted the ball in the closing seconds. And how in the world did he get that rebound?

Of course it was difficult to make any meaningful assessments from a frosh-soph game. The best freshmen and sophomores were already on varsity. Some kids **burst out of the starting gate**, other kids take their time. A coach never knows where greatness will come from, he can only hope to be around when it blossoms, if it blossoms at all.

Bo couldn't get over how much Chicago had changed during the time he was away. There was so much devastation and despair. So many flourishing working-class South and West Side communities **had bottomed out**. They were ghost towns with rows and rows of vacant lots and abandoned buildings. But in his old neighborhood, around Cabrini-Green, the story was different. A professional class of young whites, yearning to be near the downtown Loop, moved in closer. There were upscale boutiques, coffee shops, and art galleries within a block or two of what was once considered the most dangerous of slums.

The encroachment of whites on black neighborhoods defied

....

cracked a smile smiled a little
burst out of the starting gate played well immediately
had bottomed out were destroyed
The encroachment of whites on White residents moving into

age-old rules of race and residency in Chicago. Whites had never voluntarily mixed with blacks and had violently resisted all attempts at integration, which went back to the beginning of the century. The Chicago Commission on Race Relations, studying the causes of the 1919 race riots, concluded that "the Negro in the United States is a person of African blood about whom men of English descent easily lose their common sense, their usual good judgment, and even their powers of accurate observation. The Negro in America, therefore, is a form of insanity that overtakes white men." This conclusion was based on the results of interviews conducted by the Commission with dozens of men and women of all ages, ethnicities, and religious persuasions. The attitude of many white residents, the Commission reported, was that black people were genetically inferior. "They exhibit childish and primitive behavior and are swayed by uncontrollable, violent emotions that render them incapable of logic or reason and more disposed to crime."

In the 1940s and 1950s, white residents in several South Side neighborhoods rioted when the Chicago Housing Authority proposed to settle black families into all-white housing complexes. In the 1960s, the presence of one black family on an all-white block **precipitated** panic. And yet in 1985, when Bo got out of prison, white people with enough money to live anywhere were scrambling to buy property near Cabrini. It **boggled Bo's mind**. He thought they must be the younger brothers and sisters of those bell-bottomed hippies, or maybe they were the hippies themselves, their hair cut shorter now, blending in with the mainstream. They weren't so friendly anymore, not like they used to be. They weren't waging revolution, and they didn't want

....

precipitated caused; brought about
boggled Bo's mind confused Bo

to share their world. They barely made eye contact with him as they crossed the street or boarded a bus.

But their presence in the neighborhood changed things. They **sent rents soaring** and forced Bo and Sheila to move. The move irritated Sheila. She had always regarded the West Side as outlaw country. It wasn't like the South Side, which had a deeply rooted black community with social clubs, churches, cultural centers, and other bedrock institutions. The South Side had high schools named for black heroes and white abolitionists—like Dunbar, DuSable, Phillips, and Robeson—and from which many of the city's black business leaders and politicians had graduated. It had a thriving professional class of doctors, lawyers, performers, and even sports stars.

The West Side, in contrast, was raw and undeveloped. It had no independent political legacy. Old Jewish and Italian ward bosses clung to power until they died. It wasn't until 1979 that an independent black alderman was elected from a West Side ward. It wasn't until 1981 that the West Side had its first appointee to the school board.

It was to the West Side in 1966 that Martin Luther King Jr., having won great civil rights victories in the South, brought his northern campaign to end the slums. He called for massive economic development and metropolitan-wide open housing. Mayor Richard J. Daley didn't lock King in jail as Bull Connor did, but he regarded him as a threat to his **Democratic Machine** and treated him with polite disdain, blocking all but a few of his initiatives.

In 1968 when King was assassinated, the West Side erupted. The riots began with a student march from Austin High School to Garfield Park. The crowd **broke ranks** at the intersection of Pulaski

....

sent rents soaring made the cost of rent go up
Democratic Machine control of the city government
broke ranks started to separate

Road and Madison Street. They raced along Madison, looting stores and ransacking businesses. The long-repressed rage, which King warned of in his letter from the Birmingham jail, had been released. More than 400 buildings were burned or damaged, 163 others were completely destroyed and hundreds of people left without shelter. Whole blocks were left in ruin.

In time the West Side came to symbolize black poverty in Chicago. Shortly after the Agees moved there, the Chicago *Tribune* began "The American Millstone," a series about a poor black neighborhood not far from where Bo and Sheila lived. "A new class of people **has taken root** in America's cities, **a lost society dwelling in enclaves of despair and chaos** that infect and threaten the communities at large," the series began. "Its members don't share traditional values of work, money, education, home, and perhaps even of life. This is a class of misfits best known to more fortunate Americans as either victim or perpetrator in crime statistics. Over the last quarter-century in America, this subculture **has become self-perpetuating**. It devours every effort aimed at solving its problems, resists solutions both simple and complicated, absorbs more than its share of welfare and other benefits, and causes social and political turmoil far out of proportion to its numbers."

With the articles ran grim photographs of welfare mothers, teenage mothers, thugs, bums, and winos. "Ultimately the term 'millstone' was chosen to glue together the puzzle of what we found," the introductory article began. "No other word better describes the weight of the burden this issue places on America's ability to govern itself in the future, or conveys more urgently the need for riddance of

....

has taken root have made their home

a lost society dwelling in enclaves of despair and chaos they are people without direction in life who live poorly

has become self-perpetuating continues to grow

this burden from the American conscience." The language was less provocative than what was in the Commission's report from 1919, but the underlying themes were the same. The prejudices of those earlier bigots had become self-fulfilled prophecies. It was as though the paper was describing a loathsome subspecies, created like the diabolically failed experiment in Dr. Frankenstein's lab.

Sheila and Bo moved to an apartment about a mile from where King lived during his brief stay in Chicago, not far from where the riots started. They weren't mentioned in the *Tribune* series, but they might have been. They merged within the faceless, featureless mass of poor, black Chicago.

All of Bo's newfound humility and piety vanished with his release from prison. He emerged with dangerous **delusions of invulnerability**. "I could have been a great lawyer," Bo insisted. I beat the best the state of Alabama had to offer." He filed a multi-million-dollar wrongful imprisonment suit against Alabama, but the court ruled against him.

He found several menial jobs, but none lasted. He returned to the streets and started dealing. But the streets were more dangerous. Now guns were everywhere, even in the hands of children. And not just revolvers but high-powered automatics that fired a hundred **rounds** at a time. The disparate bands of youth gangs Bo remembered had banded together into **outfits** as sophisticated as the mob. They couldn't even be called youth gangs anymore; some founding members were pushing fifty. They intertwined whole neighborhoods, drawing police, politicians, and judges into their webs of corruption.

....

delusions of invulnerability beliefs that he could do anything
rounds bullets
outfits groups, organizations

Bo didn't realize that **a step from his stride** was lost with the years. He was like an old boxer hanging on with guile. He didn't join a gang—he was never a joiner. He intended to work around the gangs, avoiding their turf. He started dealing at playgrounds, schools, and parks near his home. To demonstrate his product's worth, he tasted it with his buyers and soon he was hooked. He consumed more than he sold, and his business fell apart. He began to break into cars, houses, and apartments, stealing TVs, tires, radios, tools, clothes, and selling them for the cash he needed to buy the drugs he desired.

His fights with Sheila grew louder and more desperate. He became more belligerent and less patient. He flew in and out of his family's life. He gave money one day and took it back the next. He was **at the mercy of** his addiction. He began to drop in on Sheila at the convalescent home. He wanted money, and he knew she would give him cash just to make him leave. He seemed to want to sabotage her efforts at improvement. Her ambitions intimidated him; they exposed his own weaknesses. "What makes you think you're so special?" he asked her. If he rotted in hell, so should she.

Bo embarrassed Sheila when he came to her work. The boss **frowned on** these visits and her coworkers gossiped. She begged him not to come, but soon he was coming almost every day. Finally she quit. She began using cocaine, too. *We have to do something together,* she thought. *This can bring us closer.* But the drug played outrageous tricks with her mind, unleashing terrifying demons. One night she lay on the bed watching Bo, and in her eyes he became **a deranged fiend,** with blood dripping from his lip and a dagger in his hand. He snarled and raised the dagger. He was trying to cut out her heart.

....

a step from his stride some of his strength
at the mercy of controlled by
frowned on did not like
a deranged fiend very dangerous

Her screams woke the children.

"You're trying to kill me," she screamed.

"Woman, stop talkin' like that," Bo yelled back.

"You've ruined me."

"You ruined yourself."

"I was gonna be a nurse."

"You weren't nothin' when I met you and you ain't nothin' now."

Sheila leapt to her feet. "Look at yourself, Bo," she said. "You said you was saved. You said you found God. You didn't find Him. You was using the Lord in one of your schemes."

He advanced toward her, but she continued. "You're a junkie, Bo. You're worse than your mother."

"Shut up."

"She was a drunk and you're a junkie."

Arthur, Tomekia, and Sweetie watched as Bo **whacked** Sheila. She spun free from his grasp, ran into the bathroom, and shut the door. He stumbled out the back door and down into the alley, where he met an old friend. They caught a bus for downtown, heading nowhere in particular. "Let's do a break-in," Bo suggested.

"I got a better idea," the friend said. He pulled a pistol from his pocket and handed it to Bo. Bo began to tremble. "I ain't never used a gun in no robbery," Bo said.

His friend snickered. "You don't have to use it, just show it. People get so scared they just give you their money."

They found themselves **snaking** around the shadows of the elevated tracks that cut through the **trendy** River North area. Clouds covered the moon. The night was dark; no one was out. The el,

....

whacked hit

snaking walking

trendy popular, rich

rumbling overhead, shook the ground. Then all was silent. A sports car pulled up to a stop light.

"Let's go," said the friend.

They rushed out of the shadows. Bo pounded on the passenger window. His friend ran around the back of the car to the driver's side.

"Open the door," Bo yelled.

The driver was a young white man, his eyes rounded with fear at the sight of Bo and the gun. He screamed, dove to the floor, and hit the accelerator as the bullet shattered the window. The car sped off and Bo stood stunned. He hadn't meant to pull the trigger. He didn't know how it happened. His hands were shaking. The ground was sprinkled with shattered glass. The receding footsteps of his friend running away were lost in the roar of another train. Bo began to run. He ran and ran and ran until he was hidden by the towers of Cabrini-Green. He stopped to catch his breath. He was trembling. He had never come so close to killing a man.

When Sheila woke it was late morning. The children had made their own breakfast and headed off to school. She climbed out of bed and walked to the kitchen, and what she saw almost made her cry. There were dishes on the counter, and dirt and mud on the floor. Her basic rules of order and cleanliness had been disobeyed. They were living **like slobs**. She blamed herself. She had failed her children. She had allowed them to leave that morning without a hug or a kiss. She had lost control of her life. If the family was going to survive, she would have to **grab it back**.

She opened up the curtains and the windows and emptied the house of stale air. She wiped the crumbs from the tabletop, washed

....

like slobs in filth

grab it back gain control over their life again

the dishes, scrubbed the sink, and mopped the floor. "No matter how low you fall, you still have to be clean. You still have to respect yourself," she told herself.

It felt good to work hard, it felt good to sweat. She found enough money to buy some hamburger meat for dinner. The kids would eat well tonight.

She didn't know where Bo was and she didn't care. She couldn't depend on him. She would have to do it alone. She went to the bedroom, knelt on the floor, and prayed: "Lord, I feel things **pulling me down**, but I have to rise. I have to be strong. I have to keep my family together. Lord, Lord, please give me strength."

....

pulling me down becoming extremely difficult; making me unhappy

BEFORE YOU MOVE ON...

1. **Comparisons** Reread pages 132–136. How was Marshall High School different from St. Joseph?

2. **Conclusions** After Bo got out of jail, he returned to a life of crime and drugs. Why?

LOOK AHEAD Did William help his team get to the championship game? Read pages 163–177 to find out.

WILLIAM

· · · · · · · · · · · ·

In the moments before the Gordon Tech game, William sat alone in a corner of the locker room, his eyes closed, **regulating** his breathing, trying to **chase the butterflies from his belly**. He would have preferred to soothe his nerves with music, but Pingatore didn't allow radios or tapes in the locker room. He fiddled with his wristband, placing it where Michael Jordan wore his, just below the elbow. He folded his socks over his sneakers and adjusted his shorts so the hem came almost to the knees.

Ten minutes before tip-off, Pingatore slipped into the locker room. "Remember, tight defense," he said. "Tight defense." Then he was gone, leaving pregame speeches to the players.

The players sat on facing benches with William standing in the middle. "I'd like to dedicate this game to the seniors," he said. "This is for you, this is your moment. Let's go out there and take care of business." The team gathered in a circle, put their hands together, and chanted: "One, two, three—defense!"

They ran down the hallway into the gym and circled the floor. The fans on the St. Joseph side rose as they entered; the band **kicked into** the *Rocky* theme; some student with his face painted red and white was running around waving a big St. Joseph flag. Catherine, as round as the moon and waddling when she took each painful step, was in the crowd tonight, along with Curtis, Alvin, David, Peggy, Latanya, Randy, and Emma.

I'm a lucky fool, William thought as he waved to Catherine. *The*

···

regulating controlling
chase the butterflies from his belly stop feeling so nervous
kicked into began to play

baby could come at anytime, maybe even today. Wouldn't that be something, having a baby right here in the stands? That would give Pingatore something to talk about.

William turned to the other end of the court and saw Kleinschmidt, waiting his turn in the layup line. He was a **chunky blond with a flattop**—a white kid who picked up a basketball early and couldn't let go. He was a great shooter. On the playgrounds they called him Little Larry Bird. Kleinschmidt nodded at William and William nodded back. They wouldn't cover each other—Kleinschmidt was a forward—but everyone would compare their performance: The two super sophomores in their first **matchup**. *Probably been thinkin' about me all day—like I been thinkin' about him,* thought William.

Up in the stands, Curtis was nervous and edgy—standing, sitting, almost jogging in place. "William's got it tonight," said Curtis.

"My boy's ready," said David. "I can tell."

"Welcome to the Prep Game of the Week," the television play-by-play announcer was saying. "You've got the **guru**, the legend, in Gene Pingatore."

St. Joseph won the tip and William began with a burst, driving past Kleinschmidt for a reverse layup. He hit a three and then stole the ball, hit point guard Greg Orr on the fly, took a return pass, and drove for the middle. Out of the corner of his eye William saw Cunningham slipping out from behind his man. But instead of passing, William charged harder to the basket, spinning between two players and banking the ball off the glass.

Gordon called a time-out, and the Chargers **engulfed** William

....

chunky blond with a flattop fat boy with short blond hair
matchup game against each other
guru wise leader
engulfed surrounded

as he made his way to the bench. His team led by five. The St. Joseph fans were on their feet, chanting "Go, Chargers, go." David and Curtis were hugging one another and Catherine struggled to her feet to cheer.

I love you, Deryl, thought William, *but I want to win and go downstate.*

At halftime he had seventeen points, and his team led by one. "Keep workin' the ball," Pingatore told them. "Get it to William. Play defense."

But in the third quarter Gordon Tech adjusted its defense. They ran a defender at William wherever he went; they kept a hand in his face. Unable to pass it to William, the Chargers forced the ball inside. But the big men were cold. Shots rolled out. They missed free throws. The lead slipped away, and William, struggling, began running harder, circling the floor, trying to lose his man on picks. But the picks were weak. It was harder **to shake** the defenders. And once he did, they weren't getting him the ball. Deryl wasn't passing out. The system had fallen apart. They needed someone to take command. "Take the ball, William," Curtis bellowed, "and shoot it."

Kleinschmidt got hot. The Gordon Tech strategy was so simple, they ran him off of screens and got him the ball, and he had the same fluid motion on every shot. Their system was working; Gordon was **feeding its go-to guy**, but William was starving.

Pingatore called a time out and once again told them to get the ball to William.

William started bringing the ball up the court and making his own shots. But he was off. The touch was missing. He put back a

....

At halftime By the middle of the game

to shake to move past

feeding its go-to guy getting the ball to its best player

layup, muscling past Kleinschmidt. He batted away an errant pass, fed Orr who fed Cunningham, and now they were down by one. With a minute left Cunningham stepped to the free throw line with a chance to give the Chargers the lead, but his shot **clanked off**. Curtis moaned. Pingatore dropped his head in his hands. William fouled Kleinschmidt, who had rebounded the ball. "Damn," moaned Curtis, "this cat don't miss." But Kleinschmidt **rimmed** his free throw and Orr grabbed the rebound. "Get it to William," yelled Curtis.

Orr never got out of the paint. The ref whistled him for traveling, and the ball went back to Gordon. Pingatore's face resembled a big, ugly blood vessel ready to burst. With twelve seconds left, Gordon Tech added two free throws to take a three-point lead.

Pingatore called a time out. "My guy's William Gates," the play-by-play announcer said. "I'd like to see him get it, just get to go one-on-one, pull up and ice it."

The play was set for William. The crowd rose, someone was beating a drum. The student with the red and white painted face ran around with his flag. Catherine couldn't look. "You gotta want it, man," Curtis mumbled. "This is it. You gotta want it."

William caught the inbounds pass and ran up the court. He crossed the half-court line and **let fly**. The ball slipped as it left his fingers and clanked off the front of the rim. Cunningham pulled it down, raced to the three-point line, turned and fired. It bounced off the rim as the buzzer sounded.

And that was it. For the second year in a row William walked off the court as another team rejoiced. "Congratulations to the Gordon Tech Rams," the play-by-play announcer concluded. "They're on a

....

clanked off did not go through the basket
rimmed missed
let fly shot the ball

joyride—to Champaign."

In the locker room the press surrounded William. "What happened?" a reporter asked. "You had seventeen points in the first half, but only six in the second. Why didn't they get you the ball?"

"Well," William began, trying to be **diplomatic**. "I guess they did what they thought was best for the team."

Pingatore was drained. "What **did us in** all year, did us in tonight—missed free throws and too many mistakes," he told reporters. "We didn't take advantage. We had our chances at the end of the game. You have to take advantage of the opposition's mistakes because you don't get many chances."

William slipped out of the locker room to the parking lot and into David's car. They drove back to Cabrini in silence. When they got home William went straight to his room to lie down. His head felt numb and empty. Then the phone rang. It was Catherine calling from her sister's house.

"It hurts, William."

"Do you have the contractions?"

"Yeah, they're coming all the time."

He went right over. The room was only **illuminated** by the glow of the TV. He sat beside her on the couch. The TV sound was turned down.

"Well, William, you think things gonna work out?" Catherine asked.

"Yeah, we'll be okay."

They stared at the silent screen. "I'm glad you got to play in that game," Catherine said.

....

diplomatic nice
did us in gave us trouble
illuminated lit up

"Yeah." The last play was still replaying in his mind.

"I wish you had won—I really do."

"Ah, it don't mean nothin'."

"It's too weird, though," she said. "You got a secret life. No one out there knows what you're going through. They don't know about us."

William shook his head. "I never did tell Pingatore," he said. "I'll have to tell him now. I can't go on havin' two lives. Ah, I don't want to talk about it."

Early the next morning **Catherine's water broke**. William called David, who rushed over and drove them to the hospital.

During the delivery William held Catherine's hand and told her when to breath in and when to push. He laid a wash cloth over her face and gave her ice water, and watched as his child slowly came into the world.

"It's a girl," the doctor said.

"Aw, God," said William.

"Do you have a name?" asked the nurse.

"Alicia," said William.

The doctor handed Alicia to Catherine. William's heart raced and his eyes filled with tears.

"Her eyes are so big," William said.

Catherine smiled, and Alicia started to cry.

"Look at that—she recognized my voice!" William nearly shouted. "When I said somethin', she knew who I was." He leaned over the bed and played with Alicia's tiny little fingers. Tears ran down his cheeks.

"Hello, little baby," he said.

....

Catherine's water broke Catherine was ready to give birth

"I swear she knows my voice," he exclaimed. "I'm tellin' you, she knows who I am."

"Of course," said Catherine, "you're her father."

In the days after the season ended, William and Curtis were **at opposite ends of their luck.**

William was moving, a young man in a hurry, up early and to bed late, always with someplace—school, practice, Catherine's—to go. Curtis slept late and spent his afternoons watching TV. William played in the morning, afternoon, and night—honing his shot, working on his moves. Curtis, his skills **rusty**, didn't have the spirit to return to the court. William was in the best shape of his life, his muscles rippled when he walked; Curtis's belly sagged over his belt. William had a clerical job with Encyclopedia Britannica, obtained through Mrs. Weir and her connections. Curtis lost his job at the hospital after quarreling with his boss.

Pingatore had William playing in tournaments and spring leagues all over the city and suburbs. Letters of gushing praise poured in from college recruiters and summer all-star camps; he stashed the growing pile in a box in his closet. He was, they told him, the center of their solar system, never mind that they said the same thing to many others.

Curtis stopped playing basketball and no colleges wrote or phoned, he **had dropped out of sight** as far as the basketball world was concerned. "It don't matter how good I *was*, it's how I am now," Curtis said.

It was a tense time for the brothers. Curtis's **down-fall** strained

....

at opposite ends of their luck living very differently
rusty weak; out of practice
had dropped out of sight was no longer important
down-fall failure

their relationship. Curtis had always been his hero. It wasn't easy for William to see him slip. At the same time, William wanted Curtis to treat him with more respect. "Don't be tellin' me what to do all the time," William pleaded.

"You got to show me something more," Curtis told him. "You got to take it to next level."

"If you were so great . . ." He wanted to say something nasty, but he held back.

William decided to keep his distance from Curtis. David drove him from one tournament to the other, from one playground to the next. On weekends David got up early to take William to Catherine's so he could see the baby. He never complained about it, either. Mostly he drove in silence while William sat in the front and fiddled with the radio dial and moaned about the pressures of his life, of working and going to school and seeing Catherine, and of caring for the baby and all the games, the ceaseless games, and Curtis.

"I'm so sick of Curtis being on my case. If he's so great, why didn't he do it?" William said.

"Curtis did do it, William," David said softly. "Could nobody do it like Curtis. I mean, William, I know you're on top and you're **flyin' high** and we all hope you make it. But you got to remember something: As good as you are, Curtis was the best. If he had gone to St. Joseph, if he had a coach that **stuck on his ass**, if he had your opportunities, man, it would have been frightening what Curtis could have done."

One gorgeous day in May, William, Curtis, and David got together

....

flyin' high feeling good about yourself
stuck on his ass trained him well

to watch a Bulls game. The team's fortunes had changed with Michael Jordan. Before Jordan, the Bulls drew their support from a small **band of cultists**. They played in funky old Chicago Stadium in the heart of the West Side, not far from the epicenter of the '68 riots, and only a few blocks from where the Black Panther headquarters used to be. There were always black kids hanging around in the front, begging money, trying to sneak in. There were always black guys in the second balcony, where tickets were cheap. It was said that there were too many black kids in the front and too many black men in the second balcony and not enough white players on the court, and that what the Bulls really needed was to cross over and reach white Chicago—with a white superstar like Larry Bird.

Well, Michael Jordan proved them wrong. Jordan crossed over—he smashed Chicago's racial barriers and brought the whole team with him. The same city that demonized Harold Washington turned right around and **showered Jordan with adulation**. He was exalted; the beneficiary of endorsements, money, and praise. His face was pasted on Chicago billboards, his name was heard on radio and TV. He was the lucky recipient of white society's eagerness to prove its own generosity and benevolence. Only in America, it was said, could a black boy rise to such fame and fortune.

It wasn't just the points he scored or the shots he blocked, it was the acrobatic ease with which he sailed through the air. He was the latest and greatest in a long line of playground superstars once disdained by purists who said there was no place for showboating in a team game. Now the purists were regarded as old fuddy-duddies, and **showboating** was the marketing strategy. The playground went over

....

band of cultists group of loyal basketball fans
showered Jordan with adulation praised Jordan
showboating doing fancy tricks; showing off

big on TV.

Jordan played with a blinding aura that dazzled the high-rollers in their silky suits and gold watches. They flocked to the Stadium in their sports cars and sedans and brushed past the beggars, willing to pay whatever it took to get in and see Michael play. They drove up ticket costs and ran the black guys out of the second balcony.

Curtis, William, and David satisfied themselves with the games on TV. The Sunday game in May was the deciding game in a best three-out-of-five series against the Cavaliers. It was in Cleveland and all the experts, the Gates brothers included, predicted the Bulls would lose. Cleveland, a young team **on the rise**, had three go-to scorers: Ronnie Harper, Mark Price, and Brad Daugherty; the Bulls had Jordan.

"I ain't gettin' into this game 'cause I know the Bulls just gonna lose," Curtis said.

But the Bulls played scrappy defense and Jordan was unstoppable. Each time it seemed Cleveland might **pull away**, he scored a basket to pull the Bulls back. It was like a tennis match, the way Jordan and the Cavs exchanged baskets; even Curtis couldn't help but get **sucked in**. By the start of the fourth quarter he and his brothers were on their feet, cheering every Bulls basket.

With about six seconds left, Jordan banked in a jumper to put the Bulls up by one, and the Cavs called time-out.

"They're goin' to Daugherty," said Curtis as he watched the Cavs huddle around their coach, Lenny Wilkens.

"No, look for Price," said David.

"I'd get it to Harper, man," said William.

....

on the rise that was playing well
pull away get a lot more points than the Bulls
sucked in excited about the game

"And have him face Jordan?" said Curtis. "Man, you crazy."

The Cavs didn't work the ball to any of those players. Instead, Craig Ehlo, a backup guard, inbounded to Daugherty, took a quick return pass, lost his man on a pick, and laid it in. The camera shook with the roar of the Cleveland fans. Curtis, David, and William collapsed on the sofa. There were three seconds left.

"Man, I shoulda known better than root for the Bulls," said David.

"They **stink**," said William.

"Chicago teams always lose," said Curtis.

The Bulls broke from the huddle and returned to the court. "Brad Sellers will be inbounding the ball," the announcer said.

"Come on Sellers, man. All you got to do is get that ball to Michael," said Curtis.

"Come on, Mike," pleaded William. "Please, Michael, please, Michael, please."

Sellers held the ball over his head. And held and held and held. "He's got five seconds to get it in," said the announcer.

"Someone get open," yelled David.

The Cavs rushed Larry Nance and Ehlo at Jordan. Jordan froze them with a fake, and Sellers **lofted** him the sweetest little inbound pass. Jordan caught it, dribbled toward the basket, and jumped. Ehlo jumped with him, but unlike Jordan, he couldn't hang in the air. While Ehlo fell to the ground, Jordan released his shot. It slipped in at the buzzer. The Bulls won 101 to 100.

William, David, and Curtis were jumping up and down and howling. They knocked over a lamp shade and tumbled on the couch. "Be quiet," yelled Emma, "you're wakin' up Alicia."

....

stink are not a good team
lofted threw

"I told you, man," yelled Curtis.

William dropped on the couch in a daze. The shot kept replaying in his mind as it replayed on the screen. "Man, that was amazing," William said. "If he makes the shot, they win; if he misses, the season's over."

He turned to his brothers: "Do you know what kind of pressure that is?"

"Michael Jordan don't think about pressure," said Curtis.

"He wasn't even nervous," said William.

"It comes from inside you," Curtis continued. "The great ones don't never think about missin'."

William kept staring at the TV and shaking his head. "Man, that's what it is," he said softly, "that's what it's all about."

"If I was out there, I woulda taken that shot," Curtis declared. "*Damn, I* wish I coulda taken that shot."

On the TV, a man in a headset stuck a microphone in Jordan's face and asked him how he felt.

"I live for this moment," Jordan gushed.

The Gates brothers quivered with **untapped** energy. They grabbed a basketball and **jetted** out of the house. All over Cabrini, people were pouring out of their houses and running up the sidewalks, laughing and shouting and exclaiming, "Did you see that shot?" Everyone was a Bulls fan now.

It was a beautiful, sunny afternoon. The Gates brothers got to The Avenue as fast as they could. "Come here, William," yelled Curtis. "I'm Jordan and you're Ehlo."

Curtis faked William in the air and banged in a jumper that

....

untapped a lot of

jetted ran

174

rolled around the battered rim. "Bulls win," he bellowed as he stomped across the court, arms raised like a triumphant boxer. "Bulls win at the buzzer!"

William fell on the asphalt, kicked his legs in the air, looked up at the big blue sky, and burst out laughing.

Each one pretended he was Michael Jordan, each one recreated the shot. They were still laughing and shooting and romping and running when the street lights **flicked** on.

That summer William was invited to the prestigious Five-Star Camp, held in Pittsburgh.

On the plane he scanned the roster of other talented sophomores, juniors, and seniors coming to the camp from across the country. Aside from Kleinschmidt, Sean Pearson, and Marty Clark, a new player on the Chargers, he knew none of the names.

The camp was held on outdoor courts in the sweltering sun, and beneath the watchful eyes of the great college coaches—Bobby Knight, Mike Krzyzewski, Dean Smith—all restricted to the bleachers and prevented, by NCAA order, from contact with the players.

They put William at off-guard, and he barely touched the ball in the first games of the first day. He **was imbued with** the St. Joseph system—*pass, pass, pass.* But these were playground rules, and no one was passing back. This wasn't about teamwork or running plays, this was about impressing the coaches. **It was every man for himself—** shoot or take the ball to the basket. Curtis's words echoed in his ears: "It ain't in their interest to pass you the ball."

....

flicked turned

was imbued with knew; was used to

It was every man for himself Each player only cared about himself

It's time I play like Curtis, William thought.

His defender that day was a tall, skinny guard named Grant Hill. William pounded past Hill, just muscled around him for the dunk. He took it to the basket again and again, running coast to coast, coming hard like a freight train, like Curtis used to do it back at Wells. You should have seen those all-stars scatter out of his way.

He even tried **a little trash talking**, though talking wasn't his style. "Sorry, guys," he told them after one thunderous dunk, "but this is business."

He scored a run of unanswered points and felt the stares of the coaches. They were looking at their rosters, trying to find some information about this kid out of Chicago.

Oh yeah, you wonderin' about me now, William thought.

After the scrimmage, a blond-haired **water boy** approached him gingerly and asked for an autograph.

"My daddy likes the way you play," the boy said to William as he signed.

William looked at the boy. "Who's your daddy?"

"He's a coach." The kid pointed to a man sitting in the stands who looked down at William and smiled. "Your daddy's pretty slick," William said.

The next day it was more of the same: dunking, stealing, rebounding, hitting the threes. He was playing on a higher plane, playing with a purpose, playing for Curtis and Emma and David and Peggy and Catherine and Alicia and every black kid who ever dreamed to be something greater in life, playing for all the kids who never made it out of Cabrini, playing for a **gilded** future for him and

....

a little trash talking to say mean things
water boy boy passing out water
gilded better; more promising

his family. It was a transcendent moment. He had been blessed with God-given talent; to ignore it was a sin. A few weeks later he and his St. Joseph teammates drove downstate for the annual Morris summertime shootout, featuring the best high school teams from all over Illinois. In the finals they took on King High School, a dynasty from the South Side led by Johnny Selvie, a steely-chested power forward, and Jamie Brandon, a slashing guard.

William scored thirty-five points.

"He's **burnin'** you, man," Selvie screamed at Brandon. "Guard him, man. He's **eatin' you up**."

Brandon had no response; there was nothing he could say. William *was* eating him up. Guard him close and he slashed past; give him room and he buried his shot; send in a **posse** of defenders and he hit the open man. It was going to be a great season, William thought, as the pasting continued. **He was invincible**—the best guard in the country.

....

burnin' playing better than
eatin' you up beating you; defeating you
posse team, group
He was invincible No one could beat him

BEFORE YOU MOVE ON...

1. **Conclusions** William did not let Catherine know how much he was upset about losing the big game. What does this tell you about William?

2. **Inference** How did basketball help and hurt the bond between Curtis and William?

LOOK AHEAD Read pages 178-199 to see what happened when Bo showed up on the basketball court.

JUNIOR YEAR
1989

"You're playing like you're in a big hurry to prove somethin'. You don't have to worry about bein' nothing but what you are. You don't have to be Isiah. You don't have to be the big star from St. Joseph. You don't have to be nothin' but Arthur Agee."
—Coach Bedford, to Arthur Agee

WILLIAM

• • • • • • • • • • •

By the time William arrived at the Loyola University fieldhouse, the college coaches were already in the stands, eyeing the players as they took the floor.

The fieldhouse seated a few thousand but seemed deserted. Sneakers squeaked loudly on the freshly **buffed** gym floor as the players went through their layup drills. It was another game in the long autumn stretch of an unending season that seemed to run in a circle, replenishing itself like a river—the regular season into the spring leagues into the summer tournaments, and then the Loyola University Tournament of Champions. The play was ragged, the defense lax—but it didn't really matter how the teams performed. The main purpose of this tournament was to **showcase** talent for the college coaches in the stands.

While St Joseph ran through its warm-up drills, Pingatore talked on the sidelines with Digger Phelps, Notre Dame's head coach. Pingatore made a joke and Phelps laughed as they watched William bank a jumper off the glass. William was stronger, faster, more aggressive, and more confident than when the summer began—the kind of blue-chip talent who could make a college team a winner.

Romancing the high school coach was a key tactic in the courtship of recruitment, so the other coaches **wormed** closer, waiting for Phelps to leave so that they could laugh at Pingatore's jokes, too. There were more than two dozen college coaches in the stands. They were an odd assortment of lumpy white guys in ties and

....

buffed cleaned, polished
showcase display, present
Romancing Being very nice to
wormed tried to move

suits, joking, laughing, pounding one another on the back, discussing plans to share dinner in town, and all the while trying not to be too obvious about which player they were watching. As if it wasn't clear.

A stocky, nattily dressed young man with his hair slicked back walked into the gym. The coaches nearly fell over each other getting to him. It was David Kaplan, whose scouting service specialized in Chicago-area prep stars. Kaplan flashed the latest issue of his newsletter, which was crammed with important tips on who scored what on the latest college board exams, and indicated to his readers who would be eligible to play as a freshman. Kevin O'Neill, head coach at Marquette University, whispered something into Kaplan's ear and they guffawed.

The game **meandered**. William caught a pass, spun past his man, switched the ball from his left to his right hand, and laid it in. The coaches neither cheered nor clapped, they just kept talking. Nothing William did, no matter how spectacular, surprised them anymore. They were not there so much to see William as to be seen by William, so he would know of their interest.

William dribbled up court, faked left, went right, and slipped on a pool of sweat. He fell to the floor and rolled from side to side, his face **contorted with pain, clutching** his right knee in his hand. Concerned players gathered around him.

"You okay, William?" asked Marty Clark.

"The pain, man," William gasped. It felt as though someone had ripped his knee with a knife and dropped salt in the wound. He had to bite his lip to keep from howling. A few of the other players helped him up. William circled the floor, shaking out his leg, testing the

....

meandered continued slowly
contorted with pain, clutching twisted with pain, holding

limits of the pain, trying to wish it away. He had suffered bruises before—twisted ankles and jammed-back fingers—but this was the knee, the axle on which his body pivoted. "Please, please," he whispered beneath his breath. "Not the knee, not here, not with these coaches."

He walked from one end of the court to the other and then waved the other players away. "I can play," he announced.

The coaches took it all in, settled back into their seats, and resumed their conversations, assured that for the moment there was no better guard to pursue.

Play continued, and William's pain persisted. At halftime he **hobbled off as discreetly** as he could. "I think I'll give it a rest," he said.

After the game two teammates carried him to his car, and he drove to the nearest hospital. He sat in the emergency room and watched as ambulances carted in the wounded, many of them children. Worried mothers huddled in their overcoats, and nurses and doctors dashed about.

His X-rays **were negative** and the doctors sent him home.

"Don't worry," he told Pingatore when he called. "I'm fine."

William wrapped his knee in ice, stretched out on the couch across from David, and watched a football game on TV. Players were chasing passes, but William's mind was on his knee. To the outside world nothing had changed: he was the envy of every player and the desire of every coach. But he feared that inside his body, where no one could see, something was wrong.

"I was too close for this to happen," he said.

....

hobbled off as discreetly walked away in pain as quietly
were negative showed that there was no problem

David looked up from the game. "How's it feelin'?" he asked.

William shook his head. "It feels like it's hangin' by a thread," he said.

ARTHUR
* * * * * * * * * *

Arthur dashed down the front steps, palming the basketball as he ran. His brother, Sweetie, tagged behind, his thick little legs trying to keep up.

It was a dark, dreary Sunday morning in September. Rain clouds hovered over the city, and the West Side was still sleeping—shades **drawn**, no kids or cars on the streets. The Agee house was also quiet this morning, for which Arthur was grateful. It had been turbulent lately. His older sister, Tomekia, and her infant daughter, Jazz, had moved back from Virginia, where they had gone to live with her husband, a sailor based in Norfolk. His old friend Shannon had also moved in, because he was fighting with his stepfather. And Bo had vanished again, this time after a vicious fight in which he hit Sheila with a metal pipe. She **filed for divorce after that and pressed charges for battery**, vowing to have Bo thrown into jail. That was a few weeks ago. No one had seen Bo since.

Arthur dribbled through his legs, a scissors move he was trying to perfect.

"Isiah Thomas with the ball," he called out.

"Can I be the Bulls?" said Sweetie.

"Shut up," said Arthur with a look of annoyance.

....

drawn pulled down

filed for divorce after that and pressed charges for battery
decided to leave Bo and go to the police

Arthur was trying to imagine himself as Isiah: He wore a red jersey with Isiah's name and number on the back, and pretended to walk the ball up court in the closing moments of a game at the Stadium against the Bulls. But it was hard to concentrate with Sweetie talking so much.

"How come you don't never want to be the Bulls?" Sweetie asked.

"I done told you, boy. The Bulls ain't no good. They still can't beat the Pistons."

"Man, is that true what Mamma said. You gonna **audition for** a movie about Isiah Thomas?"

"You got that right," Arthur said. "They're lookin' for a guy to play Isiah when he was a teenager goin' to St. Joseph, and you can't find no one better than me. The way I see it, Isiah's life's been my life."

"Only you ain't at St. Joseph."

"Don't worry about that, boy."

Arthur dribbled harder, feeling the bounce of the ball in his hands.

"Watch this, Sweetie," he said, and he bounced a pass toward his brother with so much spin that it jumped back to him, as though it were on a string.

"Ha, ha," Arthur cackled, "fooled ya."

"Come on, Tuss," pleaded Sweetie, "gimme the ball."

"Boy, go home if you gonna cry."

There were five guys playing on the Delano court, and some dope dealers were hanging around the perimeter fence. Arthur began a full-court game of three on three. The players had to weave between little boys on their sting-ray bicycles **popping wheelies** as they rode across the court. Arthur dribbled low, like coach Bedford had taught

....

audition for try to act in
popping wheelies doing tricks

him, and was careful to avoid the bits of glass and clumps of grass on the asphalt. He was looking right, preparing to pass left, when he got a notion: if I can palm the basketball, I can dunk it. When he reached the lane, he jumped, stretching his arm as far as it would go, reaching the ball up and around the rusty rim. He roared like a tiger when he hit the ground.

"I did it, man," he bellowed. "I dunked."

The game stopped. "Do it again," someone dared.

This time he brought the ball out from his side, sweeping his arm through the air like a windmill, twisting toward the basket from the left and—*wham*—he crashed the ball through the rim. He dunked three times in a row, leaping higher with each jump. He was a young boy but growing strong. The clumps of grass, the shards of glass, the gang graffiti on the walls, the boys on their bikes, the other players, the dope dealers—all faded from his mind as he ran and jumped and reached for that rim.

He didn't even see Bo coming up the sidewalk.

"Hey, son," Bo called out.

Arthur **reeled** at the sound of Bo's voice. When he turned, he saw his father standing under a tree. Bo had been on a binge. He was shirtless and **gaunt, his eyes bloodshot**, and he carried his clothes in a bag strapped across his back.

"I dunked," Arthur said, not knowing what else to say. "Watch this, Dad."

He stepped about ten feet from the basket, which looked to him to have grown six inches since his father was watching, caught his breath, ran, jumped, and jammed. The rim rattled against the

....

reeled turned around suddenly

gaunt, his eyes bloodshot very skinny, his eyes red

scarred backboard.

Arthur turned toward Bo, hoping for **accolades**. But Bo looked annoyed. "Gimme that ball," he demanded.

Sweetie and the kids on bikes closed in around them.

"You gonna dunk?" asked Arthur.

"What's this, a dunkin' contest?" Bo snapped.

Bo tried to still the queasiness in his belly. He'd been up all night. A wad of bills was wedged into his pants pocket. He couldn't remember how he got the money. His head ached; he craved the drug.

"I ain't touched a ball in years," Bo said. "But once you great, they can't take it away." He broke for the basket, but his legs had no push. They creaked as he ran and the best he could reach was the lower edge of the rim.

Bo curled his upper lip, baring his teeth. "One mo' time, little man," he said to Arthur, who had rebounded the miss.

But his second jump was shorter than his first.

"You got old legs, Dad," Arthur **chided**. "Old legs."

Bo turned toward Arthur. "Lookie here, son. You do the right thing, the right thing will follow you." The words tumbled out of his mouth, propelled by an old reflex. Bo wasn't even sure of what he was saying. He pulled a twenty-dollar bill from his pocket and continued, "I found a three-thousand-dollar check and gave it to a lady, and she give me seven hundred."

Bo spun away from Arthur, his mind suddenly **switching to a different track**. The craving was bad. He needed that drug. He wandered toward the dope dealers, waving his twenty in the air. He staggered as he walked and disappeared with a few dealers down a

....

accolades praise, compliments

chided sounded upset; said angrily

switching to a different track thinking about something else

walkway. When he came back, he came roaring back. "I got to be goin'." He slipped his bag across his back, wiped his nose, hopped the fence, and took off. Arthur stood alone. Watching his father walk away Arthur thought, *Why's he got to do that in front of everyone? Why can't he be normal? And who the hell is he to tell me what to do?*

"Say, Tuss," someone yelled.

Arthur turned around. Everyone on the playground was staring at him.

"Wake up, boy."

"What?"

"We be picking teams, man. You, me, Loren, and Boogaloo."

"Those teams ain't fair," Arthur said.

"Can I play?" a little kid pleaded.

"Get outta here, boy."

It took five minutes to pick teams of comparable talent. The game began again as the ball was **flipped** to Arthur, the image of his father staggering toward those dealers still **burning in his mind**.

WILLIAM
. . . .

William was waiting on the sidewalk outside Peggy's house when David pulled up.

"Look at this, you're on time," David exclaimed. "Usually I gotta drag you out of bed."

It was 7:30 A.M., half an hour before one of Pingatore's infamous Sunday morning practices. Even David, an early riser,

....

flipped thrown, given
burning in his mind in his memory

wasn't fully awake.

But William had been unable to sleep and had been up since five. He was bursting with excitement. The school's doctor had ordered him to spend at least three weeks on the sidelines, and this was the day he returned to the court. There was no more pain in his knee, the swelling was gone. Maybe it was some sort of **fluky sprain**.

William climbed in the car with David. They drove past bare trees and piles of leaves. The car windows were raised against **winter's first chilly edge**. They rode in silence; it was too early to be chatty. William studied his brother. David was the quiet one, the loyal one. He was a good but not great basketball player, **overshadowed first by** Curtis and now William. He made a living working in a factory; in his free time he had been driving William to games and tournaments throughout the city. William wanted to thank him for those rides, but he couldn't find the words. He had never thanked his family for anything.

David drove quickly, hurrying to make Pingatore's deadline. They reached the gym just as Pingatore, his keys jangling from their chain, was opening the door. David nodded hello to the coach and climbed up to the balcony. He stretched out on a bench, rolled his jacket under his head like a pillow, and tried to sleep.

As cocaptain it was William's duty to lead the team in exercises, and he began, at Pingatore's signal, with leg stretches. Pingatore was wearing shorts, sneakers, and a T-shirt, and his whistle around his neck. He wandered through the players, restless and grumpy, in no mood for play. He kept peering nervously at the clock. This was his finest team since 1978. Winning conference wasn't good enough for

....

fluky sprain accidental injury

winter's first chilly edge the cold air that was beginning to feel like winter

overshadowed first by less talented than

this bunch: to live up to their number one **billing**, they'd have to win the state. But they didn't seem ready—their defense was **hollow**, they weren't doubling down, following their shots, sliding off the open man, or running the floor. They seemed lazy and lethargic; their minds seemed to wander, forgetting the basic things, the simple things, in the middle of play. And then there was Gates and his leg. So much depended on his knee.

William sat on the floor and stretched. The gym floor felt cool on his legs. He felt no pain or stiffness in his knee.

"Jumping jacks," Pingatore ordered. Then he made them run wind sprints, shoot free throws, and practice left-handed layup drills. "Come on," he roared. "Come on, you're half asleep. You guys are going in slow motion."

The louder Pingatore yelled, the faster William ran, jubilant that his leg was **holding up**.

Pingatore called a halt to the wind sprints and stood at midcourt, the whistle dangling from his lips, his face frozen in a frown. He had them practice a half-court play. When Gerald Eaker grabbed a rebound and stumbled on the put back, Pingatore waved his hands in disgust. "Just run and shoot, would you. Quit thinking about where your feet are," he bellowed. "You people are a joke. We've got two or three people who can play and the rest of you are in slow motion."

He set up a drill where the center rebounds and throws an outlet pass to the guards streaking up court. It was a new play, requiring a complicated crisscross move that none of the guards had mastered. The more they **mucked it up**, turning the wrong way or breaking at the wrong time, the louder Pingatore shouted and the harder it was

....

billing place, position
hollow weak
holding up feeling good
mucked it up got it wrong

for them to understand him.

"Is that clear?" he **thundered** after one incomprehensible explanation. "Let's try it."

Of course it wasn't clear. Of course they got it wrong—one guy bumping into another, the ball flying out of bounds. No one knew what he was talking about. It was so early in the morning and some had been up so late. Their mouths were parched, their heads pounded, their chests heaved, and their ears rang with his **relentless barrage**.

"You've screwed up!" he screamed as a rebound fell to the ground uncontested. "Hey, look—pussy willow, you go in and you crash!"

Even William, just back from an injury, was not **exempt** from the yelling. "Come on, let's go, you're playing soft, William. Does it bother you? Don't be afraid, though. Don't favor it."

He had them run the play again and again and again, until they started getting it right. At last he gave them a break. They sat on the sidelines, chests heaving. "Man, he must have sucked gasoline for breakfast," Layton whispered to William.

"Give me a good reason why I should keep you on this team, Corey," Pingatore raged at one player. "How about you, Reed? Give me a good reason." He turned to William. "What do you think, William? I mean, how many of these people work hard?"

William looked at the ground. "Not too many, Coach."

"You want to stay home when the state tournament comes?" Pingatore continued. "All right, go on in."

The players stumbled off to the showers, weary, but William was happy. His knee was still in place.

The next day at practice William was stretching his leg when he

....

thundered yelled loudly
relentless barrage constant yelling
exempt excused, free

felt a sharp tear, like bone ripping, and his knee stuck in place. "I can't move it!" he screamed.

Pingatore ran over. "Can you get up?"

"I can't move," William exclaimed, starting to panic. "Help me. I'm stuck."

They dragged him to the side and laid him on a bench with his leg extended. They iced his knee until the cold **numbed** the pain and the swelling subsided, and he could move it a bit. He watched his teammates practice the half-court press. At first the guys looked his way or winked or smiled. But as practice continued and Pingatore ran them harder, they stopped looking his way. It was as though no one could see him, as though he had already disappeared.

He watched them shoot layups, free throws, and run sprints. The sweat dried under his arms and he felt a chill. His teeth began to chatter. He threw a sweatshirt over his shoulders to stop shivering.

"Run 'em again," Ping barked.

His teammates dashed across the floor. *Will I ever be able to run again?* William thought.

After practice Mark Layton sat beside him and rubbed his back, and Marty Clark made jokes, and some of the others tried to **cheer him up**. "You'll be fine, man," said Layton. "It's probably just a sprain."

They helped him to the locker room where he showered and dressed. Pingatore came up to him and touched William's shoulder. "I can't let you play until you get it checked," he said.

William started shaking his head. "But coach . . ." his protest **trailing off** as he began to think, *This is serious. I'm gonna have to go*

....

numbed made William stop feeling
cheer him up make him feel better
trailing off ending, stopping

to the doctor first thing in the morning.

William sat on the examining table, legs dangling over the side, and listened white Dr. Wolin talked about the **innards** of a knee. Wolin was a tall, amiable man, whose wavy brown hair hung almost to his shoulders. He had an easygoing voice and a calming manner and could talk on and on. He told William he was a major basketball fan, played the game himself, and, as a surgeon specializing in sports medicine, had operated on dozens of players all over the city.

It was hard for William to follow Wolin's words because he didn't want to hear what he had to say. Wolin had stopped talking about basketball and was discussing the cold, cruel medical facts. He handed William a model of the knee. William looked on as Wolin talked and twisted its bendable parts, explaining **the mechanics and physiology of the knee**.

"The pain could have several sources," Wolin explained, "but most likely it's a tear in either the cartilage or the ligament. In the most basic terms, the ligament is the band of tissues that holds the knee together, and the cartilage is the shock absorber that cushions the blow when you jump.

"If it's the cartilage that's damaged, that's not as serious. We can either stitch the tear or remove the cartilage, and you will be back to play in a matter of weeks."

"And if it's the ligament?" William asked.

"That means major **reconstructive surgery**. It means at least two days in the hospital and four to five months before you do any running or cutting. And even longer before you play basketball."

....

innards inside parts

the mechanics and physiology of the knee how the knee works and what it is made of

reconstructive surgery surgery to fix your knee

"But I'm willing to play in pain," William said.

"That's not the issue. The issue here is whether you will have full use of your leg."

Wolin went on with his explanation about the ligament and the knee. William looked at the floor, his mind **drifting** from the conversation. He started counting up the days and weeks. *It's November. Twelve weeks takes me to January or February.*

"Coming back from knee surgery," Wolin explained, "requires a different kind of **fortitude** or patience." It's not like practicing your jump shot; you have to have the patience to let some of the healing take place on its own."

I'll miss the Thanksgiving Tournament, the Proviso West Christmas Tournament, and the first games of the regular season.

"We'll have to do an MRI, a Magnetic Resonance Imaging, which will give us the most precise picture of your knee."

It was gonna be me and Marty and Jamal and Chris. We was gonna be the best team in the state.

"Now it's possible, William, that you may not need all of this. But if it needs to be done, my recommendation is to do it all, **miss the season**, and get ready for next year."

"Miss the season!"

"I know junior year is important, but if you come back strong and play well in your senior year, they can't ignore you."

*Maybe this **was my fate**. Maybe this was the ending to the story that God wrote for me.*

He stepped down from the examining table, put on his trousers and jacket, and limped out to where David was waiting. During the

....

drifting moving away

fortitude strength

miss the season do not play basketball this year

was my fate is what was supposed to happen to me

ride home, he barely lifted his head.

At the house, he sat around the kitchen table with his mother, Curtis, and David.

"You sure you didn't mess your knee playin' on concrete?" Curtis asked.

"I didn't," said William.

"You better hope it's your cartilage," said Curtis.

"That's for sure," said David.

"You don't want them doctors cuttin' into your ligament," said Curtis.

"You don't want to mess with that," said David.

"Those college coaches hear those doctors messin' with your ligament, and they won't want nothin' to do with you," said Curtis.

"Curtis, quit scarin' him," said Emma.

"I told you not to play on no concrete," said Curtis.

"Curtis, man, I told you—I didn't."

"Anyway, it's a good thing it didn't happen to you senior year," said Curtis. "Most coaches don't want nobody with no broken leg, no matter how good you are. They don't want to be **baby-sittin' no** broken leg."

"Aw, come on, Curtis," said David.

"First thing they gonna be saying is, 'Tell me about his knee, coach. Is he gonna be any good for me?' That's what it's all about."

They sat quiet for a moment, then David **broke the gloom** with a big smile. "Hey, William, don't worry, you get hurt bad enough, you can always get Curtis's old job as a security guard."

"Yeah, I ain't got it no more," said Curtis.

....

baby-sittin' no taking care of a; responsible for a
broke the gloom made everyone feel better

They all laughed.

"Look, son, you just gonna have to do what that doctor tells you," said Emma. "Most of it ain't in your hands now anyway."

The phone rang. It was Catherine.

"I hope I didn't **screw up**," William told her. "I was gonna use basketball to go to college and play in the pros to take care of the family."

"There are other ways to go to college than playing basketball," said Catherine.

William **hardly heard** her. "But it's my dream."

Later that night, Pingatore called. "Think positive," Pingatore said. "Just be positive. Right now that's all you can do."

As he lay in bed that night, William thought about his future. It had always been so natural, his ability to run and jump and play basketball. He never gave it any thought, never even knew the names of the muscles and bones that lay beneath his body. Now he knew what they looked like. "Please, Lord," he prayed, "let it be the cartilage. Not the ligament—anything but the ligament."

The next day he returned to Wolin's clinic for his MRI. They led him to a dressing room and had him take off his pants. He was **in his shooter's frame of mind**, like Michael Jordan preparing for those final three seconds in Cleveland, picturing the basket, calculating the distance from where he would likely get the ball. Only in this case William tried to picture the image he wanted to produce: a tear in the cartilage, not the ligament. He wanted to believe that he could take control of what was happening to him.

He walked down a **musty**, narrow corridor into a long, narrow

....

screw up make a mistake; ruin everything

hardly heard did not hear

in his shooter's frame of mind thinking about making the shot

musty stuffy, stale

room with a bed in the middle and the cylindrical MRI machine behind it. He lay on his back as a technician in a white coat strapped him to the bed.

"Are you cold?" the technician asked.

William shook his head.

"Do you need a blanket?"

"No thanks."

The technician shut the door behind her, leaving William alone with the machine. He turned his head, but he couldn't quite see the machine.

The technician's voice came over the loudspeaker, asking him to put his head down. She was sitting at the control panel behind a glass window overlooking William. He lay back and studied the ceiling's white and brown tiles. There was a clicking and a whirring, and then the bed began to move into the machine. The technician's voice returned, "The first set of pictures will take about two minutes."

The whirring grew louder. He wanted to sleep, but the noise kept him awake. He wanted to move his arms, his legs, hands, toes, and feet, but he **remained immobilized** for two full hours while the camera clicked away.

When William returned to the doctor's office, he got the news he wanted to hear. The tear was in the cartilage. Wolin explained that **his options were two-fold**: they could **excavate** a good chunk of his cartilage or sew the tear.

"If we take out the cartilage, **rehab** would take six weeks or longer, then you would be back, as good as normal. Though in fifteen years you'll have pain from arthritis."

....

remained immobilized did not move
his options were two-fold he had two choices
excavate take out; remove
rehab rehabilitation, recovery

William bit back a smile and tried not to laugh. *Fifteen years!* he thought. *Man, who cares about fifteen years. I wanna play now.*

"I recommend we sew it up."

"Just do what you gotta do, doc." *All I know is I won't miss the whole season. I'll be back to go downstate.*

William's operation was scheduled for November 22, the first day of St. Joseph's 1989-90 basketball season. Emma got him to the hospital at six in the morning. In the prep room, dressed in a **baby blue** gown and plastic shower cap, William was attended to by technicians and nurses who bustled all about, taking his blood pressure and temperature, feeling his pulse, and asking him if everything was okay.

Pingatore had called the night before. "Don't be afraid," he told him. "We're praying for you. We even dedicated the Thanksgiving Tournament to you."

William looked at the clock. In about eleven hours the team would be playing Barrington High School; Cortez Gray would be starting in his place.

"Hey, William." He looked up to see Dr. Wolin walk in, dressed in hospital blues, too. "What are you doing here?" Wolin joked, as he offered William a soul shake.

"Is your mother here?"

"Yeah."

"Look, I'll talk to you afterward in the recovery room, but you probably won't remember anything we talked about," Wolin said with a smile.

William bit his lip.

....

baby blue light blue

"It'll be all right, William."

A nurse inserted the IV into William's arm, and an orderly wheeled him down the hallways to a brightly lit operating room lined with all sorts of flashing **high-tech gizmos**, gadgets, and monitors.

Nurses and orderlies and doctors buzzed about him.

"Hey, William, remember me?" It was the anesthesiologist who earlier had given him an overview of what to expect.

"So you play hoops?" the anesthesiologist said as he bustled about.

"Yeah," said William.

"For who?"

"St. Joseph."

"I'm gonna slip you something in that IV," the anesthesiologist said, "**to take the edge off**."

"Okay."

"What year?"

"A junior."

William lay with his arms **spread eagle** on the bed, looking up into a bright light. The anesthesiologist was trying to be nice, trying to settle William, but there was something **harried** about the conversation, like he had more important things on his mind than high school basketball. *Yeah, forget the small talk and concentrate on the operation*, thought William.

"So what's third-year high school like? Getting tough?"

"Not yet."

"Any girls?"

They laughed.

"Feel that medicine I slipped in?"

....

high-tech gizmos fancy machines
to take the edge off so that you cannot feel the pain
spread eagle stretched out
harried uncomfortable, uneasy

William smiled. "Yeah."

"Takes the edge off of things."

As the drug was slipping into his blood, William's body went numb, and soon he couldn't feel the nurse's fingers on his knee, the strap tied around his waist, or the covers draped around his body. He saw the anesthesiologist approach him from behind with a gas mask in his hand.

"How ya' doin'?" someone asked. "Still with us?"

"Yeah."

"Not for long, I tell you."

The mask was placed over William's head and the lights went out. They inserted a compress in his mouth to keep his tongue from **blocking his airway** and hooked him to an oxygen machine. Then Wolin lifted William's knee off the bed and began to **knead it** like a lump of dough. Then a nurse scrubbed the area with disinfectant, and the doctor pierced the flesh and lowered in **the orthoscope**, which would flash the images on a nearby screen. Wolin stitched the cartilage by watching the image recorded by the orthoscope. He worked on William's knee for more than an hour.

In the waiting room Emma sat alone with a magazine on her lap. She looked at the pictures and read the headlines and worried: *Are those coaches gonna write him after this operation?* She knew she was luckier than a lot of mothers. This was only a knee. There were mothers in Cabrini who had to bury their children.

Dr. Wolin came up to her with a smile on his face. He shook her hand and asked her into a small office. "The ligament was **intact**, and

---

blocking his airway choking him

knead it move it around

the orthoscope a tiny camera

intact not broken

we did the cartilage repair," he said. She stared at him with no expression.

"What questions do you have, Mrs. Gates?"

"What about his future?" she asked.

"I wish I could look into **a crystal ball**," said Wolin. "The process of healing takes time, but his rehabilitation will start as soon as he wakes up."

....

a crystal ball the future

BEFORE YOU MOVE ON...

1. **Conclusions** On pages 184–186, Bo and Arthur played basketball. Why did Arthur get upset?

2. **Summarize** Reread pages 191–196. What did the doctor tell William about his injury?

LOOK AHEAD Read pages 200–242 to find out why Sheila found her house completely dark.

Above: *Arthur in his freshman year team photo at St. Joe's.*

Left: *Arthur goes one-on-one with Isiah.*

Below: *Bo and Sheila Agee at home.*

Above: *William (center) on the bench.*

Right: *Coach Pingatore.*

Below: *William (in doorway) at home in Cabrini, the summer before his freshman year of high school.*

Top: *Arthur about to play Bo in basketball the summer after his sophomore year.*

Above: *Arthur on the bench with Coach Bedford, after fouling out.*

Below, left: *Arthur (left) and Shannon.*

Below, right: *Arthur and his younger brother Joe "Sweetie" stare out the apartment window onto Jackson Boulevard.*

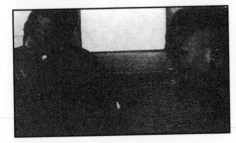

Left: *William (far left) outside his Cabrini-Green home with Emma, holding Curtis Jr., and friends of the family.*

Right: *William and Curtis watch the Bulls on TV.*

Below: *William, Alicia and Catherine.*

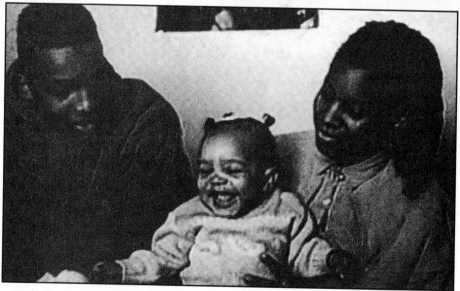

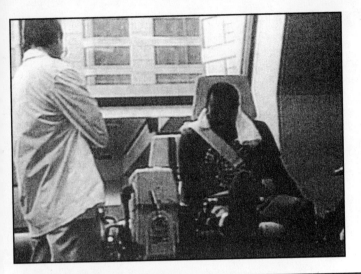

Top: *William in physical therapy at the Northwestern Medical Center.*

Above: *The St. Joe's team joins hands in prayer at halftime in a senior-year game against Carmel. Pingatore is at right.*

Right: *Arthur consoles William after the loss to Nazareth, senior year.*

Arthur scores on a fast break against Peoria Manual in the state tournament.

Left: *Arthur's eighteenth birthday.*

Below: *Arthur signs his national letter of intent.*

Bottom, left: *Arthur and Coach Pingatore talk following St. Joe's tournament loss to Nazareth.*

Bottom, right: *Sheila Agee reading a Mother's Day letter in 1989.*

Top: *Arthur graduates from high school in the Summer of 1991.*

Above, left: *Arthur leaves for college in August of 1991.*

Above, right: *Emma hugs William after his graduation from St. Joe's.*

Below: *William Gates accepts his high school diploma. Gene Pingatore is second from right.*

ARTHUR

By the start of his junior year, Arthur had emerged from his shell—no longer self-conscious about having left St. Joseph—and assumed his old role as the funny kid, the class clown. He came and went as he pleased, telling teachers he had to go to the bathroom and then disappearing in the lunchroom for fifteen or twenty minutes to chat with his friends, returning with some made-up story to explain his absence. No one seemed to notice or care, and Arthur knew the teachers had other things to worry about.

One day in Spanish he felt a sneeze coming on, only, instead of trying to stifle it, he leaned back and let it fly, sneezing all over the hair of the girl who sat in front of him. As the other kids roared with laughter, she burst into tears. Frantically she tried to wipe away the mucus, but it only stuck to her fingers and spread.

"Aw, come on, that ain't nothin' but a little booger," Arthur said.

The class howled even louder and the teacher, not knowing what else to do, called for Bedford. Arthur heard the rumble of his footsteps thundering down the hallway long before he saw him. He planned to **win the coach over** with a smile or a joke. But Bedford stormed into the room, yanked Arthur out of his seat, hauled him into the hallway, and thrust him against a locker, **breathing fire in his face**.

"You better tell that girl you're sorry," Bedford bellowed.

"But, coach—"

"Don't give me none of your bull, boy."

....

win the coach over get the coach to like him better

breathing fire in his face looking at him angrily

"But, I—"

"You pull that bull again, you ain't gonna play on my team. You hear me, boy?"

Arthur stared at the ground, his lips quivering. "Yeah."

"What?"

"Yes, coach."

Bedford paused. "You pull that bull at St. Joseph?"

"No."

"Well, you better start treating folks around here with the same respect you got for those people at St. Joseph."

He glowered at Arthur, froze him with a stone-cold glare. His jaw jutted out in anger and his cheeks quivered. Arthur **slunk back into the room** and apologized. From then on he kept his eye on Bedford, not certain what to make of the coach. Most people were easily softened; even Pingatore, for all his sternness, allowed himself to be captivated by Arthur's charm. But Bedford was a rock; his stone face never cracked. "Ain't none of you guys gonna fool me 'cause I already heard it and seen it all before," he told them.

It's gonna take awhile to figure this guy out, Arthur thought.

The audition for the role of Isiah in the Mary Thomas story, a made-for-television **docudrama**, was conducted in the casting agency office on Chicago's North Side. Arthur arrived a little early, so they gave him a script and suggested he use the time to study **his lines**. The guys in the neighborhood **kidded** him for having such wild ambitions, but Arthur wasn't afraid of mingling with white people, though now that he was here he felt a little uncomfortable. He

---

slunk back into the room returned feeling ashamed

docudrama movie that was based on a true story

his lines what he would have to say

kidded teased; made fun of

decided to keep his ears and eyes open and say nothing unless something was said to him, and to act humble and unimposing.

He took a seat on a folding chair and nodded hello to a pacing white man, another actor, there to audition for the role of Coach Pingatore. Arthur was wearing a dark blue, freshly pressed T-shirt, and had his hair puffed high on top and **cropped** along the sides. He had grown a few inches over the summer; his voice had deepened. He had his mother's deep brown eyes and his father's effortless laugh. He might have been a college kid or a student at one of the city's more prestigious private schools.

"Who you here for?" the actor asked.

"Isiah," Arthur said.

The actor nodded and lit a cigarette. "I heard they were having trouble filling that part. They've been looking all over the country."

He sucked on his cigarette. "What do you think about the Pistons losing Rick Mahorn?" he asked.

Arthur looked up. "Not a big loss."

The actor frowned. "Don't think so? He's a pretty intimidating forward for that team."

"Fighting-wise," said Arthur.

"Well, yeah, there's something to be said for that. It **puts the fear of God in people**."

The casting director, Jane Heitz, walked out of her office and called the older actor in.

He **stubbed** out his cigarette and stuck his hand toward Arthur. "Have a good one, man."

"All right," said Arthur, shaking hands. "You, too."

....

cropped cut short
puts the fear of God in people makes people afraid
stubbed put

Then he was alone in the room, quiet but for the ticking of a clock. He looked at his script—an exchange between Isiah and Mary—looked up at a painting on the wall, fiddled with his earring, and looked back at his script.

Heitz emerged from her office and called Arthur into a windowless white-walled room.

"Can you give me your name, please?" she asked as she directed him to a folding chair **ringed** by several camera lights.

"Arthur Agee."

"Age?"

"Sixteen."

"How tall?"

"Six feet—six feet, even."

"Do you have any questions?"

He shook his head.

"Do you know who Isiah Thomas is?"

He smiled. "Yeah."

Heitz explained that Mary Thomas was a hardworking woman who **persevered in the face of** poverty and made her son, Isiah, rise early and ride the trains and buses several hours each day from their home on the West Side to a Catholic school named St. Joseph, in an all-white suburb, where he played for coach Gene Pingatore and led his team downstate.

"Do you understand?"

Arthur nodded.

"Now in this scene, Isiah's about to go to St. Joseph for the first time. I'll read the part of Mary and you read Isiah." Heitz cleared her

....

ringed surrounded

persevered in the face of did not give up even though she lived in

throat and started reading, speaking in a clear, precise voice. "Isiah, are you ready?"

"I don't know," Arthur read.

"Never say, 'I don't know.' I don't know is an answer to nothing, Isiah. You have to go on your own and do your own work."

"Yes, Mamma."

"You're my pride and joy."

"White people always be using **fifty-dollar** words."

"None of that matters. You do what you have to. Be who you have to be. Just keep acting right."

"They're just a bunch of honkies."

"Don't you be calling people names. There's good and bad in every race. The real secret is you be smart enough to know the difference."

"I'm transferring to Washburn."

"You are *going* to St. Joseph."

Arthur looked up from his script and smiled. *That was nothing,* he thought, *although it did sound funny to hear a black woman's words come out of a white woman's mouth.*

"Okay," said Heitz. "Let's try it again."

They read it again, only this time Arthur read with confidence and feeling, assured of what came next.

Heitz thanked him for coming and led him to the door. He knew from the quickness with which she **dismissed** him that he would never hear from her again, and that they would **cast the part with** someone else, probably a professional. But so what. It was fun talking to that white actor, being interviewed by Heitz, and playing Isiah. He

....

fifty-dollar big
dismissed said good-bye to
cast the part with give the role to

wasn't intimidated; he wasn't going to be one of those boys who never leaves the West Side. He was his daddy's boy—afraid of nothing.

In the outer lobby another black teenager sat, waiting for his turn to audition.

In the afternoon Arthur caught the bus for Whitney Young High School, and when he got there the Commandos, playing in a fall tournament, were warming up under Bedford's **baleful** eye. Bedford sat in the bleachers, barred from the bench, as were all the coaches for pre- and post-season games. It was a prohibition intended to ensure that the official basketball season begins and ends at the same time for everyone, so teams playing in tournaments would have no advantage over those who don't.

Of course Bedford made no attempt to hide his presence. He sat a few rows behind the team, the only spectator on their side of the gym. They heard him moan, mumble, or mutter over each of their mistakes, and they made many. He waved his arms, banged the bench, and looked disgusted—nothing worked. Arthur double dribbled. "You're dribbling too much," Bedford yelled. "Stop going behind your back, you're missing the open man." Derrick Zinnerman threw the ball away. Quadell Kimble clanked a layup off the backboard. *This might be the worst team I ever coached*, thought Bedford.

Worst of all was their defense. Bedford took great pride in a dogged, full-court, trapping defense, with **hawking** guards as quick as minnows and sharp as barracudas. But this bunch lumbered back and forth on rubbery legs. "Hey," Bedford barked, "drop back on defense."

After the game, the players sat on the bottom rung of the

....

baleful scary, threatening
hawking aggressive, competitive

bleachers and looked straight ahead, not daring to peer back at Bedford sprawled across two rows of benches, showering them with harsh words of condemnation:

"I see the same mistakes over and over and over. When you gonna learn? Because your man's walking down the floor doesn't mean you walk down the floor."

The gym was empty, the other team and the referees gone. A janitor, **looking to lock up**, wandered by to see if the Marshall team was leaving. "You guys have no concept of basketball," Bedford continued, ignoring the janitor. "No concept of basketball at all. It's like playin' in an alley, runnin' up and down court doin' nothing. Nobody looked at anybody to block out."

Several seconds of silence passed. Arthur squirmed and looked over at Zinnerman sitting beside him, as if to ask: Is he done? Can we go? Zinnerman looked **perplexed**. They both knew better than to interrupt one of coach's tirades.

"It's up here," Bedford continued, pointing to his head. "You got to think about it. You're not learning anything."

Then he **bore in on** Arthur: "Goin' behind your back on the dribble—I told you a million times, we don't need a one-man show."

Arthur frowned, secretly relieved for having had enough sense to keep quiet.

"Agh," Bedford sighed, a gasp of frustration that the team took as a sign he had nothing left to say. They left from the bench, stretching their creaky limbs. Then they stuffed their shoes and shorts in their bags and wandered out into the parking lot. Robin Dunagan and Quadell Kimble started to push each other good-naturedly. They

....

looking to lock up who wanted to close up the gym

perplexed confused

bore in on started to yell at

bumped against Bedford's car, setting off the alarm just as the coach walked out of the gym.

Bedford winced with disbelief and grasped for words that might adequately describe such stupidity. "Man, how many times do I have to tell you to get off my car?"

Dunagan and Kimble lowered their heads, **perfect models of contrition**, and started to walk away.

"Where you goin'?" Bedford asked.

"Walkin'," said Dunagan.

Bedford leaned forward, his face a mask of frozen contempt. "You're gonna walk home?" he asked, each word dripping with disbelief.

They nodded.

"Come over here," Bedford ordered. He opened up his car trunk, took out cans of soda, and passed them out. "Get in the car," he ordered with mock disdain.

Dunagan opened the door and tried to squirm his way into the rear seat already crowded with three other players.

"Man, shove over," he said.

"Shut up," someone responded.

"Man, git yo' big fat ass over."

Bedford sipped his soda and shook his head. "I don't know what I'm gonna do with you all."

Sheila **kept up appearances** after Bo disappeared from home. She cleaned, hustled the kids off to school, and kept food on the table for a house full of children: Shannon, Arthur, Tomekia, Sweetie, and Jazz.

....

perfect models of contrition showing that they were sorry
kept up appearances acted like nothing happened

But her anger had hardened. She wanted Bo punished; she wanted him to rot in a cell. She pressed ahead with battery charges, and told her friends: "I'm gonna make him pay for what he's done to me."

Hating Bo was, oddly enough, a source of inspiration for her. She **was resigned to being** on welfare, and her spirit had been dulled. She couldn't find a job. She had been going to weekly job-training sessions at the public-assistance office, and did what they told her. She put on her prettiest dress, slipped on heels and nylons, and trooped all over the city in search of employment. But she had no skills or connections. There were few local opportunities—riots, crime, and decay had **run off** most of the merchants from the West Side. What was left? Small grocery stores, liquor stores, and currency exchanges, which all seemed to Sheila to be **clannish concerns** run by Arabs, Koreans, or Jews. "They don't hire black people," she decided.

One day she ventured downtown to a major department store and asked to see the sales manager. "I'd like to work in sales," Sheila said.

"Have you any previous experience?" asked the manager.

"Well, no."

"I'm sorry," she said. "We'll keep your name on file."

Sheila walked away **whipped**; she convinced herself that all white people were prejudiced, when in fact she was too self-conscious to return.

In late October she missed one of her weekly job-training sessions, and they cut her off from welfare.

Word of her cutoff came by mail. From a pay phone Sheila called the number at the bottom of the letter. First she was put on hold,

....

was resigned to being accepted that she would be

run off pushed out; pushed away

clannish concerns family businesses

whipped feeling beaten; discouraged

then she was disconnected. She dug another quarter out of her change purse, called back, and was again placed on hold. After several minutes a whiny voice, **crusted with contempt and condescension**, told her all grievances must be filed in person.

She went down to the welfare office on Pulaski, received her number from the receptionist at the front desk, and sat with all the other haggard looking people in the mustard-brown waiting room. The clock on the wall wound from nine to one, and still her name was not called.

She marched back to the receptionist, defiance in her step. "Who's your caseworker?" the woman asked, gum cracking in her teeth.

"I don't want to see a caseworker, I want to see a supervisor," Sheila said.

"I'm sorry, but no one's available."

"Listen you," said Sheila, her voice rising. "I've been waiting for over four hours."

The security guard at the front wandered by, his hand hovering above the revolver strapped to his side. "You have to lower your voice," he told Sheila.

"I'm not gonna do anything," Sheila said, her voice determined. "But I'm not gonna leave till I get the answer I came down here for."

The guard led her back to her hard metal chair, and she sat there **festering in bitter juices**. The morning's paper lay on the ground before her. There was an editorial calling for the state to get tough with welfare mothers living the good life at the public's expense, buying booze with **food stamps**, making babies with three or four

....

crusted with contempt and condescension that sounded rude and disrespectful

festering in bitter juices feeling angry

food stamps money provided by the government to buy food

men—cut them off, deny them, put them back to work. And there was another article on the latest criminal courthouse scandal, in which slimy little snitches with tiny recorders taped to their chests had fixed cases by feeding cash-stuffed envelopes to greedy judges. Those judges pled guilty. Their greed had been caught on tape, and they were sentenced to a few months in one of those low-security federal prisons without bars.

There's a little Bo, a little con, a little meanness in us all, she thought. *The white man gets a second chance. But a black woman, she's gotta pay for everything she does wrong. I'd like to see one of the rich white folks spend a day in this welfare line. I'd like to see one of them wait four or five hours for a clerk to call their name. I'd like to see them explain to their kids that they can't afford a good school. I'd like to see them rise above this.*

Her heart was racing. "Be strong," she told herself. "I didn't do nothin'. It just happened to me."

She waited another hour before she met her supervisor, **a dour** woman locked behind a gray metal desk in a **dingy office swamped** with piles of manila folders.

"As I understand it, you missed your mandatory work-training session," the supervisor started.

"Yes, but—"

"Was there a death in the family?"

"No."

"Was there an illness?"

"No."

"Then your absence was unexcused."

"You don't understand. I didn't have no money for the bus."

....

a dour an unfriendly

dingy office swamped dark office filled

The supervisor frowned. "You could have borrowed bus fare from a friend," she said.

"A friend?" Sheila blurted. "My friends don't have no money."

"Your case will be taken under administrative review."

"How long will that take?"

"Two or three months."

"What am I supposed to do till then?"

The supervisor rose from her desk. "You should continue looking for employment."

When she got home it was not yet four, but gray clouds blocked the sun and the house was dark. "Turn on the lights," she told Tomekia.

"I can't," said Tomekia. "They're broken."

It was more than the lights: The refrigerator had stopped humming, the freezer dripped icy water, the TV screen stayed black, the gas heater cool. "Our services been shut," she cried.

She banged on her landlord's door, and Willie Patrick let her use his phone. The electric company said she owed over $1,000, and the gas company said she owed $500.

"If you were **on public aid**, the state would pay your bills and we would reconnect your service," explained the gas company official.

"But they cut me off aid," she said.

"Then you have to pay it yourself."

"But how can I pay it if I'm not on aid?"

"There are local charities for cases like yours."

She hung up the phone and **broke into tears**. Willie Patrick and his wife tried to comfort her.

....

on public aid getting money from the government
broke into tears began to cry

"You been so good to me," she said.

"Bear with it, sister."

Patrick led her upstairs with his flashlight. Her apartment was **eerie**, cold, and dark, and her children stumbled about, banging into walls, following the narrow, flickering flame of a candle or a match.

"Momma, what we gonna do?" Sweetie pleaded. Jazz was wailing. Arthur pounded his fist against the table in helpless frustration.

Patrick circled the apartment, trying every light he saw. "Look here," he called, pointing to a single **unsheathed** bulb burning in the bathroom. "This outlet must be connected to my house. What you gotta do is get an extension cord and some adapters, and run as much as you can out of this socket."

By the next day thick orange electrical wires wound from the bathroom around the apartment. Sometimes they stumbled over the cords, sometimes they **squabbled** over who needed the brightness most: Arthur to study, or Tomekia to change Jazz's diaper.

Sheila tried hard not to feel sorry for herself, but it had been so long since she had enjoyed even the simplest of pleasures—a pizza, a movie, a haircut and shampoo. "I got to get off of welfare," she told herself. "It's a road that keeps on runnin'. It's set up so you can't never get off. But I gotta get off, before it kills me."

A few days later she walked over to a neighborhood missionary house and pleaded poverty. "I hate beggin'—I wasn't raised to beg," she told the nuns. "But my family's desperate."

They gave her enough money to pay her utility bills, and in January public aid ruled in her favor. A major crisis had passed. But she never forgot those dreary days of desperation: how she spent

....

eerie strange, scary
unsheathed uncovered, bare
squabbled argued, fought

nights wrapped in her bathrobe, worrying alone in the cold kitchen, watching a television hooked to the bathroom by an extension cord, and dreaming of having all the riches—Cadillacs and convertibles, diamonds and gold, silk and satin, spicy romance, and steamy hot beaches that **emanated from the greenish glow of** the TV.

Bedford began the first practice of the season with a five-on-five scrimmage. He let them run to watch them play, no sense in slowing them down and cluttering their heads with plays, at least not yet—plenty of time for that later.

Two sophomores, cut from the frosh-soph squad, shot at the side basket, playing their own spirited game of one-on-one. Bedford decided not to **shoo them from** the court. They bothered no one; better they be here than on the streets.

He turned back to the scrimmage just as Derrick Zinnerman collided with Cesare Christian. The ball bounced out of bounds. "It's gonna be a long season," he sighed.

It was, he counted, his eighteenth basketball season at Marshall. No one would mistake this team for his 1982 squad, the one that won the city title and finished fourth in the state. This team had too many juniors and not enough experience. *This is what I get for not recruiting,* he thought. He snickered at the notion. He was too old to start recruiting, to **sweet-talk high school freshmen**; too old to drive them all over town to practices and games, as some coaches did. Some coaches recruited players from one end of the city to the other. He liked to think there were enough good players right around Marshall to make any team a contender. Well, this team would test

....

emanated from the greenish glow of she saw on
shoo them from ask them to leave
sweet-talk high school freshmen try to get high school freshmen to come to Marshall

that theory. And if they lost, he wasn't going to cry. He was too old to link his identity to the ups and downs of teenagers.

Arthur caught a pass, lowered his head, and stormed the basket, knocking two men to the ground.

Bedford blew his whistle and yelled, "Charge!"

Arthur stared at him. "That's right, a charge," Bedford bellowed, rising as he spoke. "And it's always gonna be a charge, until you start playin' with your head and stop tryin' to run through the whole defense."

Arthur scrambled up the court and made a quick move, batting the ball out of Cesare's hands. But then he lost it, bouncing the ball off of his foot as he tried to dribble behind his back. Bedford buried his head in his hands.

He stood up, having seen enough. *Wheeet.* He blew the whistle and had them sit on the bench. Bedford stood above them, perusing his roster fastened to his clipboard.

"All you guys are on the team . . ."

The kids murmured.

". . . until next week when the grades come in," he said.

The kids snuck each other looks. They needed **a C average to remain eligible**. Some of them **were borderline at best**.

"Do I have all your medical cards?" Bedford asked.

The kids were silent.

Bedford looked up from his clipboard; not a face would meet his eyes. "I done told you guys, you got to have those medical cards from your doctor or the league won't let you play."

He paused at Dunagan. "Do I have your medical card?"

---

a C average to remain eligible to get mostly C grades to be allowed to play basketball

were borderline at best had a hard time getting a C average

"No."

"Why?"

"My doctor got it."

Bedford rubbed his head. "Now, tell me, what good does it do me if it's at your doctor's?"

Dunagan launched into an explanation, but Bedford cut him off. "You got to have those medical cards by next week," he said. He looked at the clock. It was after five. He'd been at the school since the early morning. The girls' basketball team, one of the best in the state, was scheduled to practice in ten minutes; he had to be somewhere at seven. "All right," he said, "get out of here. And don't forget to bring those medical cards from your doctor."

Bedford walked down the hallway to his office in the rear of the gym just **off from** the locker room. His office was tiny, not much larger than a broom closet, with a file cabinet and a desk covered with papers, and pictures and newspaper articles taped to the wall.

He looked at his watch. If he left right now he'd make his appointment. But where were his car keys?

The phone rang and Bedford answered it.

"No, Mr. Ogilvie's not here," he said. He hung up.

Zinnerman poked his head into the office, a medical form in his hand. "Here you go, coach," he said.

Bedford nodded as he pushed around the paper on his desk. "You see my keys?" he asked.

"No, coach."

Dunagan popped his head into the room. "Coach, how long I got before I get that medical in?"

....

off from next to

Bedford looked up. "I done told you two hundred times, you got to have it in next week."

"Okay, coach."

The phone rang again. It was the same guy, calling for Ogilvie. "I told you, he's not here," Bedford explained, **cradling** the phone near his ear and bending down to rummage through some files that lay on the floor. The caller put him on hold.

Cesare Christian and Arthur and Zinnerman came into the office. There was hardly room for any of them to move without bumping into one another.

Christian picked up a folder from Bedford's desk. "Excuse me," said Bedford, the phone **lodged** against his neck, "is that yours?"

Christian giggled. "No."

"Well, give it then."

Bedford's attention turned back to the phone. "Mr. Ogilvie's not around the gym. Would you like me to take a message?" He took a message, hung up the phone, and then dropped that message into the pile of papers on the desk.

"Who's got my keys?" he called out. He turned to Arthur, who stood in the doorway. "You got my keys?"

"No."

"I got to get out of here. I got an appointment," muttered Bedford.

The phone rang again.

"Aw, man," said Bedford.

Arthur picked up a folder.

"Hey, give it back," said Bedford. "This isn't public information."

....

cradling holding
lodged held firmly

The phone kept ringing.

"Derrick got one, too," said Arthur.

"Go tell him to bring it back."

Arthur slipped out of the office and the phone stopped ringing. Bedford stopped **leafing** through his papers and called Arthur back.

"You okay?" he asked.

"Yeah, coach."

"Because you're playin' **lousy**. I mean, how many times I tell you not to dribble behind your back?"

Arthur shrugged. "You're playing like you're in a big hurry to prove somethin'," Bedford continued. "You don't have to worry about bein' nothing but what you are. You don't have to be Isiah. You don't have to be the big star from St. Joseph. You don't have to be nothin' but Arthur Agee."

Arthur nodded.

"All right, get out of here."

Bedford sat and rubbed his forehead. It was the first moment of silence all day, and he enjoyed it. Suddenly he sat up straight. "I'm late," he snapped. He was halfway out the door when he remembered he still didn't have his keys.

The next day Bedford had new uniforms to distribute: shirts, shorts, and **warm-ups**, in Commando maroon and gold. They were in his office, piled on the desk next to medical slips, attendance forms, and memos from the central office. Members of the team kept running down the hallway, poking their heads in the doorway, and sniffing the gluey gleaming colors.

....

leafing looking

lousy badly, terribly

warm-ups long pants and jackets

Bedford was on the phone chatting with a reporter when he saw his players pile up in the doorway. He knew what they wanted but he kept on talking. Let *them* wait once in awhile.

"All right," he said, putting down the phone, "Line up."

They all bumped into each other, trying to be first. Five years ago, it was the Magic look. Kids wanted to wear the shirts tight and high, just like Magic Johnson. Now it was the **baggy** look, like Michael Jordan, with floppy shorts pulled down to their thighs. As a result, the little guards **snatching up** the medium and large shorts left nothing to fit the big guys.

"You think Bobby Knight's got to put up with this nonsense?" said Bedford, rubbing his hand through his hair.

"Is this large, Mr. Bedford?" asked Christian.

"I don't know," said Bedford. "You better take the extra large 'cause you're the fattest thing in here." All the kids laughed as Christian **sheepishly walked away**.

Arthur was next. "I want eleven."

"Find it," Bedford said. Arthur picked out a jersey and shorts. "Any medium shorts go with these?"

"Just small," said Bedford.

"Don't make no difference," said Arthur as he began stretching the shorts to make them longer and looser.

He went into the hallway, stripped off his warm-ups, and put on his new uniform. He ran his fingers over the bright shiny lettering, and sneaked into the bathroom to use the mirror. He adjusted the shorts so they hung low, tucked the socks into his shoes, and went down to the gym with a little hitch to his walk and the blank look

....

baggy loose
snatching up choosing, taking
sheepishly walked away walked away embarrassed

he'd seen on Isiah's face.

Bam, Zinnerman **socked** him in the arm, breaking his concentration, upsetting his flow.

"Man, don't hit me," said Arthur.

"I didn't hit you," said Zinnerman.

"Man."

"Hey, everyone—Arthur thinks he's Isiah."

The others started laughing and Arthur lunged for a loose ball, and dunked it.

"You can't dunk," Cesare called.

"Can, too."

Bedford stepped into the gym. "Hey, stop that dunkin'," he yelled. "Quit hanging on the rim."

"Sorry, coach," they **chorused**.

He scowled at them and then turned and started to walk away.

They started shooting jumpers again, and then Dunagan, perhaps unable to contain himself, put back a rebound with a dunk.

"That ain't nothin'," said Arthur. "Watch this."

He came in with a tomahawk, and soon a mini-dunking contest had erupted with about five players competing.

"Hey," Bedford bellowed. "I told you don't dunk the damn ball."

"I didn't do it," said Arthur.

"Well somebody did. I just came out and told you what to do. Will you never grow up?"

The players looked at their feet.

Bedford had them line up at center court while one of the school's teachers arranged them for a photograph for the yearbook.

....

socked hit, punched

chorused said at the same time

"I'll take about four shots," the photographer said. "I'll try to find one where nobody's blinking and we look positive. We'll do one standing as you are and one where everyone raises their index finger to make the number one sign. This one keep your finger down."

As she focused the camera, a player in the back raised his index finger.

"No," said the photographer, "not yet."

The kid in the back lowered his finger, while the player next to him, his face **knotted in** confusion, slowly raised his.

"Put your damn finger down," yelled Bedford.

Afterward some of the team members posed as though they were dunking, standing on a chair, ball held behind their head as though they were running in for a monster dunk. Then they pretended they were rimming in curling layups, the cameras flashing.

"Man, no one gonna believe that," Shannon said as Arthur climbed down from the chair.

"Hey, they don't have to believe it as long as they see it," said Arthur.

"You ain't nothin'."

"Better watch that, then."

Shannon grabbed Arthur **in a headlock** as they laughed and wrestled.

"Hey, man, here comes coach," someone yelled. Arthur and Shannon quickly separated and picked up a basketball. All of a sudden it was unnaturally silent in the gym.

"Hi, coach," called out Arthur with all the innocence he could muster.

....

knotted in showing his

in a headlock by the head

"Yeah, hey, coach," said Shannon.

Bedford glared at them for a moment and started to shake his head. "Man, they ought to pay me **double** for working with you clowns."

The last Bedford heard as he went toward his office was their laughter bouncing around the gym.

After practice Arthur and some of the guys hung around the gym. These were the slow days of a dreary winter. The sun was low before five and sinking fast, and **darkness weakly rapped against the windows**. Arthur loved these moments when the gym lights flicked on. They tried to distract the girls playing on the courts with funny faces, or they talked among themselves. Bedford let them stay, knowing they had no where else to go. While they talked Arthur stretched his legs. He couldn't believe how long and sinewy they had grown. They looked just like Michael Jordan's.

They looked at basketball magazines, particularly the glossy color photos of Jordan dunking, and their favorite photo was the famous shot of **Jordan's silhouette** frozen against a fiery sky, his arms extended, his feet appearing at least six feet off the ground.

Then they started talking about the Bulls.

"Hey, Arthur, who's gonna win that Bulls-Pistons game?" Shannon asked.

"Pistons," Arthur said.

"Bet you ten dollars."

"Boy, you ain't got no money," said Arthur.

"You don't either. Man, how come you like Michael Jordan but don't like the Bulls?"

....

double more money

darkness weakly rapped against the windows it was getting dark outside

Jordan's silhouette the outline of Jordan's body

"Hey, 'cause I like Jordan don't mean I have to like his team."

They laughed and slapped each other on the back and sat back to look at more color pictures of Jordan.

One day toward the end of January, William stopped by Arthur's house on his way to Catherine's.

"You serious about her?" Arthur asked.

"I guess," William said.

"I **ain't serious about no woman**—they get in the way of what I got to do," said Arthur.

"It's different when you have a daughter."

Arthur took him to his bedroom and showed him the new full-length poster of Jordan hanging on his closet door. He always saw it when he opened the door to get clothes. He showed William the *Sun-Times* **clipping** on the wall, an article from *Jet* heralding Isiah's new $16 million, four-year contract, and a *Sun-Times* story describing Marshall's **come-from-behind** win over Corliss, with his name—Arthur Agee, underlined in black ink—credited for thirteen points, including a big basket in the closing minute.

Arthur got excited as he described the game. Rising from the bed, he picked up a **Nerf** ball to illustrate one of his more brilliant maneuvers, a reverse layup, which he banked off the wall and through a tiny, plastic basket. *He's changed*, William thought. *He's bigger, he's grown. His arms are longer than mine.*

"How tall are you, Arthur?" William asked. "Six feet, six-one."

"Hmm."

"Ping still punch people?" Arthur asked.

....

ain't serious about no woman am not in a relationship

clipping article

come-from-behind surprising, unexpected

Nerf toy

"He sure does. Come on, man, do Ping."

It had been awhile, so Arthur's imitation was rusty. He stood on his bed and took his time **contemplating** Pingatore. "William, come here," said Arthur in Pingatore's growl. He socked William on the shoulder. "You any taller, huh? You may be gettin' taller, but you still ugly."

William laughed and then his voice **dropped**. "It's rough, sittin' on the bench. I want to play so bad. Sometimes I want them to lose, man, so they'll need me."

"I know," said Arthur. "I wanted you to lose all your games after I left."

"Sometimes I be sittin' on the bench, hoping Marty or Jamal miss their shots."

"Aw, man," said Arthur.

"If I come back healthy, this will be the year I take them downstate," William said. "I feel it."

After William left, there really wasn't much for Arthur to do. It was too cold to go out. He played a little more Nintendo and shot some Nerf basketball and then tried some homework. He fell asleep with his clothes on, his English book resting against him.

By the time the basketball season started, Bo had given up on dope dealing and moved into burglary. It hurt him, in a way, because he liked to believe that burglary was beneath a man of his intelligence. But he had no choice; he consumed most drugs that came within his grasp. He **scoped** out places by day and made his break-ins at night, slitting screens, popping locks, or climbing through open top-floor

---

contemplating thinking about
dropped became serious
scoped checked

windows. He looked for cash, but **made off with** a television set or radio if he had to. One rainy night in autumn he raced into a retirement home and told the security guard there was a suspicious man hanging around the window in the back. When the guard slipped out to look, Bo made off with the television set. He sold it to a **fence** and pocketed about fifty dollars for his trouble.

All in all he wasn't very good at burglaries. He had to be high to work up the courage, and when he came down he felt some pangs of guilt, since most of his victims were poor.

The police caught him on several occasions, but jails were filled with more violent offenders and they usually let him go free without bond. Then one night they caught him in a launderette rummaging through a change drawer. After a night in **the lockup**, Bo was taken to a drab, windowless courthouse and chained to a line of prisoners. When he was brought before the judge, to his surprise she recognized him.

"Look up, Mr. Agee," she said.

He met her eyes.

"Didn't I release you on an I-bond two weeks ago?" she asked.

"Yes, your honor."

"You have four other burglary cases pending," she said. "I'm going to do you a favor, Mr. Agee. I'm going to send you back to prison and give you some rest."

In a way the judge was right. It might be good to go back to jail. It would get him off of drugs, even if it was the hard way; it would give him time to **survey the wreckage**—skinny arms, scrawny chest, watery eyes, bleeding ulcers. *What happened to the golden boy*

....

made off with stole
fence person who would sell it to other people
the lockup jail
survey the wreckage think about his life

with the tapered waist, infectious laugh, flashing smile, and cocky walk? What happened to the singer, the athlete, the man of potential—the life of the party at Parker High? All my schemin', and I ain't worth nothin', he thought.

He lay on his cot in a crowded cell and cried silently.

"What you cryin' for, man?" another prisoner asked.

"You wouldn't understand," Bo replied.

And they wouldn't. They couldn't. None of them could know how many people he had hurt and disappointed, or the great talents he had wasted. *I got to get control,* he thought. *I got to serve a higher purpose . . . I want to serve God.*

He wrestled with strange emotions and difficult questions: Could he serve God *and* his own interests? If someone did him wrong, did he have to turn the other cheek? He vowed to free himself of drugs, if only to gain control of his life. But what about life's other urges and temptations? What about the women, the dealing, the petty scheming, his temper, the **fist he took to** his wife?

When they brought him back to court, he **threw himself at the judge's mercy.** "That wasn't me doin' those things, your honor," he said, "that was the cocaine. I'm gonna get off of coke. You can't go through life **with no accountability.** I'm gonna be accountable to God. There's a man here, your honor, begging you for a second chance."

On and on he talked, so long and hard that finally the judge gave in and gave him what he wanted: probation on the condition that he be held for several months at a South Side drug treatment facility for prisoners. He thanked the judge for her mercy.

....

fist he took to way he had hit

threw himself at the judge's mercy begged the judge to be understanding

with no accountability without being responsible for anything

Not long after, he found himself in domestic court before another judge. Sheila stood across the aisle next to the district attorney, glowering at him. The district attorney detailed the charges against Bo. But the judge reviewed Bo's file, discovered he was already on probation for burglary, and ruled he had no choice but to give Bo probation.

"You can't send a man to jail if he's already been given probation on a greater charge," the judge explained.

Sheila stomped her feet in disbelief. "Why didn't you tell that other judge that Bo was charged with beating me?" Sheila asked the prosecutor.

"We didn't know he had those other charges pending."

"You didn't know?"

"I'm sorry."

"He's smarter than all of you."

He should have felt guilt; he should have felt remorse and humility, but what he felt was smart—real smart, crafty, and slick. "God gave me a gift all right," he told himself.

Bo's **smugness** didn't last, though; soon it turned to guilt. He felt small, petty, and irresponsible. *You can fool a judge, but you can't fool the Lord.* He thought of his grandmother, Ethel Mae. She was so religious and pious. She loved him so deeply, and he brought her nothing but pain. "Please, Lord, please forgive me for what I done to Ethel Mae," he prayed. He decided his real enemy was his temper. "When I take the drugs, I lose control of it. I got to stay in control."

He was sent to an in-house treatment center, where he figured he'd have to stay for six months or so. He **bided** his time in group

....

smugness confidence, arrogance
bided spent

therapy sessions, hearing other prisoners pledge to follow the twelve steps to **abstinence**. "I don't need no twelve-step program," Bo told the others. "The Lord has freed me from drugs." He promised himself that he would attend church services every Sunday, devote the Sabbath to God, and search in his soul for answers that would help him lead a purer life.

But on the very Thursday he made that promise, his ulcers flared and they sent him to Roseland Hospital for treatment. That's where he was when Sunday came—sitting in bed, feeling **blue**, a gospel music tape playing softly at his side. "Lord, I know I promised you that I'd start going to church," he said. "Lord, please forgive me."

There was a rustle at the door and he turned to see a small, tawny-brown woman, wearing a white, flowing dress, black lace on her head, and carrying a worn, brown Bible.

"Young man, excuse me," she said. "I'm Minister Eleanor Banks, and we're having a service upstairs. Would you like to attend?"

It was a moment unlike any he had ever experienced, a miraculous moment of divine intervention—a sign that God had not forsaken him for breaking his vow. He **bolted upright** in his bed. "How did you know that I was looking for that message, minister?" he asked. "I promised God I'd go to church and now you've saved me from breaking my promise to God."

"God sent me here to make sure that you're going to be all right," she said.

He'd seen jailhouse preachers before; most of them were men, **lifers or ex-hoods**. But Minister Banks was different. Everything about her, from the sound of her voice to the lace with which she

---

abstinence living without using drugs

blue sad, depressed

bolted upright sat up straight

lifers or ex-hoods in prison for life or former criminals

covered her head, reminded him of his grandmother. "I was lookin' for a message, minister," Bo repeated. "How did you find me?"

"God sent me here."

He told her the story of his life, holding nothing back: "I've shot and been shot at. I abused myself with drugs. It's a miracle I'm alive."

"Glory to God," she said. "God has saved you for a reason."

"But why did he allow me to waste my life?"

"God has his reasons."

"I could have been a singer, a basketball player, a millionaire. I could have been a lawyer—I done outsmarted every lawyer in the state of Alabama."

"Amen."

"Look at me, Minister Banks. Look at where I've fallen. I done wasted it all."

He was weeping. "This **ain't no schemin'**, minister."

"God has blessed you, son."

"I've lied and cheated and sold drugs and beat my wife and stolen from the poor."

"But God still loves you."

"I wasted all my money."

"You may make more. God may want you to be a millionaire. But that don't make you rich. Look at all the rich men dead and gone. They had their riches but they didn't have God. To the young man in the Bible, Jesus said: 'Seek ye first the kingdom of heaven and his righteousness and all the other things will be added onto you.' Think about that, young man."

He went with her to Sunday services. Later she returned with

....

ain't no schemin' is not a trick; is not a lie

him to his room, where they spent another hour together. She held Bo while he wept and pleaded for forgiveness and accepted Jesus as his savior.

On the day of the Steinmetz game, at the midpoint of the season, Arthur slept in, rising at ten. With Sweetie watching him dress, he methodically went through his wardrobe of T-shirts, shorts, and socks, all ironed, folded and neatly arranged in his drawer or closet. He inherited his neatness from his mother. Even his collection of old gym shoes at the foot of his bed—he called it the graveyard—was organized by color and style.

On the walls around him were Michael Jordan photos and calendars and articles. Arthur was going through a quiet transition, with Jordan edging out Isiah as the great hero in his life. It was a gradual change that he was reluctant to acknowledge, given **his long-standing infatuation with Isiah**. But it was hard to love Isiah in a town where the angelic view of the scrappy little point guard who played himself out of poverty was almost forgotten. He was now known as the bratty leader of the detestable Detroit Pistons—**a conniving, duplicitous little schemer who might elbow** somebody like Scottie Pippen when the refs weren't looking only to gloat when Pippen stupidly retaliated and got nailed with a foul. The Pistons had eliminated the Bulls from the play-offs two years running—disrupting their fragile psyches with a dirty defense. When Isiah returned to his hometown, the fans greeted him with resounding boos.

The only people around Chicago to unconditionally praise Isiah were those with a close allegiance to St. Joseph. Arthur wasn't in that

---

his long-standing infatuation with Isiah that he had admired Isiah for so long

a conniving, duplicitous little schemer who might elbow a sneaky player who might hit

camp. He hardly ever thought of St. Joseph anymore. So much had happened to him and his family since he left St. Joe. His days there seemed as though they were from another lifetime. Bedford had replaced Pingatore as the consuming influence in his life. He grinned at the thought of Bedford. Old stone face had fooled him more than once, revealing his softness in gentle gestures. In the midst of the chaos, when the lights were out and Sheila had barely enough money to pay for food, Bedford showed up uninvited with a bag of groceries. He came and left quickly, embarrassed by Sheila's thanks and praise.

Arthur went to the kitchen to fix himself lunch: hot dogs on white bread. He carefully orchestrated each move in the preparation: the bread precisely sliced in half, the hot dog halved then quartered, the mustard judiciously applied and spread directly across the middle of the bread.

Then he **gobbled his sandwich down** while looking at the sports section of the morning paper. There were articles on **high school juggernauts** Westinghouse and King. Westinghouse had a point guard named Kiwane Garris, slippery quick and only a sophomore. And King, the mightiest school in the state, had two sophomores—seven-footers Rashard Griffith and Thomas Hamilton.

Arthur had seen King play in some of the summer tournaments. Their coach, Sonny Cox, usually sat by himself, away from the other coaches, permanently scowling. Guys came from all over the city to play for Sonny Cox, and he dressed them in the finest basketball outfits and sneakers and took them all over the midwest, **barnstorming** against opponents in St. Louis, Indiana, and downstate Illinois. The article said that with the demise of St. Joseph, due to the injury to

....

gobbled his sandwich down quickly ate his sandwich
high school juggernauts the powerful high schools
barnstorming playing

William Gates, King was the clear favorite to win the state. *I ain't afraid of them*, Arthur thought.

Arthur was out the door in a flash, licking mustard from his lips and moving along the sidewalks covered with snow and ice. He was tired of the cold, tired of the scenery—the old lots, boarded-up buildings, rusted automobiles. Isiah must know what it's like, living in a cramped apartment, pestered by little brothers, sick of the bedspread, the walls, the neighborhood; knowing the time will come, but sick of waiting for it, **itching to burst** out.

One day I'll play King, he vowed to himself. One day they'll know what they missed: St. Joseph, Westinghouse, King, and all the other powerhouses that picked and recruited. *By the time they realize what I had to offer, it will be too late.*

The team rode a bus to the Steinmetz game, Bedford up front with his assistants, ignoring the **racket rocking up** from the back. He turned to look once and saw Arthur and Shannon wrestling over a stocking cap. *I'm too old to worry about kids on a bus,* he thought as he returned his gaze to the front.

In the locker room, though, Bedford got serious. He rolled in a blackboard to diagram different defensive schemes. "Don't just let the guy get the ball," he said. He diagrammed a play and the players intently watched, trying to **decipher** the meaning of the Xs, Os, and squiggly arrows. They emerged from the basement locker room to a gym virtually deserted. The **inner city's chief export** would be on display for only a handful of mothers, young children, and junior-college scouts.

Steinmetz took an early lead, but Marshall crushed them with a

....

itching to burst eager to get
racket rocking up noise coming to the front
decipher understand; make sense of
inner city's chief export proud players

paralyzing press. Arthur was particularly frisky, trotting all over the court. He had one play that was **breathless**, pinpointing a perfect bounce pass to a teammate breaking toward the basket on his left. But a little later his shot was blocked, and he grew tentative and reluctant to penetrate. After Arthur sailed a pass out of bounds, Bedford disgustedly pulled him from the game.

Marshall had the lead, lost it, and then got it back again. At halftime Bedford took the team to a corner of the stands and **ripped into** them.

"You shoot it under the basket, around the basket, over the basket, everywhere but in," he said. "We set up the plays to get you wide open and you're wide open and you can't even make a layup. Arthur, you're going in there running down the floor like you're afraid to even play. And that defense is going to sleep. You work at it every day. I don't know what to tell you. Everything you run works, except you can't make no shots. You let them back in the game, and they've regained their confidence. You better get yours back."

He stopped and they said nothing, just kept staring ahead and at the floor, repressing the urge to yell back. *If we're lucky*, he thought, *we'll win ten this year.*

A few weeks later, against Crane, Marshall's season ended as it started—in the old West Side gym rocking with youthful exuberance and hopeful expectations.

There were about a hundred and fifty fans—including Sheila, Tomekia, and Jazz—in the six rows of bleachers that ran along the sides of the gym. A dozen pom-pom girls formed a line and danced

....

breathless great
ripped into yelled at

to a heavy drum beat **banging out of a boom box**.

Crane jumped to a 10 to 1 lead, and Bedford called time out. "Ain't nothin' you doin' right— ain't nothin'," he yelled. "I talk and talk and talk; you still don't do it."

He called a zone, and they slipped back to man-to-man; he asked for a press, and they backed off. Arthur took a shot and went over a defender's back, fighting for the rebound. It was the season **in a nutshell**: a waste of energy and talent. "You guys are rushing," Bedford told them. "You're just in a hurry to do nothing and that's just exactly what you're doing—nothing."

And yet whenever the lead mounted, whenever it looked as though Crane would **run away with** the game, the Commandos came back. Down by ten, Arthur hit a three. Down by seven, Zinnerman stole the ball and dribbled between two players, and Dunagan dunked.

"Come on, run. Run!" screamed Sheila.

With two minutes left Arthur fouled out on a charge. Bedford glared at him: "What the hell are you doin' runnin' wild at this point in the game?" he snarled.

Arthur sank onto the bench. Even without him the Commandos made one more rush, cutting the lead to two with two seconds left and Dunagan on the line.

Sheila crossed her fingers, and Arthur lay on the floor praying that the shots went in. The crowd rose to its feet. Dunagan eyed the basket, and missed them both. Kimble got the rebound and **put back** a shot. It rolled off; he tipped it again. "Where's the horn?" the Crane coach shouted. Kimble tipped it again, and it rolled off. Finally the horn sounded. Crane's fans ran on the court cheering.

....

banging out of a boom box playing from a big radio

in a nutshell described in a few words

run away with win

put back made

Sheila was disappointed, her voice raspy. "I got a bad headache. My head's about to bust," she told Tomekia.

That night the whole team came over to the house—twelve **brawny** guys, their long legs and arms filling up the living room and spilling into the kitchen. Sheila fed them hot dogs, and they watched videos and played Nintendo. They'd been losing all year but at least they were laughing. "There's a lot worse that can happen than losing a game," Sheila told the team.

....

brawny strong; big

BEFORE YOU MOVE ON...

1. **Cause and Effect** Sheila's electricity was turned off because she lost her welfare aid. What else happened?

2. **Inference** Why was it hard to believe that Bo was sincere about becoming a better person?

LOOK AHEAD Why was William upset that the Chargers were winning so many games? Read pages 243–267 to find out.

WILLIAM

It was weird for William to sit on the bench and watch his team while they ran the break as well, or better, than they did against Fenwick. But William had to watch from behind Pingatore, who kept blocking his view every time he jumped up to call a play or berate the referee. And he kept getting distracted from the game because parents, students, and teachers stopped by to ask how long it was going to be before he could play again. "Soon," he told them, though no one knew for sure, not even the doctor.

The first games of the season were tough on William because the team was doing so well without him. They had **swept** the Proviso West Christmas Tournament and won fourteen of their first fifteen games. He had expected them to flounder; he had even prepared an inspirational talk to keep them going until he returned. Apparently they didn't need him or his speeches. They told him: "We miss you, William," and he told them, "I'm behind you all the way." But since William knew he was fibbing, he figured they were fibbing, too. His absence meant more shots and points and minutes for them.

He didn't want to feel this way, but he couldn't help it. **Venom was squirting** through his veins, poisoning his general outlook. His grades were plummeting to Cs and Ds. He was indifferent about his classes and incapable of seeing school as **anything more than basketball's sideshow**.

The Chargers threw the ball away, and Pingatore disgustedly called time-out. The team gathered around him to be chastised. His

....

swept won

Venom was squirting Jealousy was flowing

anything more than basketball's sideshow more important than basketball

head bobbed and weaved, his face reddened, his glasses kept popping off his nose. William stifled a snicker. *Give 'em hell, Ping*, he thought.

At halftime he went to the locker room to ask each player to autograph a basketball for an eleven-year-old fan, Brian Kane, who had recently undergone emergency brain surgery. William had heard about Brian from a coach, and had visited him in the hospital. When Brian stared up from his bed, his head wrapped in bandages and his eyes huge and adoring, William nearly cried. *My problems ain't so big,* he thought. It seemed like a **noble gesture** to get the team to sign the ball, but now that he was circling the locker room at half, he felt even more remote and distant from the team, like he was a ball boy, not a star.

The Chargers pulled away in the third quarter and won by more than twenty points, but Pingatore wasn't pleased. The game was closer than it should have been, and he lambasted them in the locker room. "If you want to improve, the only way you can improve is to do the same things over and over the way we're supposed to," Pingatore told them. "There's no reason we can't win every game that we have left."

The team felt **dejected**; William looked as glum as the rest, though inside he was smiling: *Yeah, give it to them good.* He was almost disappointed when the tongue-lashing ended, and Pingatore led them in a prayer.

William was not the only one in his family struggling along a rocky road. Curtis had been out of work for almost six months.

"Sometimes I feel it would be better for my family if I just left,"

....

noble gesture nice thing to do
dejected discouraged, depressed

he told William. "I just take food from the table and don't give them nothin'."

Catherine had the exact opposite problem: she was busy almost every waking hour of the day. It was all part of an arrangement she had worked out with her mother, who had agreed to take care of Alicia during the day so Catherine could attend Westinghouse. In return, Catherine **resigned from** the swim team and gave up the cheerleading squad so she could work nights at a fast-food chicken restaurant and help pay the family's bills.

She arrived home from school at 3:30 P.M. and **checked in at** work an hour later every day of the week. They paid her minimum wage, $4.25 an hour, and made her wear a baby-blue smock and a hair net. She baked biscuits and dropped frozen lumps of chicken into boiling vats of splattering grease.

One of her coworkers was a homeless teenager. The girl spent her nights working in the restaurant and the other hours in bus terminals and parks. She had big black circles under her eyes.

The **clientele** featured a ferocious looking cast of hustlers, hookers, cops, and gangbangers, who came from **all corners of** the city to buy a late-night bucket of greasy chicken. There was a shooting one night outside the drive-through window. Catherine saw a young man lying in his blood. Wretched-looking men in tattered clothes that smelled of the street sometimes came in screaming. One night the store was robbed by a masked man who held a pistol to the homeless girl's head and ordered her to clear out the register.

"I was so scared, I was shaking," she told Catherine.

"I'd a died," Catherine said.

---

resigned from quit, left
checked in at got to
clientele people who ate at the restaurant
all corners of everywhere in

When she got home long after midnight, she was usually exhausted and coated with grease and flour. But if the baby woke up, it was Catherine's turn to tend her.

"Momma, I'm so tired," Catherine said one winter night. "Can't you take care of Alicia tonight?"

Her mother shook her head. "Maybe you won't have any more kids."

Catherine picked up the baby and staggered into her bedroom. She dropped to the bed with the baby and called William, even though Peggy and Alvin had explicitly warned her never to call after eleven. William answered the phone and she poured out her sorrows.

"All I do is work and work and work," she cried.

"It'll get better," he said.

"You don't understand. My life may look easy, but it's not."

"I'm workin', too, you know. I'm rehabilitating my knee. I'm doin' this for us and our future. So I can go to college."

It was another variation of the same old argument, and hearing it made her so angry she wanted to throw the phone on the floor. "William, I plan to go to college and I don't play basketball," she said.

Their worlds were more complicated now than during their freshman year. The little free time they had was spent separately. One Friday night William went with a few friends to the gym to **be an extra in** the Mary Thomas movie. The director made the crowd rise and cheer while the camera scanned the stands. "Don't do the wave," the director requested, "because this takes place in 1978, before people did the wave." So of course the goofy guys behind him immediately did the wave. They were friends of Layton's—kids from

....

be an extra in try to get a small role in

Maywood—who went to Proviso East, and their silly antics reminded William of Arthur.

Catherine's one **social highlight** was a dance at the Westinghouse gym where she danced to hip-hop music and chatted, giggled, and gossiped with her girlfriends. After that, she returned to her routine: school and work, work and school. As the days wore on, **her temper shortened**. She **got down on** William, blaming him for her frustrations. William took it all, even when she blatantly bossed him around.

Finally he lost his temper when she snapped at him in front of his family. "You can't talk to me like that," he said.

She apologized. William didn't deserve such abuse—he was a dutiful daddy, visiting Alicia every chance he got. "This isn't me," she told him. "This isn't who I am. I got so much pressure. I'm so tired all the time. I'll be better once I get some more rest."

On the weekends Catherine and William met at Cabrini so the whole family could be together. William loved to play with Alicia, tickling her or dangling the pacifier in her mouth. Mostly Catherine slept on the couch.

She was at the Gates's one Saturday afternoon when the doorbell rang. William limped to answer it.

It was Rankin, Curtis's old junior-college coach. "Curtis," he exclaimed. "My God, you look great."

"Coach, I ain't Curtis," said William. "I'm his baby brother."

Rankin was shocked when he saw Curtis. "My goodness, Curtis, you got big."

"It ain't nothin' but baby fat," Curtis said.

....

social highlight fun evening
her temper shortened she got angry quickly
got down on yelled at

They sat on the couch with the TV sound low, **paging** through Curtis's scrapbook and **reminiscing** about the good old days, when Colby barnstormed the Great Plains and ransacked the opposition.

"You were the greatest player I ever coached," Rankin said.

"You were the best coach I ever had," said Curtis. "They loved us in that town. Man, everywhere I went, people wanted my autograph. That was the best time of my life."

Rankin took Curtis to a restaurant and got **down to business**. He was now the head coach at a small college in Massachusetts. "I want you on my team," he told Curtis. "Can you get in shape?"

"Man, I told you, this ain't nothin' but baby fat, coach."

"You haven't played in how long?"

"A year, but my skills are still here. They didn't go nowhere."

Curtis returned from that restaurant tingling with rich memories and bright dreams. He was all set to pack his bags and move out to Massachusetts. But there was a **hitch**: he couldn't enroll until Rankin's school got his transcripts, and Central Florida wouldn't release his transcripts until he paid back a small debt he owed them.

Rankin called Curtis several times during the next few weeks. "All you have to do is write Florida and they'll send your transcripts directly," he said. "I can't write the letter. It has to come from you."

"I'll take care of it, coach," said Curtis. But he never did. He picked up the pen and eyed the paper and never got any further than that. When he thought about it, he realized he didn't want to move east, he didn't want to work himself back into playing shape or risk the humiliation of not making the team. "Sooner or later, you gotta stop playing basketball, even if you make it to the NBA," he told

....

paging looking
reminiscing thinking, talking
down to business serious
hitch problem

William. "I did all right with basketball, but I can't worry about what I might have been. I **got to get on with** my life."

Every day William strapped his leg to the weight-lifting machine at the local Y and lay on his stomach lifting up and down, up and down—until he thought his leg might burst. His routine was the same each day: the weight machine, light jogging, a brief walk in the pool, a few jump shots. Sometimes his cousin, Terrell, or his old grammar school gym teacher, Fred Robinson, **kept him company**; but most days he finished the routine alone.

In the afternoon the **old-timers** came to play full-court basketball. William went to the gym to watch and tried not to laugh at their play. They had hair on their backs and bellies, and bald spots on their heads. They tossed elbows and knees, cheated on the score, bickered over fouls, glistened with sweat, and oozed all sorts of gassy odors. *I can't imagine me looking like that—even twenty years from now,* William thought as he watched them huff and puff across the court.

Once every other week William returned to Wolin's office, **stripped to** his shorts, and sat on the examining table while the nurse measured his knee.

"On the basis of what I've seen, you're two to three weeks from being able to practice full," Wolin told him after one visit in January. "And then it would be up to Coach as to whether or not he feels you can play. It takes a substantial amount of time for cartilage to heal." William nodded and tried not to grin.

"If you practice well, then I don't have any problem with your being able to play. But that's a coaching decision, that's not a medical

....

got to get on with have to continue living
kept him company stayed with him
old-timers old men
stripped to wearing just

decision. And the last thing I'm going to do is tell Coach how to coach."

Within a week William was back practicing with the team. Pingatore asked him how he felt, and he said he felt fine. That was the magic word: "Fine." He said it so often he no longer knew or cared what it meant. He'd cut off his kneecap and scrape away the cartilage if that's what it took to return him to the team.

Alvin, Peggy, Emma, David, Curtis—they all cautioned him not to go back too early. Catherine thought he was crazy to even continue the season at all. But in the second week of February, William made up his mind that he was going to play, and he asked the coach for a meeting. Pingatore was waiting for him in his office at the end of the day

"Well, what is it, William?" Pingatore asked when William came through the door. "Remember the last time you had something to tell me?"

William **blushed**. It had taken him almost five months to work up the nerve to tell Pingatore about Alicia, so fearful was he of the coach's reaction. And Pingatore's response was not what William feared it would be. "I thought you were gonna tell me you were **transferring**," Pingatore told William. He wasn't shocked, dismayed, happy, or sad. This sort of thing had happened before, and it would happen again.

William settled in a chair in front of Pingatore's desk. "How's your knee?" Pingatore asked.

"It's pretty good," said William.

"Is there any swelling?"

··

blushed turned red because he was embarrassed

transferring leaving St. Joseph to go to another school

"No."

"Did you ice it like I told you—all night?"

"Too much."

"Too much?"

"My knee still feels cold now."

"Well, you always said you were a cool guy."

They were **bantering** like they did most of the time, when Pingatore wasn't lecturing or teaching or being the coach. William remembered the night not long ago when several players from an old team came to visit Pingatore in the locker room. The coach's eyes clouded as if he was about to cry, but he couldn't quite let go. And neither could William. *Tell him thanks*, William thought. *Thanks for sending me to Wolin and paying the hospital bills. Ah, he'll think I'm being gushy.*

"How about it, coach, can we change that play?" William said, returning to the bantering.

"What play?"

"The one you call Indiana?"

"You don't like me to call the play Indiana?"

"No."

"What do you want me to do—call it Georgetown?"

"Yeah."

Pingatore shook his head.

"It's just a play, coach," William continued. "You call Marty's 'Colorado.'"

"That's because he's from there."

"I'm not from Indiana!"

....

bantering joking with each other

"I know, but you might be."

They went on like that for several minutes until they had run out of things to say and it was time to go to practice.

His first start came in the final home game of the regular season. It was a meaningless game because they had already **clinched** the conference title against Carmel. His whole family had assembled, just like old times. Mrs. Weir was also there, as was Sister Marilyn, and even Arthur, back at St. Joseph for the first time in well over a year.

"Hey, boy," Arthur called as William circled the floor for layups. "What's that thing on your knee?"

William looked at the elastic brace and smiled.

"Hey, **gimpy** boy, you gonna dunk?" Arthur called. They both laughed at that one.

The game was delayed for a ceremony honoring Pingatore **on the occasion of his 400th career victory**, a landmark achieved earlier in the season. Players from teams representing his 100th, 200th, and 300th victories came forward to shake Pingatore's hand. The old coach stood at center court, and when the crowd rose to cheer in appreciation, his eyes misted over.

For William it was like being a rookie all over again, feeling so uncertain and nervous. He wanted mainly to blend in and play mistake free. He worried about his knee; he never realized how much pressure it absorbed, how many swivels, starts, and stops it made in the course of a game. He took a pass from Layton and laid in a shot that rolled around and in. He dove for a loose ball, jumped for a rebound; he stopped, faked, cut left—sweat ran down his back. The

....

clinched won

gimpy injured

on the occasion of his 400th career victory for winning 400 games during his career as a coach

sounds of the crowd sang in his ears, and Pingatore's barbs sailed out from the bench—and through it all his knee **held**.

They ran a three-guard offense, putting him with Cortez and Layton. They ran it well, **zipping** the ball through the cracks in Carmel's defense. William scored eleven points, dished three assists, made three steals, and when he left the court for the final time—**the rout well under way**—Pingatore was all smiles. "You don't know how good this feels," William told Marty Clark. For the first time in weeks, he earnestly rooted for his teammates. And when the game ended, he left the court to hand claps and cheers—even the opponents from Carmel were happy to see him back.

Everyone was jubilant. Mrs. Weir, casually dressed in slacks and sweater, introduced herself to Emma, who in turn introduced Mrs. Weir to Alicia.

"This here is William's baby," said Emma.

"Oh," said Mrs. Weir.

"And this is Curtis."

Curtis leaned forward, his gold-loop earring glinting in the bright light. "How you doing?" he said.

"This is Mrs. Weir," Emma explained. "She's paying for William."

"William works hard," Mrs. Weir said. "It's nice to meet you. Take care."

Arthur marched down the stairs, through the cinder-block basement hallway, and into the locker room looking for William. He swiveled to avoid bumping into Marty Clark, just out of the shower with a towel wrapped around his waist. He looked up and saw the

....

held did not fail him

zipping passing

the rout well under way St. Joseph winning the game

Who Labors Conquers sign. *Man, ain't nothin' changed.*

Coach O'Brien saw him first and extended a hand. "How are you?" he asked.

"All right."

"Behaving yourself?"

Arthur laughed. From behind O'Brien came Pingatore's **husky** voice: "Arthur."

They hugged, stiff and awkward, with Arthur **making the initial move**. As they stepped back from their embrace, Pingatore looked Arthur over, apparently calculating the exact number of inches he had grown.

"I heard you slam now," Pingatore said.

Arthur leaned back and laughed. "Yeah, a couple," he said.

"Oh, I don't know if you'd be slamming here," said Pingatore.

Arthur kept on laughing.

"If you missed one, what would you be doing?" Pingatore asked. Arthur looked puzzled.

"Running twenty-five stairs," Pingatore said. Arthur grinned and Pingatore patted him on the arms.

"They told me you were six-two, big and strong, Jimminy Christmas," Pingatore continued. "The one thing I know for sure, you didn't get any better looking."

"Ha, ha, ha," Arthur laughed.

Arthur looked at the ground, remembering to talk clearly and distinctly and to say the things he figured Pingatore would want to hear him say: that he was studying hard and taking his future very seriously.

....

husky deep

making the initial move moving towards Pingatore first

254

"Me and my mother, we were talking and she was telling me I have to **get my grades** first and then I play ball," he said.

"Now's the time to do that," said Pingatore, nodding his head. "Don't wait till next year." He paused. "Say hello to your family for me."

Pingatore stood for a moment watching Arthur walk away, and then for no apparent reason other than playfulness walked up to Layton, who was standing by a locker, and smacked him four times in the arm, turned around without saying a word, and, still smiling, walked into his office.

Meanwhile William was telling local reporters that it felt "good to be back in the game."

Arthur walked by as William continued, **doubling** back as though he recognized William for the first time. "Oh my," he said, "it's William Gates."

William ignored Arthur. "I was putting eight weeks of basketball into three weeks," he told the reporters.

Arthur bent over and snapped off William's wristband. "Oh, I got William Gates's wristband."

"At times I felt uncomfortable; I was trying to work off the other players," said William, stifling a laugh and pretending as though Arthur wasn't there.

"Oh, I got William Gates's wristband. The big G—Gates," said Arthur, talking louder and parading around the locker room.

When the reporters left, William rose from his seat and smacked Arthur who smacked him back. They were halfway out of the door when Pingatore reemerged from his office.

....

get my grades do well in school
doubling turning

"You didn't have any flow; you weren't working hard mentally," he told William. "Remember the thing we talked about at the end of the year? What you needed to do to establish yourself is to play hard all the time. Of course, I'm not blaming you. You're just coming back. But that's got to be on your mind. You have to come out and start playing hard all the time. Otherwise you're just another player, **follow me**?"

He was saying it all in an amiable way, but the message **stung**. *What does he want?* William thought. *Why won't he quit? I'm busting my ass, I'm risking my knee.*

"As long as you're physically able," Pingatore continued. "If you're not, you shouldn't be playing at all."

How come he just can't say, Nice game. How come he can't just hug me? Why's it always got to be a lesson and a lecture?

"I made some pretty good plays," William said quietly but firmly.

"I'm talkin' about on defense."

"But—"

"But, defense. You don't even know how to spell the word." By now a small group had gathered, which included Arthur, David, and Curtis. Pingatore smiled to show that he was **leavening the lesson** with humor. Only William didn't feel like laughing. *Why's he got to say this in front of Arthur and Curtis?* he thought.

Arthur watched the interchange in disbelief, amazed that his friend was violating the **cardinal** rule of getting along with Pingatore: Don't ever talk back.

"You telling me I wasn't back? I was the first person back on defense," said William.

---

follow me do you understand

stung hurt William

leavening the lesson making the lesson fun

cardinal most important

"Wait till we see the tape," said Pingatore. "I'll apologize if I'm wrong. If I'm right, I'll kick your butt. Right?" He patted William on the shoulder.

William turned to walk away. "If you're right," William cracked, "I'll run seventy-five stairs tomorrow. Seventy-five, you heard it."

William started to walk away.

"All right, William, when's practice?" Pingatore called out.

William sighed. "Eight o'clock, coach," he said as he joined Arthur, Curtis, and David in the hallway.

William was turning to his left to catch a pass coming in over his shoulder when his foot slipped on the floor and he felt a ripping in his knee.

He limped off the court, **gritting** his teeth. It was the day before the first play-off game, and he was determined to play.

They took him to a doctor, and the doctor strapped William's knee to a machine that sent soothing electroshock waves to the **heart** of the pain.

The next day he scored fifteen points as the Chargers slipped passed Fenwick—poor old Fenwick; they hadn't defeated St. Joseph in fifteen seasons. Fenwick came out **revved up, running off** the game's first nine points and taking a 57 to 48 lead with about seven minutes left. But William scored six straight points **down the stretch**, including one basket on a twisting reverse layup.

"Gates was a key during the fourth quarter," Pingatore told the reporters.

The press treated him like a wounded hero. They surrounded him

....

gritting biting down hard with
heart area
revved up, running off full of energy, scoring
down the stretch later in the game

while he sat on a stool next to his locker, stripped to his waist, his knee resting in a bucket of ice. "Tonight I knew I would play," William told them. "My knee felt good in the first half. It began to hurt in the fourth quarter. I knew I had to suck it up and continue to play."

The next day he returned to the doctor for more soothing waves of electricity. He spent two hours hooked to the machine, returning to school in time to hear Pingatore conclude practice with a passionate, almost angry speech.

"If you **let it slip**, and I emphasize the you—if you let it slip, it's your fault," he told them. "It's your fault. Because you got control of it right now. You can do as well as you want to do. There's no greater time than to play in the state tournament and going downstate." He went around the room, pointing at different players: "You been there? You play there? You play there? Anybody play there? I've been there."

His voice dropped. "You want to go. You have to do what you have to do. It will be something you remember for the rest of your life."

William shared Pingatore's passion. But his hunger was suppressed by his worries about his knee. The sound of the rip echoed in his ear. As he rode the train home he stared at his pants leg, as though some secret might be revealed. *Why does it seem that every time I come to this moment of the season, it isn't completed?* he thought. *As a freshman I didn't appreciate it 'cause I was too young to understand. Last year I was preoccupied with Catherine and the baby. And now it's the knee. It seemed all Isiah thought about was basketball. But me, it's like basketball's the last thing on my mind.*

On March 7 they **stymied** Proviso East 71 to 60, by far their most impressive win of the season. Proviso was a talented team with

....

let it slip do not play well
stymied beat, defeated

two quality juniors—Sherell Ford and Michael Finley. But St. Joseph ran its system **with clinical precision**, racing to big leads and then stifling Proviso's belated runs and rallies. Marty Clark was brilliant, scoring twenty-one and blanketing Ford, holding him to nine points. Jamal Robinson scored thirteen points and grabbed nine rebounds.

Down the stretch, the game belonged to William. With the lead cut to three in the final minutes, William drove, stopped suddenly, pivoted toward the basket, and drew a foul. His knee was aching, but he blocked the pain, as well as the sound of the crowd and Proviso's players telling him not to choke. He allowed himself to see only the basket, as though to make the free throw were as simple as dropping a ball in a bucket that lay at his feet. The ball fluttered from his fingertips and slipped through the net. He hit both free throws and two others to **ice the win**.

"Out of all the wins, this one tops them all," he told the reporters. "I think it was a matter of us wanting it more. We had the attitude that we weren't going to leave here without a win. I'm not going to say this is where it ends. We have some more business to take care of."

The business was the great rematch against Tommy Kleinschmidt and Gordon Tech. William **tossed and turned** at night plotting strategy and imagining happy results. In all of his fantasies, St. Joseph won, though the method varied. Sometimes he imagined himself hitting the game-winning basket; sometimes he made the game-winning block, steal, or rebound.

"I've got nothing personal against Kleinschmidt," he told reporters. "I don't really know him." But it *was* personal. William's

....

with clinical precision very well
ice the win win the game
tossed and turned could not sleep

reputation **was at stake**. He had started three years ago at the head of the line with only Kleinschmidt closing in, and now the chunky forward had passed him. "Man, every time I open the papers, there's something about Kleinschmidt," he told Curtis. "It's Kleinschmidt this and Kleinschmidt that. What about me?"

"You gonna have to get them to talk about you," Curtis said. "You score a few baskets and everyone will be talking about Gates."

On the night before the game, he was gripped by a dreadful nightmare in which his knee **gave way** as he was driving for the basket. He woke in a panic, the rip of cartilage still sounding in his ears. "Please hold," he prayed. "Please just for this one game."

They filled the stands an hour before the game. The students from St. Joseph and Gordon Tech sat on separate sides of the gym, wearing bright reds, whites, blues, and golds and exchanging loud, boisterous chants. Someone pounded a drum, a trumpet blared, the mascot Charger, his face painted red, waved a rubber sword. When Kleinschmidt jogged on the court, the Gordon Tech fans cheered and the Charger fans held their noses and waved the air as though a sickly smell had **wafted their way**.

St. Joseph had an elaborate routine for introductions. After each name was called, the player ran the length of the bench, slapping hands with coaches and teammates before running to the center court. The last hand William slapped belonged to Brian Kane, the kid recently out of brain surgery, whose great wish was now fulfilled. Pingatore had allowed him to join the introductions and sit on the team's bench.

....

was at stake depended on how well he played
gave way did not support him
wafted their way entered the gym

William had tears in his eyes when he **took** the court; his knee throbbed with a pain steadily advancing to his thigh. I won't make it, he thought. *It's gonna give out. Please don't give out.*

The lead bounced back and forth in the early going. Kleinschmidt drove for a shot; William held his position and they collided, with Kleinschmidt banging his eye against William's leg. The shot bounced to Clark who passed to Layton who passed to William, who could see out of the corner of his eye that Kleinschmidt still had not gotten up. Time-out was called and two trainers and the coach ran onto the floor.

Kleinschmidt lay on his back breathing hard. His chest heaved, and he clutched his right eye. Coaches and trainers approached him and offered their hands, but Kleinschmidt pushed them away. "Get your hands off of me," he cried. "Let me go. I'm all right. I'm fine, man. I'm fine." He staggered to the bench, blood dripping from his eye. "Forget it. I'm fine, man. I'm fine," he said angrily.

The sight and scent of blood **ignited a fury in the fans**. Their **racket** rose like a rocket, banging against the ceiling and bouncing off the walls. Pingatore was screaming, but his players could barely hear him. He brought in one substitution after the other, called every play from the bench, and the score kept bouncing back and forth, back and forth, the crowd more desperate as time ticked away.

William, meanwhile, was exhausted. "Keep going, man, keep going," he told himself. But his legs **were leaden**, his body lifeless. It was the knee, the damn knee, it had no pick-up, no spring.

He took the ball, pivoted, threw up a shot, and when he landed his knee buckled and he crashed to the floor. He heard a whistle blow

....

took came out onto
ignited a fury in the fans made the fans very angry
racket noise
were leaden felt heavy

and the ref call foul as he rolled on the floor clutching his knee.

"You all right, man?" He looked up to see Kleinschmidt hovering over him, blood stains on his shirt, his right eye puffy and purplish red.

O'Brien and a trainer helped him limp off the floor. He lay on the ground behind the bench. The crowd was chanting: "Defense! Defense!" And O'Brien was stretching his knee.

"Can you move it?" O'Brien asked.

"Defense, defense."

"Does it hurt?"

"Kleinschmidt, Kleinschmidt" —*clap-clap, clap-clap-clap.*

"Can you feel the pain?"

They were shouting to be heard over the crowd, and William didn't know what to tell them. *I'm tired,* he thought. *I don't wanna go back. I gotta go back. The knee's gone. It will hold. I gotta get back in the game.*

"Can you come back in?" Pingatore yelled.

No.

"Yeah," he yelled back.

"How does it feel?" Pingatore asked.

Like crap.

"It feels okay."

He jogged up and down, each step excruciating, talking to himself, telling himself: "This is the time to be great. This is for the team. This is for Brian Kane. This will be one of those big moments Pingatore will be talking about for many years—like he talks about Isiah—when William Gates limped back into the game on **a bum** knee."

....

a bum an injured

He checked in with just under four minutes left, his team was down by three, and the crowd on the St. Joseph side rose to its feet. Kleinschmidt was **on fire**, banging off screens and tossing in twenty-footers.

Clark hit a basket to cut the lead to one. With thirty-three seconds left, Layton stole the ball and passed it to William, who called time-out.

"Don't feel the pain, don't feel the pain," he told himself. He didn't want to be in the game, but he couldn't ask to leave. They wouldn't understand. The great ones never asked to go out.

"All right, listen, listen here," Pingatore bellowed. "I want to go Blue. I want to go Blue. So we can get it to one of our good shooters."

Pingatore was yelling as loud as he could to be heard over the crowd. William kept pressing his knee, trying to rub away the pain, trying to send it somewhere else. Up in the stands his family was watching him closely.

"Somethin' ain't right with William," said David.

Don't pass it to me, William thought. *I don't want it.*

"He's limpin' bad," said David.

Go to someone else.

"He shouldn't be there," said Alvin.

Marty, Layton, anyone.

"If he can't play, get off the court," said Curtis.

The ball went to Marty who dribbled, looked at Layton who was covered, and then tossed it in the corner to William.

I can't believe they passed it to me. William faked right and shot just as a player from Gordon slapped his hand. The shot bounced out and

----

on fire doing great

the ref called foul. He was going to the line.

He looked at the clock: six seconds left. It was funny! All those games as a freshman and a sophomore when he wanted the ball, he never got it. And now, when he didn't want it, the pass came right to him.

He reached the line. The ref bounced the ball. Out of the corner of his eyes he saw Kleinschmidt waving his arms in the air, **stirring his fans to bedlam**. *I don't want to be here*, William thought. He took the ball and bounced it once. *Concentrate, man*. He tried to focus in on the rim, but all he could hear was the crowd. The rim seemed to be shaking. The ball flew out of his fingers and banged hard off the back.

Gordon called time, their fans were like a mob. Emma put her head in her hands. "I can't look," she said.

Curtis stared straight on: *It should be me on that line*.

William limped back to the sidelines.

"Make him think about it," Kleinschmidt yelled.

After the time out, William returned to the line. *Concentrate*. He looked up, and for one moment the pain left his knee and the noise receded, the crowd disappeared, and he was back on The Avenue with Curtis and David. He let the ball go and it flew for the basket. It was going in. It would **tie the score**.

It **clanged** off the iron—*No, No, No*—and Kleinschmidt, *damn him*, pulled down the rebound. Gordon Tech had won.

When the buzzer sounded, the Chargers walked off in single file as Gordon's players paraded Kleinschmidt across the court on their shoulders.

....

stirring his fans to bedlam getting his fans excited

tie the score make the teams' scores the same

clanged bounced

Emma held Alicia, Curtis put on his jacket, and David stared straight ahead.

"He shouldn't have been out there," said Alvin. "He shouldn't have been playing."

"If he was hurt, he shouldn't've got out there," said Curtis.

"I'm disappointed in this system," said Alvin. "If winning is that important you need to **reevaluate** the program."

"His knee ain't got nothin' to do with him missin' those free throws," said Curtis. "That's just pressure."

"He's playing on emotion. He's trying to psyche himself up so he's not feeling the pain," said Alvin.

"It was terrible coachin'," said Curtis. "I've been tellin' you all year—Pingatore's a terrible coach. No way Kleinschmidt's the best on the floor. What he's doing, that's what William should be doing: Come down and shoot the ball. But they want to get into a slow-down turtle game. You can't beat anybody in a turtle game."

Then they got tired of talking and stood there silently, thinking of the final free throws.

In the Gordon locker room the players yelled and cheered and sprayed each other with cups of water.

"I took a beating at the beginning," Kleinschmidt told reporters. "But we wanted this game a lot. Kids who go to Gordon are **thoroughbreds** who want to win every year."

Over in the St. Joseph side, the players **were sober** and sad as they dressed. William sat on a stool and cried. Pingatore walked up and put his hand on his shoulder. "It wasn't your fault," Pingatore said. "We should have put that game away a long time ago."

....

reevaluate think again about; review
thoroughbreds strong players
were sober became serious

By the time the reporters arrived, many of the players had left. "Kleinschmidt is a man among boys," Pingatore told the press. "That's what you can say about this game."

"What about Gates and those free throws, was his leg bothering him?"

"Someone said the knee was buckling a little bit. I know he's hurting . . . but I don't know," said Pingatore. "They just played harder than we did."

Brian Kane walked up to William. "I'm really sorry," he said.

William looked up. "Hey, thanks."

William was one of the last to leave the locker room, and when he reached the gym most of the spectators had gone, except for the **Chargers fanatic** with the painted face, who stood alone in the stands, dejectedly flipping his plastic sword.

When he saw Emma, William collapsed against the wall, tears flowing. Emma hugged him, as did Peggy and Catherine. They all walked out of the gym together—the Gates family of Cabrini-Green, with Emma leading the way.

He had his choice of drivers, but William went with David. He sat up front, and as the radio played he stared out of the frosted window into the blinking lights of the passing stores, and his tears **streamed** slowly down his cheeks.

When they stopped at a red light, David pulled out a box of tissues and wiped William's eyes. "You got no reason to be crying," he said. "Man, everybody misses a shot. Look at Jordan—last year he missed two big free throws in that game against Cleveland."

"I was there," said William. "I was right there."

....

Chargers fanatic excited Chargers fan
streamed fell

David shook his head. "It didn't have nothin' to do with you, William. You did everything you could. You went to practice, you worked hard, you studied. But it just wasn't meant to be, man. Sometimes these things are **out of our hands**. It just wasn't meant to be."

....

out of our hands beyond our control

BEFORE YOU MOVE ON...

1. **Conclusions** On page 243, William was disappointed when his team won the first games of the season. Why?

2. **Sequence** William began to limp again during the rematch game against Gordon Tech. What happened next?

LOOK AHEAD Read pages 268–290 to discover if the changes that Bo made to his life lasted.

ARTHUR

• • • • • • • • • • •

One day Bo showed up at the apartment, **clean shaven**, his hair combed, wearing a tie and slacks and carrying a Bible.

"I'm a new man," he proclaimed.

But no one believed him, particularly Sheila.

"I've seen this act before," she said.

"It ain't no act, Sheila," he said. "I have come home to ask for forgiveness."

"Don't come back in this house."

"This is my home, Sheila Gaye," he said. "You can't kick a man out of his own home."

"Don't come back here with your lies."

"These are my children, Sheila."

"Don't tell me about these children. You ain't seen them in months."

She was shouting now. "Get out of here, Bo. I hate you. I hate **your guts**. You can't just walk back in my life, not after what you did to me."

But he was persistent. This change, he told her, was different from the ones before—**it was all-encompassing**. "The Lord has come into my life, Sheila. I've been saved."

When she yelled, he prayed. When she stomped around the kitchen banging pots and pans, he called Minister Banks. "Talk to her, Sheila, pray with her." His pleading went on for days. At times his anger flashed, and the old Bo appeared. He wanted to smash

---

clean shaven his face shaved
your guts everything about you
it was all-encompassing he changed his whole life

Sheila with his fist when she **poked at old wounds**. It was then that he called Minister Banks.

"You got to control your temper," she told him. "There's an anger in you, Arthur."

His old friends from the street tempted and taunted him. "Look at ol' Bo," they said, "a preacher man."

"Hey, preacher man, I got me an ounce of cocaine." And they flashed a plastic bag filled to the top with gleaming white powder.

"I don't get high no more," Bo said. "I don't sell cocaine. You just poisoning your people and poisoning yourself."

He told them about Minister Banks, and they laughed even harder. "Minister Banks saved my life," he said.

"Bo, you so full of it," they told him. "You probably going down to that church and messin' with that woman."

But every Saturday he went south to Minister Banks's church for Bible class. "God, I made a mess out of my life," he prayed. "I say, Lord, please help me. I done ripped my family apart, but you got to help me, Lord. I may be weak, but you make me strong."

He went back to the retirement home and returned the television he had stolen. He **took to counseling**—going door to door—there being no shortage of people needing help. In almost every home on every block was a family with a loved one in jail, on drugs, out of work, or recently dead.

"Life is hard," Bo told them. "But you got to trust the Lord. You've got to have faith. I tell the children, especially, "Take the Lord now; don't wait like I did. Don't make your life a waste. Accept him now before it's too late."

....

poked at old wounds talked about the bad things he used to do

took to counseling tried to help other people

His fights with Sheila didn't end overnight. "You ain't such a great mother all the time. Look at *your* life," he declared. He didn't hit her, but she could not forgive or forget the times that he had. He was still a schemer; he wasn't dealing or stealing, but he was never without a trick up his sleeve. And, on occasion, his temper still popped. "Old ways don't die overnight," Sheila said. She still believed he prowled about with other women, despite all his **piety**. "There's temptation in life," Bo said. "I won't deny that I'm tempted. I'm a man. All I ask is, Lord, give me strength to resist my temptation."

But more and more he **wore her down**. He'd read her the Bible, and when Minister Banks called, he put Sheila on the phone. "Get on your knees, Mrs. Agee, and plead the blood of Jesus," said Minister Banks. "It's not you fighting and yelling. It's the devil working through you. You can't fight the devil by fighting Bo Agee. You got to fight the devil with holy righteousness."

Sheila didn't know if she truly believed him, but she was willing to try. After three months of him in and out, back and forth, Sheila took him in. "You got to make changes in your life," she said to her children. "It ain't easy with him, but it's harder without him. One thing about Bo, he always comes back to his family, he tries to be a provider. It's an instinct in him."

Arthur was **staggered** by the changes. He had gotten used to a house without Bo, to having his mother to himself. "Why I got to take him back?" he asked his mother.

"'Cause he's your father," she said.

"What's he done for me?"

"He made you who you are," Sheila told him. "You got to look at

....

piety holy behavior
wore her down made her listen to him
staggered surprised, shocked

what your father give you, son. You're **his living, breathing likeness**. You got his smile, his confidence. You got to take the good with the bad."

Bo and Arthur did their best to avoid each other around the house. "I can't take it when he tells me what to do," Arthur told Shannon.

But the bonds did go deep, and Bo did add life to the house. There were times they got together in the living room to watch a game on the **tube** or to listen to gospel, and Arthur laughed and felt **a glow**. "A boy needs his father," Bo told him. "You can't deny that."

In the early summer Bo talked Arthur into coming with him and Sheila to Minister Banks's South Side church. It was a brick building on a quiet residential street—a long, slender **sanctuary** with bright red carpeting, white walls, and large, shuttered windows. The night was steamy, and fans blew hot air around the room. Through the windows came the murmurs of the street.

Thirty people showed up. The men wore ties and slacks and jackets, the women, long dresses and scarves covering their heads. The organ played lightly in the background, and the audience rocked as soft and gentle as the breeze sliding through the open windows.

"When you don't have a dime in your pocket, Jesus is there," Minister Banks began. "Man may fail you, but Jesus is there."

"Amen," said the congregation.

"We thank God for Arthur Junior," Minister Banks continued, the crowd adding its "Amen."

"How God has blessed him. The biggest blessing you can get is having God by your side. You may lose a few games, but you will never lose in Jesus. We praise God tonight. And at this time we're

....

his living, breathing likeness like him
tube television
a glow happy
sanctuary church

271

going to hear a song from our brother, Arthur."

Bo stepped to the center of the church, took the microphone from Minister Banks like it was a blessing, closed his eyes, and began to sing.

His voice cracked, and he spoke as much as he sang, but his song was sweet.

Praise God, I've had my good days,

I've seen some bad days.

I've had my ups and downs

And, Lord, I've been turned around.

But you been so good to me,

The Lord has set my spirit free.

And I just want to say, thank you, Lord.

Thank you, Lord,

Lord, I won't complain. . . .

I want to thank you, Lord, for protecting my family,

I just want to say, thank you, Lord,

Lord, I won't complain.

After his father finished, Arthur slipped outside and stood on the front porch beneath the moon, listening to the wind softly whistling through the trees. He was nervous. This wasn't like joking with a teacher or coach. They were **anointing** him; he was pledging his life to a power greater than himself. He didn't know if he was ready. He didn't know how much he believed or what he believed or how much, if anything, would change. He'd still be a poor, **at-risk**, unknown, skinny black boy on the West Side. But he'd have the Lord, even if he

....

anointing blessing

at-risk troubled

wasn't sure what it meant.

He entered the church and walked down the aisle to the pulpit and stood before Minister Banks, who rose above him like a **monolith**. "We're going to take in this young man to God," she said as the organ rocked and the tambourines rattled. Bo hummed and clapped, and Sheila wept.

"Are you willing to follow the doctrine?" Minister Banks asked.

"Yes," he said.

"Praise the Lord, we thank God tonight. Do I hear **a motion to** accept Arthur into the church?"

A motion was made and resoundingly approved. "We're going to anoint Arthur Junior, in the name of the Father, the Son, and the Holy Ghost. Glory to God, we thank you for blessing him. Glory to God, give him the wisdom to understand. Not to yield to the things of the street. Glory to God we pray protect him, Lord, wherever he goes, wherever he travels. Protect him, Lord, in strange territory. Always keep his mind on you. We pray right now, Glory to God."

Her voice soared high with each recitation of the word glory. She dribbled a drop of holy oil on Arthur's head, and everyone in the church came by to shake his hand, moving on to congratulate Bo and Sheila.

"For a seventeen-year-old to give up his Saturday night is something," Bo said to one man.

"Impressive," the man said.

Bo nodded. "Yes, sir. All I can be is a good example for him," he said. "That's all I can be."

....

monolith giant rock

a motion to someone say we should

273

WILLIAM

••••••••••••

A month after the season ended the doctors strapped William to another medical cot, wheeled him into another operating room, and cut open his leg one more time.

This time they weren't even going to bother saving the cartilage—they would simply remove it.

David took him to the hospital this time because Emma and Curtis were working. Mrs. Weir had hired Curtis to work in the stockroom at Encyclopedia Britannica, paying him $5.25 an hour. He **grumbled** about the low pay, but it was a start. It allowed him to bring in money for his family.

An anesthesiologist slipped a mask over William, and he fell asleep. The next thing he saw was David hovering over him, **slipping in and out of focus**. They were in the recovery room, and William was stretched out in the bed, mouth open, arms at his side.

"The doctor said he took a big, old piece of something out of your knee," David said with a smile. "He said you should be back to normal **in no time**, and this time you don't have to hold back. You have a lot of good news."

William yawned. He didn't know what David was talking about. "Where's the TV?" he asked.

David laughed. "It's gone," he said. "I guess there's no TV 'cause people come and go so fast. Last thing they gonna be worried about is the TV."

David went to the phone and rang up Emma. "He's okay," David

....

grumbled complained
slipping in and out of focus but he could not clearly see him
in no time very soon

274

told her. "I'm surprised he's not hungry. I guess when he really wakes up he's gonna eat everything in sight."

David laughed at something Emma said and hung up the phone. William's eyes were closed, but David figured he was faking in order to **squeeze out an extra drop of sympathy**. "She says she hopes you feel better," David announced. "She said get up and get out of this bed. She said last time you had her waiting all day."

For the next three weeks William went to the hospital's rehab center, working on a plan supervised by the chief doctor. No more Ys or gyms **reeking with the odors of** flabby middle-aged men. It was a scientific and precise regimen, relying on the most sophisticated high-tech rehabilitation, using weightlifting and aerobic machines.

His days and nights were measured by routines: work in the morning, rehab in the afternoon, home for dinner. When his leg was strong enough, Pingatore would send him to spring and summer tournaments again.

Pingatore was riding William most of the time. The coach felt he had no choice. He knew William was aching for independence and anxious to **challenge authority**. But Pingatore didn't want William to fall behind, to **flunk out**, or to lose his eligibility. William needed at least an 18 on his ACT, the American College Testing program's standardized exam, to be eligible to play college ball as a freshman. His last score was 13.

"You'll have many more offers from colleges if you're eligible to play freshman ball," Pingatore told William.

"Aw, coach."

....

squeeze out an extra drop of sympathy get more attention
reeking with the odors of that smelled because of
challenge authority argue with the coach
flunk out fail in school

"This is for your future."

Pingatore registered William for ACT study class; he even drove him to class. But William didn't see why he had to study so much—not with a suitcase in his mother's house filled with letters from college coaches almost begging him, bum knee and all, to come to their school. *I ain't no freshman anymore*, he thought. *I don't have to listen to everything Pingatore says.*

The talk between Pingatore and William was like the talk between a father and his adolescent son. Common sense and experience told Pingatore that he knew what was right for William, but the more Pingatore pushed, the more William resisted. "You can't avoid the big decisions in your life, William," said Pingatore. "They won't go away."

You just want to tell me what to do for the rest of my life, William thought.

They bickered over matters big and small, like the upcoming play-offs between the Pistons and the Bulls. Pingatore remained loyal to Isiah and the Pistons, while William announced he was rooting for Jordan and the Bulls. He even paraded around school in a Bulls jacket.

"The Pistons play **dirty**," William said.

"They play like a team, not a one-man show," Pingatore replied.

"But you live in Chicago, not Detroit."

"I'm loyal to Isiah."

"How can you root against Michael Jordan?"

Finally Pingatore got **exasperated**: "Everything I like, you don't like," he said.

....

dirty unfairly
exasperated frustrated, annoyed

The biggest issue between them was over which college to attend. Pingatore wanted William to at least consider Indiana, and neither William—nor any of his brothers for that matter—**wanted any part of** Bobby Knight.

In May, Pingatore arranged a meeting with David, Randy, Emma, Curtis, and William to discuss recruiting.

William mentioned nine schools he'd like to consider: Michigan, Michigan State, Kansas, Oklahoma, North Carolina, Maryland, Syracuse, Seton Hall, and Marquette.

Georgetown was off his list because they had shown little interest in him. Besides, they had not contended for a title recently and were no longer the rage of the neighborhood.

"Any others?" asked Pingatore.

"Kentucky," said William. "I like their style."

Pingatore chuckled. "William, if you took that many shots you'd **have a hernia**."

Citing a variety of reasons, Pingatore eliminated Michigan, Oklahoma, Syracuse, and Seton Hall from consideration. "There seems to be something missing," said Pingatore after rereading the list.

Randy and David smiled. "I can see one school that's not there," Pingatore added. "Which one?"

William shrugged, "I don't know." But he did know. And so did his brothers.

"A school with a terrible coach," said Randy. "A guy who likes to holler and scream."

Pingatore looked up. "You could be talking about me."

....

wanted any part of liked

have a hernia be in a lot of pain

He looked at William. "You don't think you should be interested, William, honestly?"

William swallowed. They were talking about Knight and Indiana. But William wanted no more **disciplinarians or regimentation**; he wanted to break free and play a wide-open, **run-and-gun game** for the kind of coach who stroked and hugged his players and made them laugh. "Honestly," William said, "if I would be interested, it would be because you said I should be interested."

There was silence. Pingatore bit his lip. "Well, there are schools I think you should be interested in only because of play and style and the people," he said. "There are a number of schools where I know the people. And I know they're good people. Obviously Indiana is one of them. I think you'd be foolish not to look at them. Duke is another one."

So Pingatore added Duke and Indiana to William's list.

"I want you all to have an open mind and don't make **rash** judgments," Pingatore said. "You have to be a sponge and take it all in. Our goal four years from now is to sit down and say, William's graduating next week. And maybe he has a shot at the NBA, but he's got his college degree."

Pingatore looked at Emma. "I told William he's got to make **big bucks** so he can come back and donate to the school and help some other kids come out."

He chuckled, but no one laughed with him.

A few weeks later, Curtis, David, William, and Randy gathered around Emma's TV to watch the seventh game in the Bulls-Pistons

....

disciplinarians or regimentation strict coaches or practices
run-and-gun game less structured game
rash sudden, quick
big bucks a lot of money

play-off series. The series was tied at three, the winner going to the finals to play the Lakers. The Gates boys were tense before tip-off, having so many hopes riding on the game.

"I'm sick of the Pistons **eliminatin'** the Bulls," said Curtis.

"I'm sick of seein' Isiah and Rodman and Laimbeer celebrate."

"For once I want my city to be a winner," David said.

A few nights earlier, the Bulls sent the series to a final game with a thrilling win at the Stadium as Craig Hodges knocked down four threes.

But this game was different. The Bulls were intimidated. Hodges, so hot in the previous game, couldn't hit a thing. Horace Grant was shoved out of the paint. Isiah burned John Paxson. And within a few minutes Scottie Pippen was on the bench, an ice pack to his head.

"What's he doin' on the bench?" bellowed Curtis.

"He got a headache," said David.

"A headache!" roared Curtis. "This is the play-offs, man. Ain't no time for no headache."

The Detroit lead grew to twenty.

"Michael ain't gonna let them go down," said William.

Indeed Jordan did what he could, but the Pistons attacked him with three or four defenders, forcing him to pass, and scoffing at the **inept** attempts of his teammates to score. The Pistons won 93 to 74. For the third straight year, they had eliminated the Bulls.

On the screen, the Pistons were rejoicing.

"Seventy-four points," said Curtis. "Man, Michael coulda scored that himself."

The others shook their heads.

....

eliminatin' beating, defeating

inept useless, unsuccessful

"Michael shouldn't even pass them the ball," said Curtis.

The others nodded.

"Man, if I was Michael, that's what I'd do. If Pippen complains, I'd say: 'Make a basket and I'll pass you the ball.'"

On the screen Isiah was hugging Dennis Rodman.

"Wanna play some ball?" said David.

"Na," said Curtis. "I don't wanna do nothin'."

On the screen Isiah was hugging Bill Laimbeer. "Aw man, get this off," said Curtis.

They snapped off the tube and sat in silence, staring at the soundless, blank screen.

William had heard coaches and players describing the wonders of the Nike summer camp for the last three years, and that summer he was one of one hundred twenty-five invitees from the premier high school players in the country. They flew him to Princeton, New Jersey; outfitted him with a warm-up suit, gym shorts, T-shirts, socks, and sneakers; fed him, taught him, entertained him; and let him play basketball on **an immaculately kept** court.

But mostly he was bored. He and the others were led from one classroom to the other. Seated in rows of chairs, they listened to lectures by a variety of entertainers, teachers, coaches, and broadcasters who thought yelling was the best method to **pierce the adolescent mind**.

"While you're sitting here today, you should feel like a million dollars," said sports announcer Dick Vitale at one lecture. The more he talked, the louder he talked, until eventually he was shouting.

....

an immaculately kept a very clean

pierce the adolescent mind get the boys to listen

"You should feel so special. You are one of a hundred of the best high school players. In this country, the United States, my mother—God bless her, she's in heaven today—she used to always say to me, 'This is America. You can make something of your life.'"

And film director Spike Lee told them: "You're black, you're a young male, all you're supposed to do is deal drugs and **mug** women. The only reason why you're here is because you can make their team win. If their team wins, these schools get a lot of money. This whole thing is revolving around money."

For William the best part of the camp was the glossy booklet **profiling** all the players. Of course, he turned to his profile first. There it was, on page fourteen: "Played in only eight games last year because of knee injury. Now fully recovered. Outstanding offensive player and scorer with three-point range. Superb penetrator, using strength, speed, quickness, and jumping ability to get to the hoop. Coach Gene Pingatore praises his knack of reading well defensively and his reaction to the ball. Has played both guard spots in the past, but will play the point this year. Solid student. Plans to study Business Administration."

Hmmm, he thought, *that's me all right.*

He leafed through the booklet to look at the names of some of the other players: Sherell Ford, Rashard Griffith, Juwan Howard, Jason Kidd, Tom Kleinschmidt, Donyell Marshall, Lamond Murray, Howard Nathan, Cherokee Parks, Sean Pearson, Glenn Robinson, Jalen Rose, Chris Webber. Except for the kids from Chicago, most of them were strangers.

They roomed him with Kleinschmidt and Pearson. He and

....

mug steal money from
profiling with descriptions of

Kleinschmidt managed to avoid any discussions of the last two play-offs. *He hasn't* **rubbed it in**, William thought. *I gotta* **give him credit** *for that.*

Mostly they sat around the room at night and complained.

"The food's no good," said Kleinschmidt.

"They say you're gonna learn, but you really don't learn much," said Pearson.

"I'd just as soon stay home," said William.

It was the same old thing in the games. No one passed the ball, and everyone tried to impress the coaches watching from the stands. What they expected to see that they didn't already know was a mystery. These were, after all, the country's most well known and studied players. But the coaches dutifully took notes, read their **dope sheets**, talked to scouting experts, talked to each other, and talked to reporters. It was, they all agreed, **a meat market**. Or as camp recruiter Bob Gibbons put it: "It's already become a meat market, but I try to do my job and serve professional meat."

On the second to last day of the camp, William banged a muscle in his leg and limped off the court, deciding not to play anymore. *It really doesn't matter,* he thought. *They all know what I can do.*

He spent most of those last few hours watching from the stands. He overheard two coaches talking: "I've been watching that guy," they said of one player, "since he was in the sixth grade."

God damn, that's weird, he thought, *spending your life watching kids play basketball.*

He saw Rose dribble coast to coast for a dunk, Howard drill home back-to-back threes, and Webber block three successive shots.

....

rubbed it in *talked about how his team won*

give him credit *respect him*

dope sheets *papers with facts about the players*

a meat market *like a market for coaches to buy players*

These were his peers; the guys who played varsity as freshmen. The guys who broke fast from the gate. He remembered what the TV announcer said about him three years ago: "I've found the next Isiah Thomas."

I'm as good as any of them, William thought. *I guess.*

The first thing he did when he returned to Chicago was to pick up Alicia at Catherine's. He took her down to Lincoln Park, on the shore of Lake Michigan, and pushed her in a stroller along the riding path that went by the zoo. It was a sparkling day, and the lake twinkled in sunlight. They wandered by a gravelly basketball court where shirtless boys played a ferocious full-court game. But he didn't stop to watch. They strolled by games of softball, frisbee, rugby, soccer, and football; past lovers in the grass and old men playing chess under **the pavilion overlooking** the lake.

They sat on the edge of the bike path that ran along the beach and watched water **lap at** the rocks. He was supposed to be playing in a summer game. He was supposed to be **gearing up** for the next season. But he was tired of the game, tired of chasing the ball, tired of being in the race. "I got one more year to go, baby," he said to Alicia as if she understood. "Just one more year, and I'm done."

ARTHUR
· · · · · · · · · · · ·

It was **far and away** the best summer Arthur ever spent. He and Shannon got a job at the local Pizza Hut, but most of his time was spent playing basketball in any game, on any court, in any gym or

---

the pavilion overlooking a building next to
lap at rise up to hit
gearing up getting ready
far and away definitely

playground he could find. He played with the Marshall team or by himself, he played one-on-one, three-on-three, H-O-R-S-E, full-court, half-court, or in the alley. He carried his ball almost everywhere he went. He perfected the behind-the-back spin move, the herky-jerky jump shot, the crisscross dribble, the tomahawk dunk, and the no-look pass. At night he came home to find Shannon, Bo, Sheila, or Tomekia sitting around the kitchen table, making jokes and talking dreams.

"I ain't gonna make it in basketball," Shannon told them one night. "But I'm **figuring on doing** something else."

"Like what?" asked Sheila.

"Invest."

"Invest in what?"

"In land. I'm gonna get a ranch."

"A ranch?"

"Yeah. You know my grandfather had one. My grandma and my granddaddy, they had a big old house and a big old yard with cows and stuff."

"Really," said Sheila.

"And a big old lake. That's what I'm gonna do."

Arthur had even bigger dreams. "I'm still **fixin'** to play in the NBA."

"Still think you gonna make it?" said Shannon.

"Hey, man, nothin' I seen gonna stop me."

The only **downside** came in the mornings when he had to go to summer school, and even that wasn't so bad because Shannon was sitting next to him in class.

....

figuring on doing planning to do
fixin' planning, hoping
downside bad thing

The class was a riot. The teacher **was a bespectacled, wiry man** with lots of wavy brown hair. He liked to walk around the room while he talked, and he talked long and hard. Spittle gathered in the corners of his mouth, which the kids got a big kick out of.

He tried so hard, but no one seemed to care. The class was English, but he introduced complex topics like abortion and teenage sex and birth control. There was no air conditioning, only an old fan propped on a chair blowing sticky, hot air.

"Does every woman have a right to control her body?" the teacher started one discussion.

Some kids chewed gum or blew bubbles, or took their gum out of their mouths and waved it in front of their eyes like they were practicing self-hypnosis.

"Most people who advocate pro-choice are not people who want to get rich running clinics."

Or combed their hair, or slathered on lipstick.

"There are two ways you can eliminate unwanted pregnancies. One way is birth control, which is advocated by Planned Parenthood and is taught in sex education classes."

Or fell asleep, or gazed out the window.

"The other way is the new modern way of birth control. **Abstinence.**"

The mention of sex **perked Arthur's interest**.

"It still ain't gonna change nothin'," he said.

"Change what?" asked the teacher.

"What the woman gonna do."

Suddenly Shannon was inspired to take part in the discussion.

----

was a bespectacled, wiry man wore glasses and was thin
Abstinence. Not having sex.
perked Arthur's interest interested Arthur

"They'd suck it out themselves if they had to," he said, pretending he was cleaning out his crotch with a vacuum cleaner. The class laughed and **came to life**. The buzz of conversation filled the room.

Undeterred the teacher spoke louder, trying to rise above the din. "There's a misconception here," he said, his reedy voice as high as it would carry. "A lot of people believe that a lot of people your age have no self-control."

"We don't," a girl called out.

"We do," a boy responded.

"Let me say this," said the teacher. "When you're out on a date, do you have to have sex?"

The class erupted in giggles and guffaws.

"If I take you out you do," said Shannon.

"Yeah," agreed Arthur. "Who says I ain't got to have sex?"

"You don't got to," said a girl. "You can have fun."

"What's fun?" asked Shannon.

"Going to McDonald's. Going to the lakefront."

The teacher was inspired; it was the Socratic method at its best. This discussion was precisely what he had hoped for.

"If you're really honest with yourselves. . . . Please, you got to do this, stop a second and think about this. When you are out with somebody. . . . All right, quiet down. When you're out with somebody, and you're out to have a good time, there are certain things you naturally want to do. The human being craves companionship, but companionship is also fulfilled with conversation."

"But you didn't answer my question," blurted Arthur.

....

came to life started to pay attention

Undeterred Not bothered

"Restate your question."

Arthur opened his mouth, and then realized he couldn't remember what he had asked. "What'd I say?" he said with a puzzled look that caused another eruption of laughter.

"You said, 'Why I ain't got to have sex?'" a girl said.

"Yeah," said Arthur. "Why I ain't got to have sex?"

"Well, who told you you had to have sex to be a man?" asked the teacher.

Arthur looked **indignant**. "Sometimes it be the girl's idea," he said.

"Sure do," Shannon **seconded** as he and Arthur slapped hands.

After that there was no more real discussion, although the teacher tried. He talked on and on about sex and love and unwanted pregnancies. He talked so long the spittle returned and his voice grew raspy, and time ticked on and soon class was over.

"Hey, you take care of yourself," Arthur told the teacher as the class ended. He wasn't so bad, that teacher. There were worse ways to spend a summer morning.

Bo spent an extra ten minutes in the bathroom pressing his white golf shirt and shining his shoes. Sheila and he had business to take care of. **At long last** the time had come to settle their problems with St. Joseph. There was no getting around it. The message was clear: If they didn't retire at least some of their debt, St. Joseph wasn't going to **release Arthur's transcript**, and without the transcript Arthur couldn't graduate for another two years.

"I don't want to do it," Bo told Sheila, "but it's got to be done."

He had already explored the matter with O'Brien, Arthur's old

---

indignant angry, annoyed
seconded agreed
At long last Finally
release Arthur's transcript give Arthur his school record

coach and, coincidentally, the school's new director of finance. "A **payment schedule** can be arranged," O'Brien had said, "and if **you're faithful on** the first few payments, maybe we'll release the transcript before all the debt is retired."

That's all Bo had to hear. As he saw it, this was another business deal with a white man, and he had been making deals with white men all of his life.

"Look here, Sheila, each of us got something the other one wants. They got Arthur's transcript."

"Yeah, and what do we got?"

"They just want to be rid of us, that's all. Do you think they want this thing hanging around? This a Catholic school, Sheila Gaye. They don't want to be messing with this black boy forever."

Sheila wore slacks and a white shirt, and they brought along Tomekia's baby, Jazz. "Look humble," Bo told her. "Look grateful."

"I'd **just as soon let them have it**," she said.

"This ain't no time for that," said Bo. "We did what we did. Now let's get it over."

They rode the expressway to Westchester, just like in the old days when they went to St. Joe to watch Arthur play ball. O'Brien greeted them and **ushered** them into his office. His desk was piled with papers and financial statements.

The Agees sat before him, Jazz in Sheila's lap, looking meek and gentle.

O'Brien apologized for the mess and found his file. He cut straight to the point: "Okay, what we're trying to do is work out some kind of monthly installment plan."

....

payment schedule plan to pay the money back
you're faithful on you regularly send in
just as soon let them have it rather yell at them
ushered walked with

"Okay," said Sheila.

"No problem," said Bo.

"We're looking at a total of one-eight-one-three-ten," O'Brien said as he handed Bo a financial statement. Bo studied that sheet for ten or fifteen seconds, all but scratching his head and moving his lips as he read.

O'Brien pulled out his calculator. "Starting with August as the first payment and ending in May, you'll pay $181.31 a month," he announced.

O'Brien nibbled at the end of his glasses, and Bo took a breath. "Yes sir, what I was going to ask you is . . ." Bo began, almost stuttering, "is there any way possible . . . I don't know, I'm just asking. Could his credits be released to—"

"You mean his transcript?" asked O'Brien.

"Yes, sir," said Bo, suddenly befuddled.

"Okay, here's what I'm willing to do," said O'Brien. He sighed as he said it because he knew, in all likelihood, he would never see another dime from the Agees once the transcript was released. "Official school policy states I cannot release until May, and that's not going to **do you any good**. So this is what we'll do: As long as you show me good faith in the first two months, I'll release them. And I'll send them to Marshall."

In a split second Bo totaled up the sum: $360. *Damn,* he thought. *I can scrape that up.*

"Okay, that will be fine with us," Bo said. "And I really appreciate that."

Jazz whimpered and O'Brien smiled, apparently relieved to be

----

do you any good help you
In a split second Quickly
scrape that up get that money together

done with business. "And how are you today?" he said to her. "You're so nice. You didn't make any noise."

"Say, hello," said Sheila.

Jazz yawned.

They chatted awhile about Arthur, Sheila saying she wished he'd worked harder at his books, and O'Brien saying Arthur had been a treat to coach. Sheila said she wished he still went to St. Joseph, which almost caused Bo to fall off his chair, considering all the times she **trashed** the school and everyone in it. Maybe she was acting and maybe she was revealing a tiny piece of her heart. It was a clean, well-organized school, and it had been an honor for Arthur, out of all those boys on the West Side, to be accepted there. In the end, though, not much had changed since that day, three summers ago, when Big Earl visited their apartment. They each had something the other wanted, but it just didn't work out.

As they rose from their chairs Bo stuck out his hand, but O'Brien didn't see it. So Bo wrapped his arm around O'Brien and offered him a hug.

Bo and Sheila didn't talk much on the way home. **There was a crummy taste in Bo's mouth.** He hadn't exactly **scraped and shuffled**, but he had come close. *Sometimes you gotta **bow to walk tall**,* he thought. *I did it for my son. Lord knows, I owe him as much.*

....

trashed said bad things about

There was a crummy taste in Bo's mouth. Bo was not happy.

scraped and shuffled acted like a fool

bow to walk tall *lower yourself to get what you want*

BEFORE YOU MOVE ON...

1. **Summarize** On page 268, Bo returned to his family. How did his family react to the new Bo?

2. **Comparisons** Reread page 275. How has William's attitude toward Pingatore changed since his freshman year?

LOOK AHEAD Which college did William choose? Read pages 291–321 to find out.

SENIOR YEAR
1990

*"In a way you were lucky to leave St. Joseph. You got
no more financial strain, no travel, plus you're
playing for a great coach. . . . I don't scout anymore.
I still love the game, it's the system I don't like."*
—Earl Smith, to Arthur Agee

ARTHUR

The **long-awaited transcript rolled in** from St. Joseph soon after school began; Arthur's counselor, Mrs. Mitchell, broke the news. It was a disappointment. Arthur had fewer credits than expected. All those religion classes, and not one credit could be transferred to a public school. If Arthur was going to graduate before the fall, he would have to take two summer school classes and pass all of this year's courses.

"Do you understand what this means?" Mrs. Mitchell asked. She peered at Arthur through thick glasses as he slipped lower into his seat and smiled sweetly and innocently. But Mrs. Mitchell knew better than to fall for Arthur's angelic smile. Arthur had been **acting up**. She knew he usually showed up late for classes and was chatty and disruptive once he arrived there; the teachers were tired of his mischievousness. Most of the teachers had insisted that Arthur and Shannon be split up—they were too disruptive to be in the same class—and Bedford kicked Shannon off of the team because of his shenanigans.

"If I keep getting these reports about you acting up, you're gone, too," he told Arthur. "You're not so good that I have to put up with this crap. And even if you were that good, I still wouldn't put up with it."

And there were other **troublesome threats to** Arthur's basketball future: he didn't have the credits or the grades to be accepted at college, even if he graduated.

"Have you taken the ACT yet?" Mrs. Mitchell continued. Arthur

....

long-awaited transcript rolled in record everyone had been waiting for finally came

acting up causing trouble

troublesome threats to problems with

slumped further in his chair. "When do you plan to take it?"

"Sometime soon," he said, speaking softly.

"What institution are you planning on going to? Have you decided that?"

He paused to think of some acceptable answer and recalled that Sheila had lately talked about moving back home to Birmingham. "I was thinking about going to Alabama."

Mrs. Mitchell **pressed ahead**. "But you need to take algebra and trig. Do you plan to take them?"

"I don't know."

"You don't know! So you're **just barely getting by** again."

He shuffled in his chair. "Nah, you ain't got to say that."

"But you are—you've been barely getting by all along. Now, you're going to have to do better than that if you want to go to Alabama or any other school. You're going to have to do more than just get by."

He slipped out of his chair and wandered down the hall.

St. Joe's just messed everything up, he thought. *I shouldn't have even went there. Thought I had more credits than this. That's all right though, I'm still going to make it.*

Arthur wandered passed the cafeteria and saw Shannon surrounded by three girls. Shannon waved, "I'll be right there," Arthur said.

He bolted up the stairs and slipped into his English class just as the teacher was explaining how to prepare an outline. Arthur was there for about two minutes before he raised his hand and asked if he could be excused to go to the bathroom. The teacher frowned but

....

pressed ahead continued talking

just barely getting by not doing well in your classes

consented, and Arthur took off for the cafeteria. He joined
Shannon and the girls, laughing and chatting until the period ended.

WILLIAM
••••••••••••

At the end of the school day, Pingatore called William in for a
meeting, as he did almost every day. Sitting across the coach's desk,
William fidgeted with his tie as Pingatore leaned back in his swivel
chair and lit his pipe. Pingatore wanted William in the right state of
mind for the upcoming season.

"The team should be pretty good," the coach said, running
through the roster: "Gerald Eaker, a 6'0" junior at center; Jamal
Robinson, a 6'4" junior forward; Amal McCaskill, a 6'9" senior
forward."

Pingatore swiveled in his chair. The room was quiet, almost
airless. William wanted to be with his friends, who were playing
intramural football. "You're the key. I'm looking forward to big
things from you," Pingatore said finally. "How do you see it?"

"I can picture this year as **sowing my oats**," William said. "I'm
going to attend parties that the schools throw (I haven't attended any
of St. Joe's parties), and I'll try to stay on the B honor roll all year."

Pingatore stared. "What about basketball?"

William looked up. "What's that?" he said with a smile.
"Basketball is so off to me right now, it's like a foreign language."

He was **jerking the coach's chain**. Lately, he was doing a lot
of that.

....

consented, and Arthur took off for said yes, and Arthur
went to

sowing my oats having fun

jerking the coach's chain joking with the coach

"Remember what I told you a long time ago," Pingatore said. "If you didn't work hard, you'd still be a **heckuva** ballplayer. If you don't work at it, before you know it, it's all over. It really gets down to how much you want it."

William nodded; the lesson was **ingested**.

Pingatore showed him more of the recruitment letters that had arrived for him. There was another letter from Kevin O'Neill, head coach of Marquette University. O'Neill had eagerly pursued William all summer, sending him daily handwritten letters by overnight express. "Don't let your best opportunity get way from you," the latest letter began. "Once you visit our campus, I feel confident that you will know that Marquette is the right place for you."

William stuffed it in his pocket. He used to treasure these letters, but now he barely read them.

There was a reason he spent so much of his time playing this game, but at the moment he couldn't recall what that reason was.

Emma set out extra chairs in the living room for the big meeting. Pingatore showed up first, followed by Kevin O'Neill and his retinue of assistants, Bo Ellis and Dan Theiss. O'Neill was an effortless talker, with an engaging, folksy sense of humor. "I hear you were a helluva player yourself," he told Curtis.

O'Neill was a young, ambitious man in his second year at Marquette. He showed no trace of insecurity or doubt, and he assumed control of the evening. "A coach," he began, "is only as good as the players he recruits. That's why I go for the best—that's why I want you," he told William.

....

heckuva very good
ingested learned, understood

He licked his lips, ran his hand through his hair, took off his jacket, and rolled up his sleeves. "A few things about me: I love to win, I love to compete, I love to coach. I like to think that the game is won in September with recruitment. That's why I'm here. You can help me make Marquette a winner."

Then he **turned things over to Ellis**, a legend at Marquette who had started on Al McGuire's NCAA championship team in 1977. Ellis talked about Marquette's tradition of great basketball, mentioning names from the past only vaguely familiar to William: McGuire, Dean "The Dream" Meminger, Butchie Lee. "You can be a part of that tradition," he said.

Then Ellis held up a black-and-gold Marquette jersey with William's name on the back. "This is to show you how we feel about you," he said. "This is a practice jersey. It will be hanging in your locker when you're ready to say, 'I do.'" And Dan Theiss held up another jersey that read: "William Gates/Marquette Wants You."

William wanted to **wear a poker face**, to be cool and unaffected, but he couldn't contain his smile.

"If you don't make the test score and can't play freshman year, that doesn't mean we don't want you, because we still do," said O'Neill. "If you tear your knee out again this year and you can't play ever again, you're going to have your education paid for at Marquette University.

"The **bottom line** is this: We want to win the national title. And number two: I want to make you the best player I can. I want to give you an opportunity to maybe someday be one of those guys who goes out and makes some money in Europe or the NBA. You're one of

....

turned things over to Ellis let Ellis speak

wear a poker face hide his emotions

bottom line main thing; most important message

seven guys we're recruiting right now."

Curtis cleared his voice. It was his role to **be the skeptic**, to play the protective brother.

"You say you're recruiting seven guys?" asked Curtis.

"Seven guys for three spots," said O'Neill.

"Where's he fit in?" asked Curtis.

"As soon as William tells me that he's not looking at any other schools, then I'm not looking at any other players."

"So the first one signs, that's—"

"That's what it's going to come down to," said O'Neill. "If I tell you, 'Hey, you're our guy' and this and that, and I lose you to Kansas, Indiana, North Carolina State, or something—I'm **out of luck**. And then the president's saying to me, 'Look, Kevin, I thought you were recruiting a guard.' It's a tough situation, but it's something that has to be done."

After that, there was little more that had to be said. The pitch had been made, an offer was on the table. They agreed William would visit the school as soon as possible. O'Neill offered William a soul shake and made a few more jokes, something about playing pool with Curtis. "Dr. Gates," he said, "see you around the pool hall."

Pingatore was the last to leave. "This is really a surprise," Emma told him as they shook hands. "I didn't think you were ever going to **show up**."

"I told William, I was never invited," Pingatore said with a laugh. "Otherwise I'd be here all the time."

Two weeks later William and Emma drove north to Milwaukee for their tour of Marquette. O'Neill **booked them a set of suites** at

....

be the skeptic ask a lot of questions
out of luck in a bad situation
show up come over to our house again
booked them a set of suites got them rooms

the Hyatt. William's was filled with blue and gold balloons and banners saying, "Welcome William." That night the coach took William and his mother out for a steak dinner. For dessert, a cake with "Welcome William" written on top was brought out.

The next day Emma was given a tour of the campus while William was taken to meet various deans and professors. They asked him what he planned to do with his future. He said he wanted to major in communications, and they told him how Marquette could help him achieve his goals.

That night O'Neill took Emma out for another steak dinner, and the team took William to a couple of **strip joints**. And on the final day, Ellis gave William the tour of the Bradley arena.

"This is a great place. We're getting ready for it to rock, too," said Ellis as they walked around the empty stadium. William eyed the NCAA and NIT champion banners that hung from the **rafters**. "A lot of serious ballplayers have been through this building: Junior Bridgeman, Sidney Moncrief, Bob Lanier, Oscar Robertson. Can you see yourself playing in this place with 18,000 fans in it? Big difference from St. Joe's, right?"

O'Neill was waiting for them in a carpeted luxury suite overlooking the court. At first they played what O'Neill called a "William Gates highlight reel" of his dunks and threes, set to Curtis Blow's rap hit, "Basketball."

William's face glowed with pride as he watched himself **overpower** his high school opposition.

"But that was the past. Let's think about the future," O'Neill said when the film ended. He pushed a button on a boom box, and over

....

strip joints clubs where women dance
rafters ceiling
overpower play better than

the speakers came the broadcast of an imaginary Marquette game.

"Notre Dame 77, Marquette 76," the announcer said, his voice tense with excitement. "Gates is out high-calling for the ball. There are six seconds left. The freshman spins past a defender, slicing to his left. Three seconds left, Marquette down by one. Gates launches a flying one-hander. It is on the way. It is . . . Good! Gates buries a thirteen-footer just ahead of the horn and Marquette has defeated Notre Dame!"

Everyone laughed. "If you think we care about you now, we're going to do more when you're here," said O'Neill. "We'd love to have you. The only thing I'll tell you is that there are other guards who may be coming for visits. So if you want to do it, don't let it get away. Don't let it get to a point where somebody else comes in and takes a scholarship away, 'cause it's yours if you want it."

That night, after driving back to Chicago, William and his brothers gathered in Emma's living room to **weigh the pros and cons of** accepting Marquette's offer.

William told them about the balloons, the steaks, the cake, the tape recording. "Man, they give everyone that stuff," Curtis said.

"They said I'm gonna start," said William.

"You can't believe everything they tell you," said Alvin.

"O'Neill already said he's looking at seven other guards," said Curtis. "You don't want to be left on the bench."

"Yeah, but you got to look at the fact they're offering him five years of college—free," said David.

They considered their options. They could wait for all the other offers, except the other schools were holding back on their offers.

....

weigh the pros and cons of think carefully about the good and bad things about

Apparently they considered William damaged goods because of his knee operations and wanted to wait until the end of the season before they offered him a scholarship.

"Let's face it," said Curtis, "the boy's **been under the knife twice**. O'Neill's going after you 'cause he thinks you're the best he's gonna get."

"He's hoping you make him a winner," said David.

They considered the disadvantages: it had been years since Marquette played in the Final Four or was even a serious contender for the NCAA championship; and if he signed early, William couldn't weigh offers from other schools.

They considered the advantages: It was close to home; O'Neill showed potential—years from now he might be considered a great coach.

"Take it," said Curtis. "I would." *And I did, too, once.* He thought it, but he didn't say it. His brothers were thinking the same thing.

"I agree," said David.

"The more you wait," added Randy, "the more you gotta put up with Pingatore talking about Bobby Knight and Indiana."

The others laughed. They decided William would attend Marquette.

The next day at school William announced his decision to Pingatore and the other coaches. Don't be rash, they warned him. Don't **be taken in by** one visit.

"Talk to any of the leading black people on the campus?" coach Doyle asked.

"The leading black people?" William was perplexed and a little

....

been under the knife twice had two surgeries
be taken in by decide after only

embarrassed by the question. He never talked about race with the teachers or coaches at St. Joseph.

"Yeah," said Doyle. "Well, whoever might be in charge of all the black students on campus? What kind of community life they have for the blacks there. Did you talk to anyone about it? Did you ask the players how they're treated?"

"Yeah."

"Wha'd they say?"

"They said they're treated fine," William said. "I mean, they get the best of everything."

The conversation struck William as absurd. *Doyle* **means well**, *but he could have asked me that same question about St. Joseph.*

Pingatore said he should at least hear what other schools, such as Kansas, North Carolina State, and Indiana, have to offer.

"It's all right," William said, "I discussed it with my—"

"I think you should take a few days," said Pingatore, "because you just came back. You understand?"

William was even more determined to immediately sign his letter **of intent** to attend Marquette, if only because Pingatore told him to think about it.

ARTHUR
• • • • • • • • • • •

On October 22, Arthur turned eighteen and Sheila decided to celebrate **in grand fashion**. She spent the afternoon making him a special birthday dinner of fried chicken and German chocolate cake.

---

means well is trying to be nice
of intent stating that he was going
in grand fashion with a great party

"It's his favorite cake," she commented. "He's a great kid. And some kids don't even live to get this age. That's another thing to be proud about. It's his eighteenth birthday; he lived to see eighteen— that's good! I want to show him how much we appreciate him and love him and care for him," she said seriously. "Everything you can imagine was going wrong with this family, but now everybody's together."

Sheila was optimistic about the family and her future. She was studying to be a nurse's assistant in a program at a local community center, Bethel New Life. This night was going to be more than a party for Arthur's eighteenth birthday. It was going to be a celebration of the family's rebirth. "I'm gonna get back," she vowed. "I'm gonna get back to where I should have been."

She and Bo **coexisted in a wary truce**. It was clear to her that he was off of cocaine. He spent many of his nights counseling wayward friends. "My door's always open to bring someone into the Lord," he told people.

Bo's not as bad as some, she thought. *He wants to help his family.* One morning she woke up and saw Bo and Arthur laughing and wrestling. *A boy needs a man in the house*, she thought. But she also had her doubts, as did Arthur. She still wondered whether he was seeing other women.

The living room filled with Arthur's teammates: Derrick Zinnerman, Roderico Dale, Quadell Kimble, Robin Dunagan, Cesare Christian. They **cranked up the boom box** until the walls rattled with a thumping bass beat. There were four girls in the apartment **vying for** Arthur's attention.

....

coexisted in a wary truce managed to be at peace
cranked up the boom box made the music louder
vying for trying to get

"He's quite **the lady's man**," said Bo. "Just like his daddy."

Sheila didn't laugh. *Bo's not gonna upset me today. Today is for my boy. He's a great kid.*

After dinner everyone went into the living room. The girls read Arthur cards professing love, and Bo brought in a cake as they sang "Happy Birthday."

"I want to tell you that I love you very much," Bo said. "I'm very proud of you. Seems like I was eighteen just yesterday."

A few weeks later the state called to say that they were cutting Sheila's welfare benefits because Arthur, having turned eighteen, was no longer a dependent.

"I was getting $368, now I get $268? That's it! And this is to take care of me from one month to the next? Now can you imagine a person living on that?"

She called the public aid office and was told where to report. Once there, she had to wait three hours for an appointment with a caseworker.

"He still has to eat, even if he's eighteen," Sheila argued.

The rules were explicit, she was told. There would be no appeal.

Sheila was still shaking with anger when she attended her job training session. She entered a room adorned with posters of great African American leaders—statesmen, doctors, writers, and freedom fighters. There were a dozen women—single mothers, welfare mothers, recovering addicts, and alcoholics—all of them from the West Side. They were there to practice **resume writing** and job interviewing. The instructor showed them how to sit—shoulders straight, hands in lap—but Sheila turned the class into a **rap session**.

....

the lady's man popular with the girls
resume writing writing about their old jobs
rap session time to talk with the other women

"It's a trap," she told the others. "They don't want you to have no control or power over yourself. They just give you just enough to keep you hungry and keep you coming back. I got a lifetime of experience. I'm raising my children. The things we survived would kill other people. And I can't find a job? I don't have what it takes to find a job? They just want us to be little black girls, crying and begging."

"That's right," a woman said. "I see these girls on the West Side, been on welfare all their lives. Some people never been no closer to the **Loop** than the Congress Expressway. Never been to the cultural centers of this city. Never been out to eat at a nice restaurant with **linen cloth**. It's McDonald's all the time. Don't know how to eat no steak dinner. They just want to keep us stupid and on welfare, so we won't ask no questions or do nothin' with our life."

"Well, they ain't keeping me down," Sheila exclaimed. "I got pride. My momma didn't raise me to be on welfare. She didn't raise me to beg. I ain't begging no more."

The next day Sheila got more bad news: Arthur was close to flunking out of school. She decided to go to Marshall to talk the matter over with his teachers. It was the same old complaints, though: He was late for class, he was absent, he didn't do his homework, he was acting up. He was falling behind. He was failing Spanish and science.

"As you see, he's turning in his work and only missed one assignment, but he rushes through his work," one teacher told her, as he opened the grade book to show Sheila.

"Would you do me a favor?" Sheila asked. "When you see things slipping like this, would you give me a call and let me know? So I can

....

Loop center of Chicago's business
linen cloth tablecloths

stay up on top of this boy, because he'll tell you one thing and tell me another. I'll say, 'Where are your books?' And he'll say: 'Oh, we didn't have to work on anything. They're in the locker.' See, he's going to have to start showing me something better."

Bedford was bitterly blunt in his critique: "If he doesn't bring his grades up, he won't be eligible to play. And let's be realistic. If he can't play, he's not going to hang around school, 'cause the only reason he's in school is to play basketball. He's probably on the borderline, and with all that clowning, teachers just get mad. I would, too."

"I'm gonna **stay on his behind**," Sheila said. "I'll tell him we're paying $189 to St. Joseph for his transcript and he ain't gonna get away with doing nothing."

That night, Sheila cornered Arthur in his bedroom and **gave it to** him. ". . . And coach Bedford said you almost off the team!"

"Momma, those teachers made up half of them stories. I did that homework, they probably lost it and now they're blaming me."

After Sheila left, Arthur sat on his bed with a library book and his notebook balancing on his lap. He was preparing a report for one of his classes—"The Life Cycle of the Butterfly." He liked to think he had as much **street smarts** as any boy—black or white, rich or poor. He remembered how the white boys at St. Joseph laughed at his jokes. But he had never had an interest in academics. He rarely read a book on his own, not even a sports book. As he saw it, the only reason to stay in school was to play basketball, and the only way to play basketball was to graduate. He bent over his notebook and crafted his opening sentence: "As people bloom into another year, the butterfly also blooms."

....

stay up on top of watch
stay on his behind make sure he does better
gave it to yelled at
street smarts common sense

It wasn't a bad sentence, he thought. He was proud of it.

I'm gonna do what I gotta do to stay on the team, Arthur thought. *Even though I don't like writing, and I don't like reading, and I don't like school.* He had been telling himself that for so long that he believed it.

WILLIAM

In the third game of the season, William exploded for twenty-seven points and ten rebounds as the Chargers knocked off La Grange and won the La Grange Thanksgiving Tournament.

William was in flawless control, knocking down threes, driving with power, controlling the ball's flow. He felt like a star and was treated accordingly. People watched him when he warmed up, the reporters came to him for quotes. In their stories it was always, "William Gates, bound for Marquette, one of the country's best guards."

"We make mistakes, but thank God we have William," Pingatore told reporters after a **close win**. "He's a guy who you can go to in **crunch time**."

The team was young, and they were indecisive, and Pingatore couldn't decide which lineup to stick with. For a while he tinkered with a twin-tower arrangement, starting Eaker and McCaskill, but the big guys seemed to get in each other's way. Pingatore pulled McCaskill and went with smaller players who couldn't rebound as well.

"What do you think's wrong, William?" Pingatore asked after they had defeated Collins by twenty points in the first round of the

---

close win game St. Joseph almost lost
crunch time times when the game is close

Proviso West Christmas Tournament.

"But, coach, **we're ten and oh**," William said.

"We're letting teams play us too close," said Pingatore. "We're missing too many free throws; we're making too many turnovers. It's not right."

They lost to Fenwick on the next day, and then barely **squeaked past** St. Martin. Then they closed out the tournament by losing a **heartbreaker** to Westinghouse in which they blew a nine point lead and missed fifteen of twenty-seven free throws.

Pingatore was livid. "Alabama, Alabama," he called from the sidelines at one point in the game. But half the guys weren't sure what Alabama was or where they were supposed to go when he called it. Pingatore called a time-out, gathered them round the bench, and bellowed out some instructions, which were lost in the roar of the crowd. The players nodded even though they couldn't hear what he was saying. The play was designated for Eaker. But he wasn't looking. The ball hit him in the back and bounced out of bounds; Pingatore looked like he might explode.

"What this tournament told us is that this is the worst team I've ever coached attitude-wise," Pingatore told reporters. "They have no idea of the team concept and they'll never be a good team unless they change. It might not ever happen."

By midseason, despite many moments of brilliance, William was **in a funk**. He blamed his blues on Pingatore. He remembered those days as a freshman when he absorbed Pingatore's every word. Now he barely listened to what the coach said.

....

we're ten and oh we have ten wins and zero losses
squeaked past beat, defeated
heartbreaker game they almost won
in a funk unhappy

On the bus ride to a game in January, Pingatore told them: "And, remember, think about the ball game on the way to the game."

The team rode in a heavy silence, afraid to talk, laugh, or even exchange glances. *This is so stupid*, William thought. *You don't want to make a team tight before a game. You want them to think about anything but the game—you want them to relax.* But relaxation wasn't part of the Pingatore method; Pingatore practiced reverse psychology, William decided. *He tells a guy he stinks to make him angry, to make him say, 'I'm gonna prove you wrong.'* As the bus rambled on, William recalled all the times Pingatore had told him, "The stakes are high," "It's on your back," or, "It's up to you."

His brothers told him it wouldn't be much better anywhere else. All coaches yell. Pingatore wasn't even the most strident. There were some screamers who kicked tables and threw clipboards. "What is it about basketball coaches, they got to yell all the time?" William asked Curtis.

"That's the only way to get a guy's attention," Curtis said.

"I'm a senior; I've heard it all before. It don't work for me anymore."

What bothered him most was that there was no solace on the basketball court. Something was missing, some **elementary** pleasure and enjoyment was gone from the game. He wanted to **recover it**, but he didn't know how. He **retraced his steps**, looking in familiar places. He went back to the old tapes in the St. Joseph archives and watched the old tapes of Isiah, including a news report that **aired** the day before the state tournament.

"Isiah is joined by two other starters, Ray Clark and Tyrone

....

elementary simple, basic
recover it find it again
retraced his steps did all the things he used to do
aired was shown on television

Brewer, all three recruited from Resurrection Elementary on Chicago's West Side," the reporter said. "The kids get a good education and the Chargers get one terrific basketball team."

What a joke, William thought. *I think St. Joseph got the better part of the deal.*

He reread an article about Isiah. "When Thomas was in the eighth grade, he applied for a basketball scholarship to Weber High School, but the coach turned him down because he was 'too small,'" the article read. "Seeing the boy's disappointment, Isiah's brothers pleaded his case to Gene Pingatore, the coach at St. Joseph High School in Westchester, a Chicago suburb. Impressed, Pingatore secured financial aid for Thomas, who was, he said, 'a winner.' Under Pingatore's guidance, Isiah also learned to control his **freewheeling** playground style, especially his tendency to dribble full tilt the length of the court and draw charging fouls."

He tossed the article away. *They make it seem like Isiah needed St. Joseph to be great,* he thought.

One Sunday afternoon he returned to his old grade school gym at Jenner Elementary. The gym was empty and the ball echoed as it bounced. He saw himself as he used to look, and remembered the old games. It was here that coach O'Brien spied him and recruited him for St. Joseph. *Man,* he thought, *they came a long way to find me.*

He tried a jump shot and it swished; he backed up and nailed a three. He hit just about every shot he took, and then stepped to the free-throw line and imagined himself at the line against Gordon Tech. This time the free throw swished in.

A few days later Jamal Robinson announced he was transferring

....

freewheeling wild

to Proviso East. Robinson, who had been averaging sixteen points a game, had **given no indication** of his plans, which caught everyone by surprise. **The speculation was** that he wanted to play with his old grammar school buddies, Donnie Boyce and Michael Finely, two kids he had grown up with in Maywood. "This has nothing to do with Coach Pingatore. I just didn't feel comfortable and wanted to make a change," Robinson told reporters.

Robinson's departure made William feel even more lonely and isolated. *He's doing what I want to do—he's going home*, thought William.

"You're going to have to take over," Pingatore told William. "You're the guy we're turning to."

Soon after Robinson left, they **went up** against Holy Cross in a game that could decide who would win the conference title. Before the game Pingatore pulled William to the side of the locker room: "Would you like to be remembered as the one who didn't win the conference?" he asked.

"No, coach."

"All right, then—do something about it."

William scored twenty-one points as they defeated Holy Cross 73 to 39, winning St. Joseph their eleventh consecutive conference title. "It became a challenge for William," Pingatore told reporters. "It's just a different kind of motivation."

The final home game of the regular year was against Carmel. It was seniors night, which meant a special pregame ceremony honoring graduating seniors and their parents. Emma wore a canary-yellow jump suit with a carnation pinned to it. When they announced her

....

given no indication not told anyone about any
The speculation was People guessed
went up played

name, William escorted her to center court where they stood, holding hands, while the national anthem was played. William wanted to win big for his mother.

"Thanks, Mom," he told her. "Thanks for everything."

The team raced to a big lead, but in the second quarter Eaker shattered the glass backboard with a thunderous dunk. They stood or sat for over half an hour while the backboard was replaced. Their legs softened. They **came out flat** and allowed Carmel to **chew into** their lead, and faced a **tidal wave** of criticism from Pingatore. Even when they won, William didn't feel **gratification**.

"This team drives me crazy," Pingatore screamed. "You just don't respond, it's been a struggle all year. The biggest part of it is the fact that you refuse to learn. For you people who hate the hollering it will be over next week. Then you can do whatever you want to do.

"That's what I want you to think about."

ARTHUR

It was a bouncy bus ride south to Dunbar High. Bedford sat in the front seat. In the back, some of the guys were playing poker.

"Any bets on the side?" Arthur asked. "I'll bet a nickel. If I got a nickel."

They shrieked with laughter. Every now and then Bedford shot them a look of annoyance, but let them continue.

He had already exerted so much energy in the opening game, an eleven-point loss to Hirsch. "How the hell can you lose to Hirsch?"

---

came out flat did not play well in the end

chew into take away

tidal wave lot

gratification satisfied

he exclaimed afterwards. Hirsch was slower and smaller and couldn't shoot as well. They figured to win six games all season, if that. Bedford **lambasted** the Commandos for fifteen minutes after that game. Later in the week he called in Arthur for a private meeting.

"It's a wonder I even keep you on the team with the things you do," he told Arthur. "Your mother has enough of a hard time at home without having to deal with you. You're eighteen years old; you're a man. She shouldn't have to bother."

Arthur tried to interrupt, but Bedford cut him off. "You're always trying to take the short cut, always trying to find the easy way out. If you don't have to study hard to barely get by, you won't study. If you can get by with playing basketball the way you want to, why listen to the coach? You don't know all the answers. I hate to say it, but guys who come in here with that attitude usually end up in the street talking about how they used to play for Marshall, and if they would have gone to class, they could have gone to any school they wanted to. They end up being just somebody standing on the street corner talking."

Arthur let his big eyes **go droopy**, and Bedford almost felt sorry for him. *Only ones they want to send here is the ones that they don't think have any hope*, Bedford thought. *They think I can make miracles with them, and I can't make miracles.*

"Don't give me that look," he told Arthur. "You can be **such a little slickster** sometimes."

Outside the Dunbar gym a group of students were milling. Could be trouble, maybe not. "Take your hats off," Bedford told the team. Gang affiliations were designated by the colors of caps and shirts. A

---

lambasted yelled at

go droopy look sad

such a little slickster so tricky; so sneaky

kid wearing the wrong color baseball cap could instigate a fight.

"Only way you'll beat them is playing good basketball," Bedford told the team before the game. "You have to play a whole ballgame!"

They came out flat. Arthur was sloppy. He missed a shot, and in his frustration **hacked** the man who grabbed the rebound. He missed a layup and tried to slip through two defenders, bouncing the ball out of bounds when he tried to dribble behind his back. At the half they were losing by fifteen.

"You aren't playin' smart, you aren't using your heads," Bedford raged. "I tell you somethin' over and over and over and you still don't do it."

Marshall played more aggressively in the second half, trapping the Dunbar guards. On its first few possessions Dunbar **broke the press**, but their guards began to tire. They stumbled and they panicked, and they desperately looked for help. Suddenly everywhere they looked they saw the lightning-quick hands of Marshall's defenders. No one on Dunbar wanted the ball.

"Harder," Bedford yelled, "press harder." Arthur ran all over the court, doubling down on the ball carrier and then racing back to fill his piece of the zone. Bit by bit they cut into the lead. Bedford used the press like a yo-yo, calling it on, calling it off, **psychologically toying with** Dunbar's players, keeping them confused. "They don't know what to expect," Bedford told his team at one time-out. "They're afraid of that press."

On the next play, Arthur yelled. "Look out!" and Dunbar's **jittery** guard stopped dribbling and covered the ball, even though no Commando was near him. He was called for traveling. On the

....

hacked hit
broke the press got away from Marshall's defenders
psychologically toying with misleading
jittery nervous, tense

inbounds Arthur drove left, pivoted, turned to his right, and banked in a jumper. It was a back-breaking basket, pushing Marshall's lead to five. As Dunbar called time, the Commandos hugged Arthur—even Bedford was impressed.

The kid's showing me, he thought. It was the little something extra—the fearlessness, the determination—he had seen in Arthur in the sophomore championship game against Westinghouse two years ago. It was the way he wanted the ball, the way he went after it. And even if he missed, even if it meant **a blistering tirade** from the coach, he wanted it back.

In the locker room afterward, Bedford pointed out their mistakes and **chastised** them for falling behind and then, almost grudgingly, he started to smile. "You did win," he said. "There may be hope for you yet."

Marshall won eight of its next nine games, but almost no one was paying attention. They were not ranked, and most of the local press coverage went to other schools: King, which featured two seven-footers, Thomas Hamilton and Rashard Griffith; Westinghouse, with quicksilver guards Kiwane Garris and Antoine Morris, and Anthony Davis, a tenacious rebounder; and Taft, a North Side school with Kenny Pratt, a high-scoring guard.

For Bedford and his assistants, Eli Ephram and Al Williams, it was hard to determine just how good their team would be. They might—just maybe—overtake Westinghouse to win the conference title, but go downstate? No. The city's play-off was a brutal play-off—six games in less than two weeks—from which only one of sixty

....

a blistering tirade an angry lecture
chastised yelled at

teams emerged to go downstate.

"We'd have to get by King and those big bodies," said Bedford. "Realistically, the best we might make is the final four of the city play-offs."

The only people **wise to** Marshall were the small-time, freelance scouts who prowled the dingy public league gyms, looking for unknown talent they could **peddle** to the junior colleges. They loved Arthur for his speed, quickness, confidence, and durability.

As the season wore on, more of them showed up, and soon they brought with them assistant coaches from junior colleges and small four-year schools. They sat on the gnarled bleachers trying hard not to look conspicuous, which was difficult because they were usually the only white guys in the gym.

About six or seven of these coaches attended the last regular season game, a rematch against Westinghouse. They were as ambitious and persistent as their big school counterparts who had courted William for the last two years.

Bedford was rather indifferent to **their obsequiousness**. But Bo adored their attention. It was the **payoff** he had anticipated since he held Arthur, big hands and all, in that hospital eighteen years ago.

"I know how to handle these scouts and coaches," Bo told Arthur. "They want something, and we got to hear what they have to offer. But we don't want to make no commitments."

Bo assumed that any white in the gym was a coach or scout (though there were many black coaches as well). He walked up to any white man and introduced himself as "Arthur Agee *Senior*," so there would be no doubt that he was the man to see.

....

wise to who knew about
peddle take, show
their obsequiousness the nice things they said
payoff reward, result

The coaches and Bo sat in the stands while the bleachers filled with students, the band swayed, and the cheerleaders shimmied—and Westinghouse, led by Garris, **took the floor**. They gave Bo their cards, and he told them his philosophy of **child-rearing**: "You got to stay on these children while they're growing up." And when Sheila came by, Bo all but shooed her away. "I'm takin' care of business here," he told her.

"Your son is a helluva player," one scout from Elmhurst College told him.

"Oh, thank you."

The scout pulled out a brochure. "This explains a little about our program, where our program's heading."

It was a small college in a nearby suburb. Bo flipped through the glossy brochure. They couldn't even offer a full scholarship, just a little off the tuition. But Bo reckoned this was just the start of negotiations, and he was willing to listen to all offers. "I like what you're saying, and I want him close to home, you know," he said. "I'm kind of leaning your way because, I just thank God, he's getting into it."

He made virtually the same statement to an assistant coach from Northeastern, another local college.

Then a coach from a nearby junior college came by. "I'm Arthur Hester," he said, shaking hands with Bo. "Us Arts got to stick together. I'm over at Kennedy King."

"Kennedy King?" said Bo. "Okay. May the best man win."

Oh, he loved it. They chatted about the Bulls and Jordan and whether King could be beat. Bo excused them to stand and cheer as Marshall took the court.

....

took the floor came onto the court
child-rearing how to raise children

The crowd started a rhythmic applause: "Marshall, Marshall—*clap-clap, clap-clap*." Five girls jumped from the bleachers and began to dance, stepping forward and back, twisting, spinning, and finishing with a split. Everyone was standing, clapping, chanting: "Marshall, Marshall." Into the gym strode Bedford, wearing team colors—a maroon sweater over a gold turtleneck.

The courtside announcer, his voice trying to break through the feedback buzz, introduced the starters: "Quadell Kimble . . . Cesare Christian . . . Mozell Williams . . . Derrick Zinnerman . . . and senior guard, six-foot-one Arthur Agee!"

Arthur skipped to center court, hands raised. The remaining team poured off the bench and crowded round him. They chanted: "One, two, three—defense!"

The game was **a bullet shot out of a gun**—go-go West Side ball. Each team played hands-in-the-face trapping defense. Westinghouse **pulled ahead** as Garris nailed long jumpers, but Marshall **roared back**. At halftime they were down by one and they trailed by five midway through the final quarter. By then the fans were standing and rollicking for almost every play. The first row of the bleachers almost touched the inbound line, and students who sat there were never more than a few inches from the action. When a call went against Marshall or when Marshall made a great shot, they **surged** onto the court. The referees had to stop the game to shoo them back.

With two minutes left, Derrick Zinnerman put back a layup to give Marshall a one-point lead. The scent of triumph stirred the crowd to bedlam.

Garris's shot rolled off; Robin Dunagan grabbed the rebound

....

a bullet shot out of a gun noisy and full of action
pulled ahead scored more points than Marshall
roared back played well also
surged ran, moved

and fed the ball to Arthur, jetting for the basket. He was fouled on his approach and went to the free-throw line, where few players want to be with less than a minute left and the game at stake. But Arthur had no doubts. He bounced the ball, he eyed the basket, and he drained two perfect free throws.

"Yeah, that's my boy," screamed Bo, "that's my boy."

Arthur waved his hands triumphantly when the shots swished in. "Yes!" he exclaimed. "Yes!"

Those points sealed the win, and just in case there was any doubt, Arthur stole the ball and roared in for a sweeping dunk as the buzzer sounded.

Bo was one of the first fans on the court, running past Westinghouse's stunned players. He grabbed Arthur in a **bear** hug. "We did it." Arthur cried, "We beat Westinghouse."

The celebration spilled into the locker room, where Arthur and Roderico Dale, a backup guard, broke into **an impromptu dance**. They quieted as Bedford walked in, turning to the coach and hoping for praise. There was none. Bedford had decided **to downplay** the win to keep them from thinking all of their goals had been reached.

"Arthur Agee, you got seven turnovers—even for a guard that's too many," Bedford said, his voice cautious and calm. "This is a good win for you, but it doesn't mean anything. You got to do better than that."

The team nodded solemnly—until Bedford left. Then they began to celebrate again.

"The big games are coming up in the play-offs," Bedford told Bo. "I don't want them to think this is their whole season."

....

bear very big

an impromptu dance a dance they made up

to downplay not to say too much about

After the game, Bo introduced some of the college coaches to Arthur. "Us Arts got to stick together," Hester said as he shook Arthur's hand.

Hmm, Bo thought, *not bad—even the second time around.*

Then Bo introduced them to Sheila. "You the mom?" said one coach. "I thought you were a cheerleader."

"Thanks," said Sheila.

Oh, very slick, thought Bo, *very slick indeed.*

The win gave Marshall a share of the conference title—quite an achievement for a team which had won nine and lost sixteen the year before. They went on to win their first two games of the play-offs, **blasting past two lesser foes**: Metro High and Manley. Each game drew more coaches and scouts. Another familiar figure who showed up was Big Earl Smith, the playground scout who had spotted Arthur at Delano. He looked a bit sheepish hovering in the corner away from the action.

"Where you been, man?" asked Arthur.

"Where I been? I've been working," said Big Earl.

"You talk to Ping?"

"About what? You're here, not at St. Joe."

"Yeah, I had to **break out**."

Arthur brought Big Earl over to Sheila. "Hello, Mrs. Agee," he said.

"Well, hi, Big Earl," Sheila said.

As he talked he put his hands in his pockets and looked around uncertainly. His voice didn't rumble with its old **bravado**, not like

....

blasting past two lesser foes beating two teams that were not as good as Marshall

break out leave the school

bravado confidence, boldness

when it filled her living room almost four years ago.

Big Earl offered Arthur a ride home, and as he drove he started to talk, the words pouring forth as though he had some confession to make. "In a way you were lucky to leave St. Joseph," he told Arthur. "You got no more financial strain, no travel, plus you're playing for a great coach."

Arthur nodded.

"I don't scout anymore," Big Earl continued. "I retired."

I got a bitter taste in my mouth about a lot of things that happened, he thought, but did not say aloud. *A lot of people accuse me of taking youngsters out of the inner city and sending them out to St. Joe. And they ask, what did I get out of the deal? I got a lot of racial* **slurs** *and so forth from my own people about me, about what I did. I felt, I still feel, that I was doing the right thing for that particular time. Sometimes I have* **second thoughts** *when I see the net results of what happened with youngsters.*

"I still love the game," he said to Arthur. "It's the system I don't like."

"I love the game, too," said Arthur. "No matter what happens, I always love the game."

"I wish young black kids would do other things than just play basketball."

"That's all I wanted to do."

They reached Arthur's house, and Sheila and Bo were already home. Sheila invited Big Earl into the living room.

"This is where it all started," he said.

"You have no idea of what we've been through since the last time you were here," she said.

....

slurs *insults*
second thoughts *doubts, regrets*

Almost as an afterthought Big Earl asked Arthur if he wanted to go with him to see St. Joseph play that night. "They're playing Nazareth in a play-off game."

Arthur's first **instinct** was to say no, but then he thought—*It would be real good to go back as a winner.* "Yeah!"

He put on his gold and maroon Marshall High jacket. "Let's go. I hope they win," he said. "I hope they win them all, until we beat them downstate."

....

instinct idea

BEFORE YOU MOVE ON...

1. **Conclusions** William chose to go to school at Marquette. What were some of the reasons he chose this school?

2. **Comparisons** How have William's feelings about basketball changed?

LOOK AHEAD Did the Chargers finally play in the championship games? Read pages 322–342 to find out.

WILLIAM

· · · · · · · · · · ·

On the night of the Nazareth game, round two of the playoffs, David had to work late, so Curtis and his **longtime** friend, Louie Wilson, drove William to the game.

They had to be there by six for a 7:30 tip-off; they left Emma's house at quarter to five. The night was rainy, the roads slippery, the **arteries crowded with rush-hour travelers**. It took forever to get from Cabrini to the highway, and then it was bumper to bumper once they got there. On the radio the announcer said it was 5:20.

"We should be at Oak Park by now," said William. "Get off at Pulaski and try Roosevelt Road. God, I can't be late—he'll kill me if I'm late."

Nazareth wasn't a great team—undefeated, but from a weak conference—but they were a threat. They had Sean Pearson. One great player can take a team a long way in the play-offs if he gets hot. And William knew from the Nike Camp that Pearson could get very hot.

We should be there by now, William thought as he looked out the window. The traffic wasn't moving. *I should be in the locker room; I should be focusing on the game, not sitting in the back seat of a car.* This **maddening scene** was a replay of the season—running late from city to suburbs, always in a hurry, always late. *Pingatore's gonna kill me.*

At ten after six, William bolted into the locker room. He raced into his uniform, **foregoing** his elaborate pregame rituals of focus and concentration, and dashed up the stairs.

···

longtime old
arteries crowded with rush-hour travelers highways crowded
maddening scene frustrating situation
foregoing without performing

Both teams were warming up, the stands were slowly filling, and the band was setting up. He saw Sean Pearson and waved. He bent for a loose ball. "William." It was Pingatore, his voice cold and hard. "You aren't starting. You were late. You can't do that to the team."

William stood silent and still until Pingatore walked away, then he slammed the ball on the ground. "In four years I was never late for a game—not once," he muttered. "This is some time to teach me a lesson."

"Hey, boy." It was Arthur, standing by the side of the basket near the entrance to the locker room.

"Arthur, man, what are you doin' here?"

"Came to see you, boy. You better win."

"He ain't startin' me, man."

"What?"

"He says I was late."

From Arthur **the word spread throughout the gym**, though most people couldn't believe it. "Pingatore can't be real," said Curtis. "You can't mess around with a play-off game."

When the starters were called, it wasn't William who jogged out but a reserve named John Musachio. The Chargers scored the first three baskets; Nazareth was uncertain and nervous, Pearson cold.

William sat on the bench, two down from Pingatore, and cheered his teammates. But his mind was scrambled. He had never come off the bench before, his routine had been toppled. He was cold, he wasn't ready. *I can't believe he didn't start me*, he thought. *Why would he want to embarrass me?*

The lead pushed to ten.

....

the word spread throughout the gym everyone in the gym found out that William was not starting

When's he gonna put me in? he thought. *In the first quarter? In the second? What are people gonna think?*

Pingatore called William's name with about a minute left in the first quarter. He staggered into the game and **got rid of the ball** as soon as it came his way. He felt like one of those scrawny kids forced to play basketball in gym class—the kind of kid who runs to the corner and hides. He wanted to hide. The great William Gates, and he didn't want to touch the ball.

He scored on a layup, but felt more relief than exultation. The game should have been **a blow out**, but the Chargers were **stagnant**. They played without passion and the crowd was listless. Pearson was cold—what would happen if he were hot?—and yet the lead was not building. The Chargers couldn't score. Nazareth sent two defenders at Eaker and forced St. Joseph to take outside shots, but the shots weren't falling. They led by nine at the half.

During the break Arthur wandered out of the gym and down the hallway to the cafeteria, bumping into people he knew from St. Joe. Some barely recognized him, he'd grown so tall. Others were delighted to see him. In the cafeteria were three of his old buddies, including the fat kid they called Ox. They gave him hugs and high fives. These were the kids who roared at his jokes, who begged him to do impersonations, who slipped him five dollars, who wanted him to stay. Now they had little to say to one another except for, "Good luck."

Arthur returned just as the second half began, with William in the starting lineup. William hit a jumper, pushing the lead to thirteen, but then they slipped back to bad habits. Bad shots, no rotation. The crowd began to murmur, and—it was bound to happen

....

got rid of the ball passed the ball to another player
a blow out an easy victory
stagnant not playing well

sooner or later—Pearson got hot. He hit six straight jumpers. At the end of three quarters, St. Joe's lead was seven.

There comes a time in some games between the mighty and the weak, when the roles reverse, when the good team runs on **wobbly** legs and the underdog roars. The Chargers and Nazareth had reached that moment. The Chargers had lost their rhythm. Whoever had the ball raced for the basket or took the shot. And the more Pingatore told his team not to play selfishly, the less they listened. It was every man for himself.

"Get William the ball," screamed Curtis, echoing an old lament.

Pearson grabbed a rebound, dribbled to the three-point line and buried his shot. The lead was four. The next basket cut the lead to two.

"Just take the ball, William," screamed Curtis.

Thaddeous Wordlaw, the point guard, didn't even look William's way. He **steamed for** the basket, clanking off a layup; Pearson rebounded and hit another three. Suddenly, Nazareth was winning. Pingatore called a time-out and huddled the team around him.

The next play went to William. He dribbled to his left, faked, and launched a pretty little jumper. If he hit it, they would regain the lead and maybe the momentum. The ball bounced around the rim, started to roll in, and then rolled out. The Chargers didn't score another basket, and in the final seconds Nazareth pulled away.

As a freshman William thought his days of high school basketball would never end, and now they were over. **A hodgepodge of** memories flashed before him: Sunday practice, surgery, crying over free throws, shots clanking off the rim. He heard the delightful

....

wobbly weak
steamed for ran toward
A hodgepodge of Many different

squeals of celebration. He knew the scene without looking: players swarming around the star, parading him about on their shoulders—Eric Anderson, Tom Kleinschmidt, and now Sean Pearson.

He was numb. He never imagined they'd be **upset** in the early rounds in a sloppy game against a **so-so team**. If you're going to lose, you want to go down to the great ones, with fire in your eye and blood on your face. *I can't believe it's over—I never thought it would end like this.*

In the bleachers his family silently watched the Nazareth celebration. "It was bad coachin'," Curtis said finally. "This ain't no time to teach nobody no lessons. Ain't no way you put your star player on the bench. This is the play-off, man."

Mrs. Weir stopped by. "You've got a lot to be proud of," she told Emma.

"Me and William roomed together at Nike," Pearson was telling reporters. "We used to joke about this game. I said we were gonna **do it to** them, and we did."

The St. Joseph locker room cleared out quickly. William dressed in seconds. "I never felt right," he told reporters. "I never felt in the flow."

He didn't start crying until he walked upstairs and saw his mother. "I'm sorry Mom," he told her.

He hugged Emma, Catherine, and Mrs. Weir, and then his tears stopped. But when he saw Arthur he **broke down** again.

"Hey, boy," Arthur said.

William hugged Arthur as hard as he could. He wanted to disappear in his arms. "I ain't never wanted to go out this way," he said.

---

upset beaten, defeated
so-so team team that played well but not great
do it to beat
broke down started to cry

"You played a good game," said Arthur.

"We were gonna go down there together," said William.

"I love you, boy," said Arthur.

"I love you, too."

The locker room was empty except for Pingatore, sitting on a table with a Coke can in his hand, talking to reporters. His face was **drawn** and pale.

"I'm just curious about the starters?" a reporter asked.

"William was twenty minutes late. The team was dressed and he came strolling in," said Pingatore. "Maybe he has to learn something from that."

"Even in a big game?"

"Even in a big game."

Pingatore put his Coke down and pursed his lips. These things were difficult to talk about after a hard loss. "William's a nice young man who is going to move on, and I'm sure he's going to do well," he said. "Whether he becomes a great player or not—that's not important. He accomplished what he set out to do. He's got a college scholarship and a means of going to school."

As he talked, Arthur slipped into the room and stood in the corner. He thought he might enjoy watching Pingatore suffer, but he felt no satisfaction. Pingatore looked old and tired. *He never meant it personal*, Arthur thought. *He made a mistake. It was his mistake. If he had kept me they'd be going downstate.*

"Do you feel a little sad?" Pingatore was asked by one of the reporters.

He smiled **faintly**. "It's always sad when you lose something that's

....

drawn sad

faintly a little bit

been with you for four years. A lot of good things have happened over the four years. A lot of **remembrances**. That always happens. You don't **dwell on it**. To quote Isiah—the toughest loss he ever took was the De LaSalle game in 1979, when we got beat at the buzzer. Now I look back at it as just one of those great moments in our high school scene. Our toughest loss to take, and yet we talk about it now. So that's the way I look at these things now."

Pingatore looked up and saw Arthur. "Arthur!" he said. "Could have used you tonight."

"Yeah," said Arthur.

Pingatore rose to greet Arthur. This time there were no jokes or playful punches.

"Good luck," said Pingatore. "I'm gonna be watching. Don't forget to stay in touch. . . . How are your grades?"

"They're all right."

"Good," said Pingatore. "We missed you."

"I missed you all, too," said Arthur.

And he did, he really did.

"Well, I'm proud of what you've done. Mr. Bedford said a lot of good things about you. You be in touch. Okay? Good luck."

Arthur walked out of the locker room and up the stairs. He stood beneath the basket and counted the conference championship banners on the wall. *They still don't have one for the state championship,* he thought. *They had their chance, and they **blew** it.*

Then he dashed out to the parking lot where Big Earl was waiting and caught a ride back to the city. There wasn't any traffic by then, and he was back home and in bed by midnight, which was good

....

remembrances things to remember
dwell on it think about it all the time
blew lost

because he needed his sleep. His season wasn't over, and he had practice in the morning.

ARTHUR

Marshall's next game was against the Rough Riders of Roosevelt High, **a peppy bunch of overachievers** coached by Manny Weincord, the same man who coached against Curtis in the 1980s.

The two teams had never played, and Marshall knew nothing about Roosevelt's players. The school was known for soccer not basketball; its team was not acclaimed. They were one of the few integrated teams in the public league—blacks, whites, Hispanics, and Arabs. They didn't engage in theatrical warm-ups; their uniforms were old and faded. "Man, we're gonna kill these chumps," Arthur told his teammates.

But Roosevelt came out steaming. Senior guard Moe Ghanimah, a Palestinian kid, opened with two long jumpers; the husky front line of Tim Davis and Kenric Mattox dominated the boards; a spindly junior named Terrell Redmond lost Arthur on a pump fake and scored on a finger roll. It was 11 to 2 and Bedford called time. "Would someone cover that guy?" he said of Ghanimah. "You gonna let him shoot all day?"

The Rough Riders led 15 to 13 at the end of the quarter. "We can beat these guys," Weincord told his players. "They thought they were gonna **run all over** you, now you got them worried." The Rough Riders put their hands together and chanted, "One, two,

....

a peppy bunch of overachievers an energetic group of smart kids

run all over play better than

three—defense!"

It was a role reversal that Bedford had feared. All year long his team had been the **underdog**, now they were playing **fat and sassy**— like pampered bullies. The gleam of determination was in Roosevelt's eyes. On a hunch Bedford brought in Rico Dale to work the press with Arthur and Derrick Zinnerman. Roosevelt valiantly fought on, but Bedford kept moving men in and out of the lineup, wearing them down. Mattox tired, Ghanimah's shot fell flat; Weincord turned to his bench, bringing in Ronnie White, Mario Ramos, and Herman Carey, but they were young and inexperienced.

Rico scored eleven points in that quarter as the Commandos mounted a twenty-three-point lead. The rest of the game was a formality, a blast to play for Marshall. They alley-ooped and jammed, blocked shots, and ran the break. Bedford emptied his bench, not wanting to run up the score, but even the benchwarmers piled it on. The whole team knew its role—five players at a time playing as one. They won 90 to 57.

"Your team was excellent," Weincord told Bedford after the game. "Really magnificent. I wish you all the luck. I hope you win it all."

By now the city was waking up to Marshall. The next day's *Sun-Times* carried a **blurb** about the game. The team was so unknown, the paper got their names wrong. They called Arthur, "Anthony Agee," and spelled Derrick "Derek." Everyone had a laugh. "Hardest name is Quadell's, and they got that right," said Arthur.

Despite the growing **hype**, Bedford was worried about the next game. They were playing Taft, the fourth-ranked team in the city, featuring Kenny Pratt, a hot-shooting guard. The winner would play

....

underdog team that everyone thought would lose

fat and sassy as if they were not trying very hard

blurb short article

hype attention

the winner of a game between Simeon and King. "I know what you're thinking—you're thinking about King," Bedford told his players. "Take it one step at a time."

For Taft it was an emotional game. Pratt's mother had died the night before and the team wore commemorative arm bands. Through three quarters, the lead had bounced back and forth seven times with twelve ties. By the fourth quarter, though, the Marshall trap had tightened and Taft went the way of Roosevelt—**falling prey to** the press and to the waves of players rolling in from Bedford's bench. Arthur scored eighteen; Cesare Christian had nine rebounds. The Commandos won by nine points.

"You're in the final four," athletic director and assistant coach Williams told Bedford.

"I predicted that—didn't I?" he laughed.

When the team entered the locker room they discovered something new: reporters from both downtown dailies, the *Tribune* and the *Sun-Times*.

Arthur had been waiting for this moment ever since his freshman year at St. Joseph. And he didn't waste it. He **issued forth on** a range of subjects, opening with a reminder that greater challenges lay ahead, and closing with a tribute to the valiant opposition. "We tried to deny Ken Pratt the ball and take him out of the game," Arthur told them. "He's a great player."

While the team dressed, **word shot** through the locker room: Simeon had been defeated. Marshall's next opponent was the mightiest of them all—King.

···

falling prey to having a hard time with
issued forth on talked about
word shot news spread

Bedford wasn't much for pregame speeches, but he couldn't resist this moment.

The two teams, King and Marshall, and their coaches, Sonny Cox and Bedford, were **polar** opposites. Cox recruited from all over the city; Bedford coached who came through his doors. "Everybody says King's a bunch of all-stars that can't be beaten. They got those two seven-footers—Well, we didn't come this far to be scared," Bedford told the Commandos as they gathered in their gym. "You gonna beat these boys if you play smart."

He pointed to the banners on the wall. "In the old days there wasn't recruiting. It was just neighborhood school against neighborhood school, and Marshall was the best," he said. "We got a tradition of greatness here. Let's carry it on."

They rode a bus to the International Amphitheater, a huge pavilion some sixty years old. They dressed in one of several basement dressing rooms, **a catacomb rimmed** by rusty lockers and mildewy overhanging pipes. "The way to beat them is to **deny** the big men," said Bedford. "You got to frustrate them, attack them. We're gonna build a wall around them. Quadell, Mozell, Cesare— stay in their faces."

The Commandos were well into their warm-ups when the Jaguars, the defending state champions, made their entrance. Hamilton and Griffith led the procession. They weren't big, they were enormous, with **mountainous** shoulders and husky arms. They wore silky warm-ups and shiny-new gym shoes. The last to emerge was Coach Cox, rotund and barrel-chested, and strutting arrogantly. He grunted hello to Bedford, scowled at the officials, and stood, arms

....

polar complete, total
a catacomb rimmed an underground room surrounded
deny keep the ball away from
mountainous huge; very large

folded, by his bench while his team **swooped in for** dunks. The Jaguars, undefeated last year and ranked the best team in the country, were twenty-six and one.

Arthur watched their arrival with growing anticipation. This was his dream, his chance to beat the best. *You ain't nothin'*, he thought.

The Commandos rallied around Bedford for final instructions. "Double down," he told them. "Opposite man fall back in the paint. Remember, build a wall."

Arthur broke from the huddle, tucked his shirt into his shorts, wiped his hands on his shoes, located his family in the stands—Bo, Sheila, Tomekia, Sweetie, and Jazz—and gave them a wave. "They gonna win," said Sheila.

"Twenty-six and two, that's what King gonna be when this game is done," said Bo.

Arthur moved to center court and saw a camera focused on him. The game was being **televised live**. *The whole state's watching Arthur Agee!*

From the start King tried to get the ball to their big men, and from the start Marshall built their wall. Robin and Quadell surrounded whichever big man came closest to the basket. They grunted and shoved and pushed, their heads bobbing at Hamilton and Griffith's shoulders.

The game was slow and filled with dreadful shots. King became preoccupied, almost obsessed, with getting the ball down low. All effort was focused on the shoving match in the paint.

At the half, Bedford had what he wanted—a lead. "You've given me one good half, don't stop now," Bedford told them.

....

swooped in for practiced

televised live shown on television as they played

King hit a few jumpers at the start of the third quarter and took a four-point lead. Bedford called time.

"You don't play with no confidence whatsoever," he bellowed. "None. None! Get your heads in the game!"

On the next play, Arthur skipped through the lane and banked in a layup. Then Derrick stole the ball and hit a three. **King's run had ended**; Marshall regained the lead. The game went back to its **turtle-paced pattern**. Another team might have adjusted its strategy, but King was too proud. They were not going to let some unranked bunch of losers from the West Side make them change. Again and again they hammered the ball into Griffith or Hamilton, and again and again their big men **churned and jerked** and tried to break free. A few minutes into the third, Hamilton got called for his fourth foul and had to sit on the bench. Now the Commandos focused on Griffith, running three, even four men at him. He was only a junior, only sixteen, and he got flustered and angry. He began complaining to the refs about fouls. Mozell put back a rebound; Cesare hit a three; Rico hit a jumper. Marshall's lead was ten with 3:09 left.

"They're gonna do it, they're gonna do it," screamed Sheila.

Now it was Cox who called time out to yell at his players.

"We got a long time to play," Bedford warned the Commandos. "If we can force them out of their zone defense, we can **run it up**. They can't keep up with our quickness."

With a minute left Arthur took the ball up high. His team led by four, and he stood there as the clock ticked down. "Let them come at you," Bedford called from the bench. "Don't move until they break the zone."

....

King's run had ended King was no longer playing so well
turtle-paced pattern slow pace
churned and jerked struggled; had a hard time
run it up get the ball to the basket

It was a war of nerves between Bedford and Cox, and as the seconds slipped away, Cox broke and called off his zone. Hamilton stepped up to Arthur, and Arthur dribbled right around him, drove to the basket, and passed off to Dunagan who buried a jumper. Cox dropped his head—the lead was **insurmountable**.

When the game ended Arthur fell on the floor and wept. They had beaten one of the best teams in the country. They had **torn down the twin towers**. If they won tomorrow they were going downstate.

Arthur's teammates **converged on** him. They prayed and hugged and laughed and cried.

Bo and Sheila ran onto the floor screaming his name.

"I love you, Dad," Arthur told Bo.

"I love *you*, son," Bo said.

"Can you believe it, Man? Can you believe what we've gone through?" Sheila cried.

Bedford remained cool; he didn't gloat or taunt Cox. "It was an ugly win—poor shooting, poor free-throw shooting, everybody was especially tight," he told reporters.

"Is this your biggest win?" a reporter asked.

"No," Bedford said. "Tomorrow's would be bigger."

The championship game was against Westinghouse, and William decided to come. "I gotta support Arthur," he said. "He supported me."

He saw Bo and Sheila in the stands. He hugged them and congratulated them and read the sports sections they showed him, featuring pictures of Arthur.

....

insurmountable too great

torn down the twin towers defeated King's two tallest players

converged on surrounded; crowded around

He sat by himself and watched the Commandos warm up. He waved to Arthur, but Arthur didn't see him. The arena filled, reporters crowded into the press table, bands started playing, TV announcers did their pregame stand-ups at center court.

I wonder what would have happened if I hadn't left Chicago, if I hadn't gone to St. Joe? William thought. *That might be me out there.*

The game wasn't close—Westinghouse **was ragged**. Marshall took an early lead. *It used to be when we were freshmen, Arthur watched me play,* William thought. *Now, I'm watching him.*

Arthur was brilliant, harassing Garris on defense, throwing the highly **touted** sophomore off his game. The lead built to twenty. William watched Bo and Sheila; as the seconds ticked down, they were dancing in the aisle. Marshall won 58 to 38.

The Commandos ran on the court and danced and hugged and held their fingers in the air while chanting "We're number one." Photographers buzzed about them. The superintendent of schools gave them the championship trophy. It was all in slow motion for William, almost a dream.

I shoulda never left the city, he thought. *I shoulda played for the home team.*

The celebration continued in the locker room where the Commandos happily answered every question **thrown their way**. By now they were **adept at handling** reporters—wasn't nothing to it, especially when you win.

"Last year and earlier this year, we were our own worst enemies," Cesare told reporters. "We used to fool around in practice. It was like the coach decided to show us what would happen if we didn't

....

was ragged played terribly
touted praised
thrown their way that they were asked
adept at handling skillful at talking to

take basketball and him seriously."

"Before the game," Derrick said, "Coach Williams told us, 'You remember what Westinghouse did to you as sophomores? I think it's pay-back time.' We said, 'We think so, too.' So we paid them back."

"They always played hard and they always played together," said Bedford.

At last, Arthur saw William.

"I told you," Arthur said as they hugged. "Told you what I was gonna do!"

"I told you, boy," William said.

Then someone began to pull Arthur in another direction. William watched him walk away.

The next day's papers were filled with accolades. "Marshall doesn't do anything fancy," read the lead story by Taylor Bell in the *Sun-Times*. "No slam dunks, no behind the back dribbles, no intimidation, no talking trash.

"The Commandos do all the things coaches appreciate. They clog passing lanes, put hands in your face, block out, slap at the ball, press, penetrate, distribute, disrupt, and take charge.

"'They've learned to play together,'" Bedford was quoted. "'They try to adjust with me yelling at them. They get closer together when I yell at them. They rebel against me as a group. That's fine with me—as long as they do what they're supposed to do.'"

Arthur read that article many times. It was, he thought, the finest writing he had ever read. He **clipped it from** the paper and taped it to his wall. When he woke in the morning, he read it again. Marshall's progression to the state tournament began on a Thursday

....

clipped it from cut it out of

morning with a pep rally in the gym, which was decorated with banners and bunting and packed with students, parents, and faculty. "What are we gonna be?" Bedford called to the crowd.

"State champions!" the crowd responded.

Team members ran though a **gauntlet** of supporters to Adams Street where the bus was waiting. Bouncing along the expressway past steel mills, factories, and warehouses, the bus rolled beyond even subdivisions and malls to rural Illinois and the prairie land of corn, cows, barns, and silos—downstate.

Bedford **gave them a recitation on the significance** of their achievement. The first all-black team to play in the state finals was the legendary DuSable Panthers, led by Sweet Charlie Brown and Paxton Lumpkin. They might have won the state title, if not for controversial calls in the fourth quarter by a white referee. The first all-black team to win the state title was the 1958 Marshall Commandos, coached by Spin Salario and led by George Wilson, a 6'7" sophomore center. Wilson and the Commandos repeated in 1960.

But Bedford gave up on the history lesson: no one seemed to be listening—it was ancient history to them.

They rolled into Champaign that Thursday night. On Friday they won their first game, beating the Batavia Bulldogs the way they defeated Roosevelt and Taft: They wore them down with defense.

The university campus was buzzing with high school students and their parents, **ablaze with** letter jackets and sweaters of the brightest oranges, reds, purples, and whites. The arena was a cylindrical cave made of concrete where sound bounced back and forth and reverberated like thunder. A huge, overhanging scoreboard

....

gauntlet crowd

gave them a recitation on the significance made a speech about the importance

ablaze with wearing

flashed the names of players and their numbers. The court was ringed by reporters, photographers, and play-by-play announcers. The game was **broadcast statewide** on TV.

The Commandos stayed in a nearby motel and wore their maroon and gold warm-up jackets everywhere they went. People kept coming up to them and congratulating them for upsetting King.

Bo, Sheila, and Sweetie drove down for Friday's game and spent the night in a motel. In the morning they ate breakfast at McDonald's, where they, too, got the celebrity treatment when people found out they were Arthur Agee's family.

"You all are playing the number one team and we're playing the number two team," Bo said to a couple from Libertyville who were sitting in a nearby booth.

"This is the first time in the history of the school that we've gone this far," the woman said.

"It's just like the Commandos," smiled Sheila. "We're the underdogs. I'm glad we are, because it just shows you how you can come up. And then beat your opponent." They laughed together and exchanged high fives.

After breakfast the Agees strolled around the campus. It had long flowing lawns and intimidating buildings of marble or brick. "I'd always wanted to go to a college like this," said Sheila. "I could have done it. I could have had my chance."

Bo was quiet, not used to the academic environment. It wasn't what he expected. Because it was spring break, the campus was quiet. A few students **lounged about on the quad** in the sun's warm rays, with nothing but time on their hands.

....

broadcast statewide shown across the state
lounged about on the quad relaxed on the lawn

"This would be a good place for Man to come," said Bo.

"Yeah, this is really something that a child shouldn't miss out on," said Sheila. "Like a whole different world."

"It's beyond different," said Sweetie, summing it all up.

That night Marshall played against Peoria Manual, the second-ranked team in the state. Peoria was as fast as the Commandos, and just as deep. They had a **bullet-quick** point guard named Howard Nathan, who zipped through the press, scoring twenty-eight points and dishing seven assists, and then he turned right around and applied a press of his own. He **hounded** Arthur and Derrick, and harried them into mistakes.

William watched the game at home on TV, with David by his side. They drank soda, ate chips, and cheered when Arthur's name was mentioned.

"Arthur Agee, spinning inside—tough shot!" the announcer said.

"Get 'em, Man," said William.

"Little penetration move by Agee," said the announcer.

"I taught him that one," William said. In the next instant Nathan slapped the ball away.

"Teach him that one, too?" David asked.

Their grandest cheer came when the camera **cut** to the overhanging scoreboard flashing Arthur's name and number in huge bold print.

"That's my boy," said William, "You did it. Goddamn it, you said you would and you did."

With a few minutes left in the game Arthur fouled out. "He just never quits," the announcer said, "He just kept going for the

....

bullet-quick very fast
hounded stayed close to
cut went

basketball."

Arthur sat on the bench, his head in his hands.

"Don't get down, son."

Arthur looked up in amazement to see Bo sitting on a bench next to Sweetie, just a few feet away.

"How did you get down here?" Arthur asked.

Bo grinned. "I told the guards I was part of the **film crew making that documentary** about you."

"How did Sweetie get here?"

"I told them the same thing," Sweetie said.

"Oh, man," Arthur moaned.

Peoria won 68 to 55. But Sheila kept cheering long after the buzzer sounded, not willing to acknowledge that Marshall's glorious run had ended.

"Number one!" Sheila yelled. "We're still number one."

There were no tears in the locker room—there wasn't time. The consolation game against Libertyville would begin in two hours. Marshall won it on a last-second jumper by Mozell.

Afterward there wasn't much to do before the championship game between Proviso East, the school Jamal Robinson left St. Joe's for, and Peoria. Arthur wandered over to the press room filled with reporters, coaches, and scouts, including Bob Gibbons, who was updating his list of the country's top seniors (Glenn Robinson, Chris Webber, and Juwan Howard—William **had fallen off** the top-fifty list). Arthur had bite-sized **quips** on subjects ranging from Marshall's tradition ("We used to scare everyone in the '70s") to Bedford's philosophy ("You just gotta sacrifice; if you love the game of

....

film crew making that documentary group making that movie

had fallen off was not in

quips statements, comments

basketball, you just go out there and **give all your heart**"). He was still talking when the championship game started and was a little disappointed when the reporters had to leave.

During the half-time intermission of the championship game (which Proviso East won), Marshall accepted its third-place trophy as the crowd stood and cheered. At the center of the court, tears in his eyes, a smile on his face, and his hands held high over his head, was Arthur—little Arthur Agee, triumphant at last.

....

give all your heart play the best you can

BEFORE YOU MOVE ON...

1. **Conclusions** If basketball was not important to William anymore, why did he cry when the Chargers lost the big game?

2. **Inference** Marshall won third place at the championship tournament. Why was Arthur "triumphant at last"?

LOOK AHEAD Read pages 343–377 to find out if Arthur was able to leave Chicago.

WILLIAM

• • • • • • • • • • •

In the spring Catherine joined her classmates at Westinghouse for the senior trip. They went to an amusement park in Cincinnati, Ohio, and spent most of their time in the motel eating pizzas, **guzzling** pop, playing cards, and gossiping.

Many of the girls on the trip were girls Catherine had seen almost every day but never gotten to know—girls she had dismissed as being too **brassy, or boy-crazy**, or not her type. "You mean to tell me you were in this school all year, and we just got to know each other?" they asked Catherine incredulously.

"I didn't realize you all were so much fun," she said. "I just **wrote you off** without knowing you. I won't make that mistake again."

They had a grand time, but those days of play in Cincinnati left a residue of melancholy. Gone before they started, they reminded her of all the many high school functions—dates, proms, and dances—she had missed.

She came home determined to get out of Chicago and move on with her life. "I don't want to look back ten years from now and say, 'Damn, I missed it all,'" she told William.

William felt the same way. As far as he was concerned, school could not end soon enough. "I'm so damn sick of going to this place."

In April the team had its basketball banquet. They sat in a mirrored room of a suburban supper club with glittering chandeliers and dazzling white tablecloths. The featured speaker, a local college coach, droned on until William was drowsy. Then Pingatore made

....

guzzling drinking
brassy, or boy-crazy loud or only thinking about boys
wrote you off decided not to be friends with you

his remarks.

"We had a difficult year; most of you are aware of that," he said.

The coach ran down a list of William's accomplishments—all-conference, all-state, four-year starter—before presenting him with the team's Most Valuable Player award. The boosters and parents and players applauded, but William was a bit embarrassed to accept the award, linked as it was to so much expectation. He walked to the front and returned to his seat as quickly as he could. *They think I'm a disappointment*, he thought. *They think it because of the knee—that after the injury I wasn't the same. But it's not the knee. I just never felt right here. They made basketball more of a business, more of a job, than a sport to play.*

He still had **the ACT hanging over his head**. The best he had scored was 17. If he didn't score 18, he would be ineligible to play as a freshman. Marquette's coaches were concerned. Is he taking his preparatory courses? they asked Pingatore. When will he take the test again? If they didn't have to, they didn't want to waste a scholarship on an ineligible player, promise or no promise.

Just before graduation Pingatore called William into his office for a final chat. They sat across the desk from each other. William looked at the floor.

"Well, how's it feel—to be finishing?" Pingatore asked. He was smiling, as though he expected William to make a joke.

William paused. Here was his chance to **let it all out**. *You never really understood who I was, Coach*, he thought. But he couldn't get the words out of his mouth. Pingatore was still too formidable, even though William was almost a graduate, with a college scholarship **beckoning**. At times like this, he envied Catherine; she would have

---

the ACT hanging over his head to take the college entrance exams

let it all out say everything he was thinking

beckoning waiting for him

told it to him straight.

"I enjoyed my four years. I mean, we had our **run-ins**," William said.

"Who had run-ins?"

"Me and you."

"We did?"

"Yeah, like that time you made me run seventy-five stairs," William said.

"You never forgot that. See, you should have been happy and enthusiastic about doing your punishment. But someday you're gonna learn that everything done was for your benefit. So that you come back four years from now and say, 'Coach, you were right. Everything that happened at St. Joe helped me a lot. And as a result I got a degree.' That's what I'm hoping for."

William paused. "I'm going into communications, so when you start asking for donations I'll know the right way to turn you down."

The crack was instantaneous—had he taken time to think it over, he might not have made it. Pingatore **bridled**; it had to have hurt. Then he smiled. They shared a nervous laugh.

"I'm sure you'll never turn us down," he said.

William walked away feeling an odd mixture of satisfaction and regret. He wanted to say something much more important that might never get said. *It's always gonna be like that between us—gonna be back and forth,* **gettin' in our digs,** he thought.

Two weeks later, William walked across the stage to receive his diploma. It was like a Friday night game in the gym; almost everyone in his family showed up. Emma broke into tears as she watched her

....

run-ins problems, disagreements

bridled looked upset; looked angry

gettin' in our digs *saying mean things to each other*

son. He looked so alone and fragile. *Everybody's been throwing their dreams into him*, she thought. *He's got to follow his own dreams now.*

After the ceremony, Curtis and William hugged. "I love you, William," Curtis said. "I'm so proud of you. We think you're the greatest, William. And I'm gonna love you to death." They hugged again.

William broke into tears. "Thanks, man," he said. "Thanks for everything."

William gave Emma his diploma, and the next day she hung it on her living-room wall right next to all the others. *Everyone of them's a high school graduate*, she thought. *My baby's the last.*

Then it was William's turn to see Catherine graduate. The Westinghouse gym filled with parents, families, and friends. He recognized a few of the players—Antoine Morris and Anthony Davis. Catherine's graduation cap was **outfitted** with a gold ribbon. Despite her **travails**, she was sixth in her class.

In those last few weeks, William spent as much time as he could with his family. He and his brothers watched every game of the Bulls play-offs, including the most glorious day of all: the 1991 play-off finale between the Pistons and the Bulls.

It was game four—Bulls up three games to none—a Memorial Day **matinee**, which meant everyone had the day off. They watched it at Emma's, the TV cranked high. They popped open soda and brought out the chips and stared in joyous wonderment as the Bulls systematically **worked away at** an early Piston lead.

"He ain't soft now," Curtis chortled, when Scottie Pippen stole the ball from Isiah. "He ain't got no migraine now."

....

outfitted decorated

travails difficulties

matinee game that was shown during the day

worked away at took away

The Pistons did what they could to **rattle** the Bulls: hacking, holding, tripping.

"Can you believe that?" cried David, after Dennis Rodman shoved Pippen out of bounds. "That's no foul; that's battery."

But the Piston tactics failed. The Bulls had seen it all before, and they didn't try to retaliate as they had foolishly done in the past. They ignored Detroit's bad-boy antics, and it was the defending champions who **came undone**. It was pathetic, actually, watching the Pistons fall apart. They whined over calls and bickered with the referees. The Bulls won 115 to 94, to **complete a four-game sweep**. As the game ended the Piston starters—led by Isiah—shamelessly filed off the court, unwilling to congratulate the new champions.

"Call Pingatore," Curtis roared. "Ask coach what he thinks about Isiah and his Pistons now."

From there the Bulls advanced to the NBA finals against Magic Johnson and the Lakers. "I've been livin' with this team through all its struggles on the way up," David said. "It's like I'm in the play-offs now."

In game two, Jordan brought the Gates brothers out of their seats when, on a drive to the basket, he switched the ball from his right to his left hand in midair.

"I didn't see that," said Curtis. "Did I see that?"

"Oh, man, Michael. I love you, Michael," laughed David.

When the series was won, they danced around the living room and ran out into the street. Cabrini was alive with happy noises—cars honking, firecrackers popping, people bursting out of their homes. "We won, we won—Bulls win!"

....

rattle bother, upset

came undone did not play well

complete a four-game sweep win four games in a row

In the middle of it all, William decided he just had to get over to Catherine's. He borrowed Curtis's car and headed west on Division, but the streets were blocked with celebrants dancing across the hoods of cars. He sat in the traffic honking his horn, radio tuned to the postgame show, and watched the sky of his city **aglow with** the firecrackers of jubilation.

ARTHUR

Most of the scouts and coaches left Arthur alone once they learned he wanted to attend a junior college in Chicago and didn't have the grades or test scores to play for a four-year school.

He was recruited by a junior college called Mineral Area in Flat River, Missouri—a school he had never heard of until the coach, Tim Gray, contacted him at a postseason all-star game.

In April he flew down for a visit **at Mineral Area's expense**. He followed Gray around campus and took in the sights: a series of low-lying pre-fab buildings dug into the flat southeastern Missouri landscape.

He was led from one dean to another, **an endless stream of white faces**. He sat before them in their offices and they asked what he wanted to do with himself. He said the first thing that came to his mind.

"Uh, communications," he told one professor he met.

"Are you more interested in overall communications?" another asked.

....

aglow with lit by
at Mineral Area's expense that was paid for by Mineral Area
an endless stream of white faces who were all white

"Uh, I like that and accounting—like business."

"Oh. Okay."

They even took him to meet the president. "We enjoy winning things, but the primary purpose is your education," the president told him. "May I ask what are some of your career goals?"

He might as well have asked Arthur if he wanted to fly to Mars. His only career goal had always been to play in the NBA. But Arthur knew that wouldn't be the sort of responsible answer the president wanted. He cleared his throat. "I want to have my own business, like real estate," he answered. The president looked impressed.

Gray ended the tour at the gym, which was covered with picnic tables for an upcoming social function. "Try to picture it without the tables," Gray told him. "This is where it all happens. It's a beautiful place. And it gets to rocking."

Arthur tried on a team warm-up.

"That's about a hundred and twenty dollars apiece," the coach said. "You need to be very careful with this decision. You know if you come in and act right, you're going out of here with two years of your college finished, and a scholarship to a Division I university. Exactly where you'd want to be—**on track** to graduate in four years."

Gray drove Arthur through the towns around the college. "I know you think it's another world 'cause it's not like Chicago. But it's really not that isolated," Gray told him. "It's not that small. There's 34,000 people around here. We've got some movie theaters."

They passed a farm. "Maybe it'll be good for you to get away from the city," Gray continued. "If you had the grades, you could have gone to a big school, but . . ." They pulled up to a **squat**

....

on track ready, prepared
squat short

one-story house at the edge of campus and got out of the car.

"This is the basketball house," Gray said. "This is where the students on basketball scholarships live." It was **cramped** and tiny—six big guys in three little rooms. They were all black men from inner city neighborhoods, doing their best to adjust. "You know what a bonfire is?" one guy asked Arthur.

"No.

"I didn't, either. They get a big old pile of sticks and start a fire." Arthur looked perplexed.

"Don't ask me; it's **big around** here," the student said.

The key to survival, they told Arthur, is to play ball, build your reputation, and move on. "After awhile you get used to it," one player told him.

Their walls were decorated with posters of Jordan and Malcolm X. They had radios and boom boxes, and the latest rap and hip hop discs. *I just want to be where I'm going to play*, Arthur thought. *I can get the grades. It's only two years. I can put up with this—I put up with worse.*

Five days later Gray visited Arthur in Chicago. Sheila showed him the trophies and the articles from the papers, and pictures of Arthur playing ball. "If we can take care of business, I'll have to swipe one of these pictures and put it in the paper," Gray said.

Sheila snickered. *It's gonna take more than a picture in the paper to get my boy to commit*, she thought.

Bo walked in the room and Gray rose to greet him.

"How many of your players that leave there ended up going to a four-year college?" she asked Gray.

"Thirty-one sophomores in a row," he said.

....

cramped crowded
big around very popular

"Every last one of them he coached," Arthur added.

"I'll show you what the scholarship entails—"

"Is this a full scholarship for two years?" Sheila asked. "The reason I'm skeptical is because of promises made in the past."

"From the time he comes down there until he leaves, he will not have **a financial need**," said Gray.

It was Bo's turn to talk. He sat on the arm of the sofa looking down at Arthur. "Now when you make this decision, you got to live and die with it," he said in a fatherly tone of calm, serious concern, "'cause it's your decision to make. Now I'm here to support you if you done researched this whole thing—"

"And it's what you really want," Sheila said. "Not because Momma said this or—"

"Or because you're saving Momma money," said Bo. "'cause if we have to, we will pay—have to try to pay—if we must **put up** something."

Arthur frowned and **wiggled** in his seat, and kept looking at the floor. He wanted to laugh at that one. *Pay for college?* he thought. *Man, how are you gonna pay for my college?*

Bo continued. "I'm just saying you should understand what you're saying, you want to save somebody money, but still—"

"You have to still do what's best for Man," said Sheila.

"But still we want the best for you, even if we have to **go into the hole**. Do you understand what I'm saying? But still the decision is up to you."

Bo stopped talking, and Gray leaned forward, pushing the letter of intent toward Arthur. "Well, what do you think?" the coach asked.

....

a financial need to worry about money

put up pay for

wiggled moved around uncomfortably

go into the hole owe a lot of money; go into debt

"Ready to sign it?"

"Yeah," Arthur said quietly. Bo had taken much of the pleasure of this moment away from him.

Gray sat back and watched as Arthur and then Sheila signed the paper.

"Oh yes, we're happy about this," the coach said. "I mean, we're really happy about this."

Well, you ought to be, thought Sheila, *'cause I'm giving you my son!*

All summer long, Sheila **trudged** through her classes. They **bombarded her with** the details of therapy: how to care for the aged, the infirmed, the weak. She completed a residency at a neighborhood clinic, working with survivors of strokes, accidents, beatings, heart attacks, and degenerative diseases.

"You got to believe in yourself," she encouraged her patients. "Look at me. My whole life people told me I can't get it done, and I'm working to get my nursing certificate."

She got no pay for her efforts, just credits toward her certificate. Tired, she came home and cleaned the house and made the dinner. She **stretched the family's resources**, and she kept Arthur focused on his books—he still had to endure another stifling hot summer-school classroom to get his high school diploma.

On the day of her own graduation ceremony, she pressed her white nurse's uniform to make sure it was smooth and perfect. She spent at least five minutes in front of the mirror combing her Afro with a pick.

"Man, you remember I told you, 'Whatever I start I finish,'" said

....

trudged slowly went
bombarded her with taught her a lot of
stretched the family's resources spent the family's money carefully

352

Sheila, gently needling Arthur. "I'm not like some people I know; I don't need nobody to push me. All I got to have is the goal and the motivation, and I'm ready."

Arthur and Sweetie walked her to the ceremony at Bethel. She felt so proud, parading down Pulaski with her two boys. She was determined to go through the ceremony **with her head high**, dignified and proper. But then Mrs. Martin, one of her counselors, called her into Bethel's kitchen to break some surprising news.

"Sheila, you scored 89 on your exam and you're gonna get the highest grade-point average," Mrs. Martin told her.

"Really?" Sheila shrieked. "Really! No, no, no, no, no! Oh, I love you, I love you, I love you! I'm so happy. Oh, thank you."

She jumped in the air and did a little dance.

"You did it yourself," Mrs. Martin said. "I knew you could do it."

"Yeah, I did," said Sheila. And she started to cry. "You gave me that belief in myself. You really inspired me to go on. Not to just stop right here, but go further. And people told me I wasn't gonna be anything."

She couldn't stop crying—"It took me twenty years to get here, but I'm here," she told Arthur. "Lord, I'm here."

The ceremony was held in a narrow room with several dozen folding chairs, most of them empty. The graduates sat along the wall behind Mrs. Martin. A gospel singer and a choir provided musical accompaniment.

When Mrs. Martin called Sheila's name, the tears started **anew**, washing away years of heartbreak. She stepped forward and took her certificate. Arthur and Sweetie waved at her. Sheila smiled and

....

with her head high and show that she was confident
anew again

clenched her fist and raised it in the air.

The chorus broke into song:

I sing because I'm happy

And I sing because I'm free,

His eye is on **the sparrow**, and I know he watches over me.

His mother's triumph made Arthur more ready to leave Chicago. *I know she's gonna be able to take care of herself,* he thought. There was no reason to stay. His friends were either off for college, working full-time, or, worse yet, in gangs, hooked on drugs, or dealing.

Shannon had been arrested for selling drugs. Arthur was sympathetic—this was one of his best friends, a boy with whom he shared his secrets. *A bad step here or there, and me and him could have been tradin' places,* Arthur thought. *It could be me in jail and him going to college.* After the arrest he stopped seeing Shannon. He had to be careful. He had to look out for himself. "I can't mess with that," he told Shannon. "I got too much goin' on."

Ironically the whole sad scene made Arthur appreciate Bo. Shannon's problems began when his parents divorced. Shannon never got along with his mother's boyfriend. At least Bo never left—he always came back.

A week before his graduation Arthur was robbed **at gunpoint**. "The guy pulled out a gun and asked for my wallet," Arthur told his parents. "I said, 'I ain't got no wallet,' and then he just grabbed me and took what I had."

"The neighborhood gettin' too dangerous," said Bo. "You got to leave, Man, if you don't want to **wind up dead**."

....

the sparrow a little bird

at gunpoint by a person with a gun

wind up dead be killed

WILLIAM

• • • • • • • • • • •

Before he left for Marquette, William **made a guest appearance at** Pingatore's camp.

"Why **you botherin'**?" Curtis asked.

"For the kids," William said. "They look forward to this kind of stuff."

But William knew he was also fulfilling an old dream once shared with Arthur. They were going to return to St. Joseph as stars, just like Isiah. If Arthur couldn't be there, then William would go it alone.

Pingatore met him at the door. William was wearing shorts and a T-shirt and a Marquette baseball cap. He hadn't seen the coach in several weeks.

"You can't play basketball with a cap on—take it off," Pingatore told him. "It's the last time I'll probably ever tell you to do something."

William nodded, but kept his hat on as he followed Pingatore into the gym.

There were about sixty kids in the bleachers. William took a seat alongside them as Coach Doyle walked up to him. "Take off the hat," Doyle said.

"I will, coach," said William. He waited a moment or two, and then he took it off.

"William is here today to tell you about the good and the bad things that happened to him here," Pingatore said. "William Gates

....

made a guest appearance at visited
you botherin' are you doing that

was all-state. He could have been **a high school All-American**, but he had a knee injury. We didn't know if William would come back, but he had a very good season—not a great season. I think partly it was his injury. It's tough to come back. But he's the only player who started for four years."

The kids clapped, and William stepped forward to speak. "It was only four years ago that I sat in these stands, wondering if I wanted to come here or stay in my neighborhood school," he began. As he talked, he saw the kids—black and white, innocent and young, eyes big and round—**hanging on** every word. He started talking and suddenly he couldn't stop; everything he had always wanted to say to Pingatore came pouring out. He told them about being a black boy so far from home, about being afraid to tell his coach that his girlfriend was pregnant, about Catherine, and about Curtis, the greatest player who ever came out of Cabrini.

"No one really understood me," he said. "I was so alone. I was like livin' two lives."

And yet, against all the odds, he had emerged with his diploma and a college scholarship. If it wasn't for Pingatore, *I might not be going to college*, he thought. "Coach Pingatore took care of me like I was his son," he told them. "Education, fellows, it's the big goal."

He paused, looking at Pingatore who sat with his chin in his hands and his eyes misting over. What came next was **spontaneous**. Normally he would have been reluctant to share such personal feelings. "St. Joseph," William said, "was probably the best thing that could have happened to me."

One of the kids asked him to dunk, which made him laugh.

....

a high school All-American one of the best high school basketball players in the country

hanging on listening carefully to

spontaneous not planned

That's really all they wanted. They were just like him and Arthur four years ago: They saw him talking, but they didn't hear a thing, lost as they were in their dreams.

He hadn't played for a few weeks. His legs felt heavy. He missed the first dunk, and the kids groaned. But he nailed the second and the third, spinning around to slam from behind. The kids cheered **lustily**.

William met Pingatore at center court. "That's the last time you're going to dunk at St. Joseph High School," Pingatore said. "And if you tear down the backboard, you're going to have to pay for it before you go to Marquette."

Pingatore told the campers to start their workout.

"Well, I'll be seeing you, coach." William said.

They shook hands and Pingatore went back to work. He looked at his watch and wandered **amidst the throng** of campers—the next generation of Chargers stretching on the gym floor.

The night before William left for Marquette, they had a boisterous family barbecue in Alvin and Peggy's backyard.

William was nervous. He had never lived away from Cabrini or Emma or his brothers. He felt guilty for leaving Alicia and Catherine. He **was already homesick**, and he hadn't even left.

"If you gonna do it, you gotta go," Curtis told him. "Get on out of here and don't look back."

The next day Amal McCaskill, who had also accepted a scholarship at Marquette, came by to drive him to Milwaukee. William took the old suitcase filled with recruitment letters and dumped them into the garbage bin. "Won't be needing them

....

lustily loudly
amidst the throng between the group
was already homesick missed home already

anymore," he said.

A bunch of boys and girls stopped by to watch.

"What's William doin'?" one boy asked.

"He's goin' to college," David said.

The little boy nodded and watched.

William stood on the front stoop and hugged his mother. "I'll miss you," Emma said.

"I'll miss you, too," said William.

"I want you to be okay," she said. "Don't get into no alcohol, no wine coolers, none of that stuff.

They hugged one more time.

I just hope he stays in there, Emma thought. *I think he's gonna make it. Lord, I hope so anyway.*

William got into the car and turned to McCaskill. "Come on, man, let's go," he said. If he hung around any longer, he might not ever get out.

After William left, Catherine went on her own recruiting trip to Northern Illinois University.

She had applied there because Hiawatha Henderson, a student at Northern and a friend from the neighborhood, recommended it.

Hiawatha took her all around the campus, showing her the library, the classrooms, the **student union**. She introduced her to other black **coeds**, many of them single mothers. *They **got day care for** students, they got girls here just like me*, Catherine thought. *I fit in here.*

William didn't want her to go to Northern. "It's too far away," he said. "Go to school in Chicago so I can see you and the baby."

....

student union building where students ate and relaxed

coeds female students

got day care for *have a program that takes care of the children of*

358

"No way," Catherine said. "It's time I'm on my own."

In her application she wrote an essay outlining the story of her life. "I want to go to college to make sure my daughter has a secure future," she wrote. "So my daughter can say, 'My mom is a doctor or a pharmacist,' which is what I think I might want to be." Northern accepted her, and Catherine decided to go there.

At the end of the summer, her older brother Roy packed her belongings into his Buick and drove her up for the start of school. She called William that night to tell him she had settled in at Hiawatha's apartment and to see how he was.

"It's all right up here, I guess," he said. But the competition was fierce, and he wondered if he would make it to the pros. "Everybody always says, 'When you get to the NBA, don't forget about me.'" he said. "I should say to them, 'Well, if I *don't* make it, don't forget about me.'"

"William," Catherine replied, "I never could understand why you spent so much time worrying about that game."

Within a month, Catherine had an apartment of her own. *A lot of people didn't think I was going to make it*, she thought as she unpacked. *They thought I'd just get me a little apartment in Cabrini and wait for William to make the pros. But I'm gonna prove them all wrong.*

ARTHUR
· · · · · · · · · · ·

On the day before he was to leave for Mineral Area, Arthur and Bo **hooked up for** a game of one-on-one.

....

hooked up for met to play

The game started as a **playful shoot-around**, but escalated into a heated competition after Bo began taunting Arthur, saying, "You ain't the player you used to be."

At least ten people came over to watch, including Sheila and Edonnya, one of Arthur's girlfriends. They were playing **to thirty-four by twos**—winner gets the ball out.

Bo nailed a jumper. "You want to see it rain?" Bo cried as he shot another. "Let it rain!" His shot slipped in again—three in a row, like he was back at Parker High. "You want to see it rain? Let it rain." He drove for a bank shot, but it kicked off the rim.

Arthur grabbed the rebound and stood at the key, dribbling through his legs.

Bo stood a few feet away. "Peoria Manual, remember?" he taunted. "Do you know Howard Nathan?"

Arthur fired in a jumper. "And I **stuck him up** just like that."

"Uh-oh," someone yelled. "Like father, like son."

"You better stick to church music, Bo," Edonnya yelled, "and leave the basketball alone."

Arthur drove for the basket, and Bo whacked him on the arm.

"*Hack, hack,*" the crowd called as Arthur's shot rolled in.

"Got one," said Arthur.

"That's thirty-two," said Bo.

"Thirty-four," the crowd called.

"That last one don't count because he called foul," said Bo.

Arthur stomped the ground. "That's thirty-four."

The crowd was into it by now. "That's thirty-four," they chanted.

Bo **turned on** them. "He didn't hit nothin'," said Bo.

....

playful shoot-around time to shoot the ball for fun

to thirty-four by twos to 34 points, with each shot worth 2

stuck him up beat him; defeated him

turned on got angry at

"This ain't no con game," Arthur said, "I'm older now. Ain't no con game goin' on no more."

"The score is 32 to 28," said Bo.

Arthur shook his head. "The game's over with. I can con, too."

"Losers quit," said Bo. "I'm ready to play. You're a coward if you don't play."

Arthur picked up the ball at the free-throw line and began to dribble as Bo **sunk into a defensive crouch**.

"He's mad now," said Arthur.

"You ain't two years old," said Bo. "You ain't getting no **pacifier**. Your momma ain't here to give you this ball. Come on, make it rain."

Arthur dribbled toward the basket, faked, and then hit a jumper. "Game, game," he shouted. "Right there. Go get down. Go sit down." Arthur dropped to his knees and pounded the pavement for emphasis.

Edonnya and Sheila laughed, cheered, and twirled umbrellas. "Its raining, Bo," they called. "It's raining."

"Yeah, yeah, yeah," Bo said. "What he knows, he learned from me. I taught him everything he knows. And he's still got more to learn."

Coach Gray arrived not long after dawn to drive Arthur to college.

The family gathered in the living room. They knelt, held hands, and Bo **led them in a prayer**. "God, we thank you for this day, Lord. And we ask you to go with Junior, Lord, and we thank you, Lord. Go with him as he tries to better his education, Lord. And we thank you for coming this far. We came this far by faith, Lord. And we ask you, Father, when he gets in college, Lord, to keep him, Lord, keep him

....

sunk into a defensive crouch got ready

pacifier help

led them in a prayer said a prayer for the family

protected. We thank you for him, Jesus. In Jesus's name we pray. Amen."

They rose and hugged Arthur. Sheila walked him to the front porch and watched him climb into the car. She watched that car until it disappeared around the corner, and then she hurried back to her home. She had a job interview in the afternoon and maybe, just maybe, a new job in the morning.

EPILOGUE

"I've come this far, I'm not about to give up. . . . I know I can play. . . . Every step of the way someone says, 'Arthur, you can't do it,' or, 'You're not going to do it.' And that just makes me want to prove them wrong even more."

—*Arthur Agee*

"I think about what I've been through, and mostly I'm very thankful. . . . I don't think I'll chase after the dream, but if the NBA calls me, if they invite me to camp—I'll go. I guess I still have the dream."

—*William Gates*

Arthur

......

Arthur spent two years at Mineral Area College living in the "basketball house."

Initially, he had a **bumpy transition** to life in rural Missouri. He struggled in the classroom, and his teachers and coaches wondered if he would ever graduate. But he did, earning a degree in communications in 1993.

"The remarkable thing about Arthur is that he's a survivor," says Tim Gray, Arthur's college coach. "He saw what he had to do and he did it. Give him credit for that."

In his second year at Mineral Area, Arthur started every game at point guard, averaging nine points and six assists a game. He led the team to a conference title and a 26-7 record.

Almost eighty universities and colleges expressed interest in recruiting Arthur; seven offered him scholarships. He settled on Arkansas State in Jonesboro, because the coach told him he would start. He made his presence felt in his very first game, knocking down a 45-foot jumper at the buzzer to beat Texas Tech. He majored in communications, hosted his own radio show, and became quite a favorite of the local reporters, who considered him one of the more colorful and quotable members of the team.

Arthur's senior year at Arkansas State, however, didn't work out as he had hoped. For every good moment, a bad one followed: a flash of brilliance, then he'd throw the ball away. The team, **mired in mediocrity**, lost many more than they won. He was relieved when

....

bumpy transition hard time getting used
mired in mediocrity unable to play very well

the season ended.

By then he was known less for basketball than for his role in the movie, *Hoop Dreams*. On the street, strangers often approached him, hands extended, to say how much his perseverance had **moved them**. The acclaim followed wherever he went, and, thanks to the movie's popularity, he went places he never imagined. He threw out the ceremonial first pitch at a Cubs game, gave speeches to businessmen, testified before a congressional committee, and even met President Clinton—a photo of them embracing **ran on front pages** across the country.

After the season ended, Arthur returned to Chicago, just 21 hours **shy of** his degree, promising to finish once his playing days were over. There he was reunited with his two children, Anthony and Ashley, who lived with their mothers. He hired a Chicago agent name Keith Kreiter, who set up promotional appearances and got him a trading card deal. Along with Sheila and Bo, he started a foundation (the Arthur Agee Role Model Foundation) intended to help kids like him. He worked out at Chicago's most upscale health club; it was suddenly fashionable for young professionals to brag about going one-on-one with Arthur Agee.

He grew another inch, put on ten pounds of muscle, increased his vertical leap, honed his jump shot, and got **drafted by** the Florida team in the United States Basketball League, a semi-pro spring basketball association. They featured him in ticket-sale promotions— "Arthur Agee, star of *Hoop Dreams*"—then relegated him to the bench. He felt exploited and unappreciated, and so he left, finishing the season with the league's Long Island team.

....

moved them made them feel happy

ran on front pages appeared in newspapers

shy of away from getting

drafted by picked to join

On the basis of his performance (he averaged nine points a game), Isiah Thomas, of all people, came calling. Thomas was now general manager of the Toronto Raptors, an expansion team in the NBA, and he wanted Arthur to play for the club's rookie/free agent summer-league team. If Arthur played well, he'd get to try out for the Raptors.

Alas, with the NBA lockout the summer league was canceled; so went Arthur's first shot at the NBA. It seemed to him the story of his life—the next break would be his first. Tim Gray did not think the road ahead would be easy.

"Here's the book on Arthur," says Gray. "He's six-foot-one and quick as a water bug; he can get the ball from one end of the floor to the other as fast as anyone I've ever seen. What happens at the other end of the court, however, is what distinguishes him from the great NBA point guards. In other words, he doesn't always know what to do with the ball. And he's not a great shooter.

"But, the thing about Arthur—and you cannot overlook this—is he comes through in big games. Ever since high school his whole career has been about **rising to the occasion** in pressure situations. That's why I think he'll play somewhere professionally—be it overseas or in the CBA—if he sticks at it."

Arthur had no plans to quit. As far as he was from his lifelong dream (and he remains very far), he'd never been so close. He would, he vowed, play until his **legs gave out**, and all hope was gone.

So back to the phones went Kreiter, looking for a minor-league team for whom Arthur could play. He got Arthur a tryout with a CBA team in Moline, Illinois. They offered him a contract, but

....

rising to the occasion doing his best
legs gave out body could not continue playing

Arthur turned them down to sign with the Winnipeg Cyclones, a new team in a **lesser-known league**: the International Basketball Association. "The Cyclones promised him more playing time," says Kreiter. "That's what he needs more than anything else—more time."

The Cyclones's season runs through February. After that Arthur and Kreiter will get on the phone once more to see if any team anywhere is looking for a guard. "People have always **counted me out**," Arthur says. "When I got kicked out of St. Joseph, people said I'd wind up on the streets. When I went to junior college they said I'd never survive the basketball house. They said I'd never play major college ball. I proved them wrong then, and I'll prove them wrong again."

Sheila Agee is a rehab technician at the Jackson Square Rehabilitation and Nursing Center, a West Side facility. "It's an inspirational job, and it's a difficult job," Sheila says. "I work with survivors—people who have survived strokes or heart attacks or shootings or car accidents or violent beatings. I bathe them, I brush their teeth, I wash under their arms. I lead them in physical therapy. If they're depressed, I talk to them to get them motivated so they can move on with their lives.

"I try to make them see all the good things in life. If they had a stroke and they can't feed themselves, well, maybe they can wash one part of their body—that's what you encourage them about. From that point, it's on to the next thing, one little thing after another. You do the best you can, and you never give up. That's the secret to dealing with **life's tribulations**."

....

lesser-known league league that was not well known
counted me out said that I could not succeed
life's tribulations the difficult things in life

The job pays Sheila $4.85 an hour. "It makes me angry to hear people talking about women on welfare like they're dogs," she says. "People say, 'Get a job.' Well, think about this: After all these years of training and working, I'm still making less than five dollars an hour, and I don't get any benefits. You can talk all you want about people **pulling themselves up**, but you have to ask yourself: What kind of future is out there?

"Sometimes I get so frustrated, I want to give up. But I won't stop here. I'm training to become a registered nurse. And one day I hope to operate my own nursing home. I think I will make it, but, Lord, it's a struggle." In 1995, the struggle paid off as Sheila got a higher paying job as a rehab technician in a suburban nursing home. She commutes up to three hours a day, following roughly the same roads her son once took to St. Joseph, but she says the new job's worth the ride. "I'm much better off, even the driving's not so bad—it gives me time to be myself and think."

Three years ago, Sheila and Bo **remarried** in a simple ceremony at Minister Banks's church. Arthur was the best man.

"I had been married since I was seventeen all the way up until my thirties, and I just cannot picture myself being out there as a single parent," says Sheila. "I just thank God for bringing some peace to my house and to my marriage. It's very hard being the mother and the father, so I'd rather be married than be single. And Bo has changed. Believe it or not, the man has changed for the better."

They live in the same West Side apartment where Big Earl visited them in 1987, and it's still crowded with family. Tomekia has moved back with her daughters, Jasmine and Brittany, while her

....

pulling themselves up working to make their lives better
remarried married each other again

husband, LaVelle Ellis, finishes his **tour of duty** in the Navy.

"Tomekia will be going to nursing school to take the courses her mother took," says Bo. "And she'll be a nurse one day, and hopefully she'll work at Sheila's nursing home."

Sweetie is now a fourteen-year-old freshman at Marshall and built like a desert tank. "He went out for the football team, but next year I think he's going out for basketball," says Sheila. "It's his decision."

Luther Bedford is still coaching at Marshall, and still refusing to recruit. His team still plays relentless defense, though they haven't returned to the city finals since Arthur's senior year.

As for Bo, he says he has grown closer to his children, including DeAntonio and DeAngelo, Deon, Imogene, and Ishaia—sons and daughters he's had with other women.

"I like to think that I can help Arthur, let him learn from my experiences. I'm like an advisor to him. He was going through a **little slump** not long ago, and I took him aside and said, 'Son, you can't let distractions get the better of you. Now, you didn't come all the way this far, and put up with everything you put up with, to let it slide now. You got to go out there and play your game.' And he went out that night and scored twenty points. He was like a wild man— said he felt the spirit of the Lord from within. The coach asked, 'What did you say to turn him around?' And I said, 'Well, it was just something between a father and his son.'"

At a recent reception, Bo got to meet his longtime idol, former Bulls great Norm Van Lier. "I said to him, 'Stormin' Norman, man, I used to sneak into the stadium to see you play,'" says Bo. "That man was a fighter—just like me. Sometimes you've gotta fight just

....

tour of duty work, service
little slump hard time

to stay alive."

Bo says he has had a hard time finding steady work. He attends Minister Banks's church every weekend and sings with the choir and counsels friends and family members facing hard times.

"I'm a free man," says Bo. "I'm free from drugs. I don't have to look over my shoulder for the police. I talk to children or addicts about the church. I have four old friends—Jimmy Wiley, Jeffery Burch, Charles Tabbs, and Ronnie Hoskins—I'm working with. And God has **turned all of our lives around**. Jeffery gave his life back to the Lord, and he and his fiancée got married. I turned Ronnie out, and he's saved. I told him about Minister Banks, and Ronnie came to church and now he's fixing to get married to one of the sisters in the church."

Bo's larger goal is to make a living as a **motivational speaker, and to this end** he has put together a promotional flier.

"Arthur Agee Senior has seen it all," the flier begins. "He is now an active minister on the streets of the West Side of Chicago and a motivational speaker on such topics as how to build inner strength and how to overcome adversity. Sometimes a man is judged by the respect he has earned from his family. When Arthur Jr., who is widely recognized as a special young man by his peers, is asked who he admires most, without hesitation he will say: 'my father.' So, if your audience is looking to listen and learn from a man who has truly overcome all odds, then look no further than Arthur 'Bo' Agee."

On the day before Thanksgiving, 1993, DeAntonio Agee was shot dead in the **vestibule** of a Cabrini-Green high-rise by members of a rival gang. He was nineteen years old. The funeral service was held at a church near Cabrini-Green and was attended by about two

---

turned all of our lives around helped us all change for the better

motivational speaker, and to this end person who tries to encourage people, and to start doing this kind of work

vestibule hallway

hundred people, including Sheila, Tomekia, and Sweetie. Bo gave a cautionary sermon intended for the young people in the church. "I've been in and out of prison, and I've been hooked on drugs," he preached. "I've been through ups and downs. But I want to let you know—it's not too late. It's never too late. You've got a chance to turn your life around to God."

WILLIAM
· · · · · · · · · · · ·

In the summer of 1993, William and Catherine got married in a large ceremony with more than three hundred guests at a church only one block away from the one where DeAntonio's funeral was held. Curtis and David were the best men. Catherine's sister Carolyn and Charlene Gideon, an old friend from Jenner, were the maids of honor. Catherine made her own wedding gown.

"It was a white gown with short sleeves; it had lace to cover the shoulders and a long **train**. I stayed up all night working on that dress. I didn't finish it until a quarter to twelve, and I was getting married at one. That was pretty wild."

They had a three-day **honeymoon** at the Wisconsin Dells resort area. Then Catherine and Alicia moved to Milwaukee to live with William.

By then he was beginning his junior year. He had been a starter during his first two seasons and had shown flashes of brilliance, scoring twenty-five points in one matchup against DePaul. Many observers expected William to emerge as one of Marquette's

···

train piece of cloth at the back of the dress
honeymoon trip after their wedding

leading scorers.

But he was tired of the race, sick of the game. His sophomore scoring average had slipped to 3.4 points a game. He had lost confidence in his shot. The time had come to take a break. So he went to the athletic director and made sure that his scholarship was guaranteed whether or not he played. Then he took **a hiatus** from the team. Some coaches called him a quitter, but William didn't see it that way: he was going to be one young black man from the inner city who made basketball work for him.

"I didn't tell my brothers 'cause I knew what they would say," says William. "They'd be against it. All my brothers had the dream of me making the pros. When they found out, they tried to **talk me out of it**. But I knew what was best for me. I realized what mattered most was getting my degree. And I wasn't going to get it if I kept concentrating on the game."

His friends and brothers predicted William would drop out without basketball. But William proved them wrong. He kept his scholarship and continued his courses. "It was the best time of my life—I wouldn't change a thing," he says. "I never had so much free time. It felt so good to come home from class and not have to rush off to practice and get yelled at. I got to spend a lot of time with Alicia. I got my grades up. So I'll be ready to graduate in December of 1995."

While away from the game, William gained thirty pounds. But over the summer of 1994, he began to work out, lost almost all that weight, and decided to return to the team. "I realized I still liked playing the game," he says. "I saw some **footage** of myself from high

....

a hiatus a break; some time off
talk me out of it tell me to go back to the team
footage old videos that were recorded

school and I said, 'Damn, I can play this game. No reason to give it up so soon.' I figured I'd come back for one last bang."

William did not start; he was the shooter off the bench. But he's comfortable with his role. "In high school I was the starter, I was the go-to guy; I didn't even know how to come off the bench. It's different now. I'm into it—I cheer for the guys. I wave the towel. I help them out. It's just a game; I'm having fun."

In January 1995, William came home to Chicago for a game against DePaul. During one sequence in the first half, he found himself up against Tom Kleinschmidt, his old opponent and DePaul's star forward. The first time William got the ball, he hit a three—right over his old rival's **outstretched arms**. "For awhile, I thought we were back in high school," says William. "I kept expecting Coach Pingatore to be yelling something from the bench."

Emma works in a nursing home and lives in Cabrini. Peggy is a manager for United Airlines, and her husband, Alvin, is regional director for Young Life, a social service organization. They have two children, Cartel, who used to room with William, and Brandon, 3. Randy Gates works as a security guard; he and his wife, Katherine, have a son, Randy Jr. LaTonya "Tee" Gates is an after-school coordinator at a social center in Chicago.

David and Curtis are drivers for Federal Express. David plays in basketball tournaments and leagues throughout the city. Curtis is fondly remembered by veteran coaches and reporters as one of the finest North Side players of the last twenty years. "He's welcome to come back to my gym anytime and talk to the kids," says Manny

....

outstretched arms arms waving in the air

Weincord of Roosevelt. "Curtis Gates is a legend."

But Curtis says he's happy to be through with basketball. He and his wife, Beatrice, had a second child, Curtis Jr. Their daughter, Sparkiesha, is twelve years old. "I don't miss the game," says Curtis. "I feel so good about myself; I don't need it. I got a good job; I support my family. Basketball was fun while it lasted, but I'm not gonna cry now that it's gone."

"I think about what I've been through, and mostly I'm very thankful," says William. "I think about all the people who helped me, and I want to thank them: Sister Marilyn, Mrs. Weir, Tom and Mary Esselman at Cycle, Alvin and Peggy, my mom, my brothers, Cleve Lester, Theo Johnson, Terrell Chambers and all the other boys in Cabrini, Coach O'Neill and Coach Pingatore, and of course, Catherine."

The Gates family remains close. At New Year's twenty different members of the extended Gates families—husbands, wives, children, and grandchildren—came to Milwaukee to see William play. They all slept at William and Catherine's house, the kids in sleeping bags on the floor. In the morning they sat around the dining room table and **feasted on** pancakes, eggs and bacon.

Then they went to Bradley Arena to watch the game. William came off the bench midway through the first half. Soon afterward, a Marquette player stole the ball and **hit William streaking up the court**. Until then, this year's fans at Marquette had not seen the basketball brilliance in William; he had not even had an opportunity to dunk the ball all season. But this time the moment was right. His momentum carried him to the basket, and instead of laying the ball

....

feasted on ate
hit William streaking up the court threw the ball to William who was running toward the basket

in off the glass, he **cradled** it in his hand, threw his arm back, and slammed the ball down the hole.

The crowd erupted. They rose to their feet. And as William jogged back on defense the chant rolled down from the balcony until the stadium shook with the roar: "Hoop Dreams . . . Hoop Dreams . . . Hoop Dreams!"

William rode the bench in the final game of his college career, the championship round of the National Invitational Tournament in Madison Square Garden. But he was too tired to care. He had gone sleepless ever since Catherine gave birth to Will just two days before.

It was funny, thinking about the differences from when Alicia was born. Once again a birth date coincided with a post-season basketball tournament. But back then he and Catherine had been two frightened teenagers, all alone in the hospital. He had worried that the birth might make him miss a game. Basketball was his whole future in those days. Without it, they said, a poor black boy from Cabrini had no chance—he should never, ever let a girl or her baby get in his way.

Well, he had proven them wrong. He **severed the cord to** basketball (he **harbored no more illusions** about playing in the NBA), and he still would graduate from college. Catherine was right: he didn't need basketball to get his degree.

William flew from New York to Milwaukee to be with Catherine and Alicia when Will was born. It all happened in between the final two games of the National Invitational Tournament in New York City. William was at NBC's studio making an appearance on the *Today* show when he got word that Catherine had gone into labor. He

....

cradled held, carried
severed the cord to stopped thinking only about
harbored no more illusions no longer thought

flew to Milwaukee, visited his family in the hospital and returned to New York, just in time for tip-off. No one had the audacity to suggest that he belonged anywhere else but his family's side.

Over the summer, William and Catherine moved back to Chicago.

"William and I have worked out a deal," says Catherine. "I'm going to stay home and take care of the kids for awhile. But after the baby's a year or two old, I'm going back to school and William's going to pay for my college education. I plan to become a pharmacist. I have not given up on my dreams."

He makes a nice living delivering motivational speeches to college students. He has formed his own foundation. Corporations offer him jobs in public relations. He's very busy and he doesn't have much time to work out. He played against Arthur in **a pickup game and marveled at** his moves; it's hard to remember that William was once the better player. The closest William came to professional basketball was acting as the master of ceremonies for the Harlem Globetrotters during a summer tour of black colleges in the South.

He did have one last great moment on the court. It was at a Bulls game in the new stadium (the old one having been **demolished,** apparently too funky for the high rollers and their dates). The Bulls had invited William and Arthur to toss the ceremonial first ball at the opening of a playoff game against Orlando. Walking back from center court, William spied Anfernee Hardaway, Orlando's bright young star, and they embraced. Once upon a time they had played against each other in one of those high school camps. But that seemed long ago.

The Bulls lost the game, blowing a seven-point lead with two

....

a pickup game and marveled at an unplanned game and was surprised by

demolished destroyed

minutes left. Michael Jordan, only weeks back from his retirement, never looked so old. Horace Grant, who had **fled** the Bulls for Orlando, taunted the crowd. It was a rough night to be a Bulls fan—it's hard to lose when you've been on top.

Over the summer, Jordan started working out (talk is he's in the best shape of his career), and the Bulls signed rebounding champ Dennis Rodman. Grant's not gloating anymore. He and his teammates are looking over their shoulders, worried about those old guys in Chicago.

It will be, experts predict, a great season for the Bulls, one last **championship run**. And William will be there watching, most likely at home with his brothers—forever a fan, if not a player.

As a freshman, William **likened basketball to a long-distance race, pitting him** against all the other Williams and Arthurs of the world. He now knows better. He and the others are not so much runners in a race as marchers in a parade, which they must one day leave to watch from the side.

....

fled left, quit
championship run chance to be the best basketball team
likened basketball to a long-distance race, pitting him said basketball was like a long-distance race, making him compete

> **BEFORE YOU MOVE ON...**
>
> 1. **Conclusions** Reread page 354. Why did Arthur feel he could leave Chicago? Where did he decide to go?
>
> 2. **Summarize** How did William play at Marquette? What did he do after he graduated?